# The Hurt

# The Hurt

DYLAN HARTLEY
WITH MICHAEL CALVIN

VIKING
*an imprint of*
PENGUIN BOOKS

VIKING

UK | USA | Canada | Ireland | Australia | India | New Zealand | South Africa

Viking is part of the Penguin Random House group of companies whose addresses can be found
at global.penguinrandomhouse.com.

First published 2020
001

Copyright © Dylan Hartley, 2020

The moral right of the author has been asserted

Set in 13.5/16 pt Garamond MT Std
Typeset by Integra Software Services Pvt. Ltd, Pondicherry
Printed and bound in Great Britain by Clays Ltd, Elcograf S.p.A.

A CIP catalogue record for this book is available from the British Library

ISBN: 978–0–241–34895–6

To my wife Jo, for her unwavering support, my kids, for inspiring me, and my parents, for giving me the opportunity.

# Contents

1.  Meat                                          1
2.  Mana                                         18
3.  The Lost Boys                                35
4.  Outsider                                     51
5.  Heart of Darkness                            68
6.  Sixty Weeks                                  86
7.  Stone Age to Space Age                      104
8.  Dwarves, Drinks and Destiny                 121
9.  Respect                                     138
10. Rocky Road, Beautiful Destination           156
11. Slam Dunk                                    174
12. Shadowlands                                  192
13. Boys in the Bubble                           210
14. Own the Unexpected                           228
15. The Shirt                                    244
16. The Long Goodbye                             262
17. Outside, Looking In                          279
18. Hurting, Healing                             295

*Acknowledgements*                               309
*Index*                                          313

# I

# Meat

'You're fucked, mate . . .'

Eddie Jones may be a brilliant coach, but his bedside manner leaves a little to be desired. Even by the standards of the 6am texts he delivers while running on the treadmill, which make the recipient's balls tighten and the brain melt, this phone call was brutal.

I'd spent four years as his captain, confidant, pupil and ambassador. I'd accumulated ninety-seven caps over ten years, coped with controversy and survived the ebbs and flows of international rugby. I'd lived the slogan 'Leaders never show weakness' but had struggled with a knee injury for eight months. He was effectively ending my England career with three words.

Eddie is always prepared, whether he is throwing the media a bone with a smart soundbite or confirming he has written you out of his provisional World Cup squad. I was at a disadvantage, because when he delivers bad news in person you can at least read his eyes. They are sharp and penetrating, and give a tantalizing hint of his inner thoughts.

The England environment was never relaxed, by design. To quote one of Eddie's favourite phrases, borrowed from P. T. Barnum, the nineteenth-century American showman and entertainer: 'Comfort is the enemy of progress.' It's difficult to assess his mood when he is a disembodied voice, so our subsequent conversation was fractured and pretty surreal.

'I'm not fucked.'

'You can't run, mate.'

'I can. I ran this morning.'

'You ran ten sets of fifty metres. That's not fucking running.'

'There's a bit of swelling on the knee, but I'm powering through, training every day.'

'I can't pick you. You're not fit enough. Start making a decision on what you're gonna do.'

I saw a chink of light. It felt as if he was trying to get me to withdraw, voluntarily. That was never going to happen. I wasn't going to make it that easy for him. I knew him as a firm but fair man, and it was time to try to set my own agenda.

'Before you make any decisions, why don't you give me some parameters, a goal, a level that I need to run at, to be considered?'

A pause: 'OK, mate. I'll get back to you.'

Twelve days remained until the provisional training squad for the 2019 World Cup was due to be announced, on 20 June, when one of his strength and conditioning staff sent me the session that would decide my fate. It was a forty-minute beasting, repetitive shuttle runs and explosive movement, on and off the floor, with barely a minute's rest. That's manageable at peak fitness, immediately after pre-season and with a few games in the legs and lungs, but close to impossible at that stage of my rehabilitation.

Eamonn Hyland, the Northampton Saints S&C coach overseeing my recovery, studied the programme and cut to the chase: 'Do they want you to pass this?' He works methodically, in a world of protocols and professional caution. I work instinctively, in a world of pragmatism and professional urgency.

Though I understood his concern, and shared his suspicion that I had not been given the leeway allowed to others, as they sought to reach peak condition, I had no choice. 'Do you know what?' I said. 'Fuck it. I'm nearly out of time. Let's just get some running done. I'm going to have to drive this. Fuck the warm-ups. Fuck all the drills and technique work. Let's just see how we go.'

My knee swelled every day, despite my wearing compression leggings. I did an hour's round trip each morning to do low-impact work in a swimming pool. I paid for a masseur to work on me at my house each evening. I took painkillers, backed up by CBD, the naturally derived cannabis oil that elite athletes, in sports as diverse as golf, football and swimming, use to regulate sleep, the immune system and chronic pain.

My diet was ridiculously harsh since I needed to reduce body fat to underline my determination to regain and retain my fitness, but my body ultimately dictated the limits of my commitment. Everything came to a head after three days, on a Friday morning when I got into Franklin's Gardens especially early to do a running session before driving to Wales to attend the wedding of George North, my friend and clubmate.

The routine had become familiar. My knee blew up, and the pain kicked in. I silently repeated the sportsman's mantra of no pain, no gain, and went for a final push. Suddenly, I was seized by what felt like a sustained electric shock. Not for the first time, I had pulled a back muscle. I caught it before I entered spasm, and Eamonn advised me to stop.

I couldn't, wouldn't. What's that they say about the definition of insanity, doing the same thing over and over and expecting a different result? I was ready to take that particular cliché to a different level. I merely reduced my speed, closed my mind to potential damage, and got the distance in. I paid the price on the way to Wales, when I had to stop and find a doctor to drain my knee.

So-called joint aspiration is not a process for the squeamish, and involves the insertion of a needle into the knee. The doctor drew 80 millilitres of fluid into the syringe, an unprecedented amount. To put that into context, it is popularly assumed that 5 millilitres is enough to switch muscles off. The pressure on the joint was eased, but the process was as much mental as physical.

I was on my own in the hotel that night, because my wife, Jo, a make-up specialist, was attending the bride. As I lay in bed, churning over the possibilities, I had a moment of clarity and release. I'd had enough of being governed by Eddie. I was a grown man, who wasn't ready to be a semi-detached guest at my mate's wedding.

I'd keep off my feet as much as possible, but would have a drink, and enjoy the celebrations. My knee was bloody sore, but from that moment on I vowed to take things at my own pace. I accepted that I wasn't going to be announced in the initial World Cup squad, and wasn't bothered about the fall-out, the public perception of failure.

I unloaded on the Rev. Jez Safford, Northampton's club chaplain, in a quiet corner at the wedding reception. Like many men of the cloth, he has a reassuring presence. It's never about him, it is always about you. 'What's going on in your life?' he asked. 'How are you? Are you OK?' We'd both had a few – I was on pints and he was on the wine – and the barriers were down.

We talked softly about the hardest thing of all, having almost to justify myself to strangers, who would ask 'How's the knee?' with good intentions, when it was the last thing I wanted to dwell on. I couldn't tell them the truth: 'Actually, mate, it fucking hurts.' I was forced to be an actor, reciting a well-rehearsed line: 'Just trying to get it right, thanks, and training hard.'

I craved a quiet place, and would drive without the radio on, churning things over in my mind. Do I go up to someone in the street and ask them something personal? Do I ask about their health or their worries? Of course not; visibility is part and parcel of being a professional athlete. As soon as I came to terms with that, with Jez's help, a weight was lifted.

I gave thanks for my blessings. I needed to get my knee right, not for rugby, but so that I could play on the trampoline with my daughter Thea, or go on a fun-run around the park. I needed to get fit enough for bike rides with my girls, and to be able to bend down to play on the floor with Thea's toys. The transition to an alternative lifestyle, which began in the summer of 2018, when I faced the terrifying uncertainties of concussion, was fully underway.

There was no room for bitterness or self-recrimination, no point in sacrificing everything to please a bloke who, understandably enough, was no longer willing to give me a bit of wriggle room. I accepted the situation, because it made sense. High-performance environments have a high membership fee. Eddie has his way of working, which involves the imposition of pressure on those around him. It works for him.

I'd occasionally noticed the nervous tremor in the analyst's hands, hovering over the computer keyboard during team video presentations. I'd come across England coaches, surreptitiously FaceTiming their families from a nook or cranny in the hotel because they didn't want to give Eddie the impression they were anything less than 100 per cent devoted to the cause.

I was no different. I had to earn my place in the team every single day. I wasn't picked because I was the best player. As one of the oldest members of the team, I had to set the best example in training. As a figure of supposed authority, I had to be a reassuring presence in front of the media. I was the embodiment of Eddie's belief in attending to the smallest details, in order to reach the biggest goal, of becoming the best in the world.

My credit came from working harder, and longer, than anyone. Did I enjoy that? Of course not. It can be miserable, doing additional training, attending seemingly endless strategic meetings with management and support staff when everyone else is on their PlayStation, playing cards, drinking coffee and shooting the shit.

Did I like being different? No. But I'm thankful I did it all, because it enabled me to experience the highs of winning consistently, and the satisfaction of leading from the front. Trust me, a Grand Slam or a Six Nations title stirs the blood, engages the brain, and batters the body. No commemorative DVD, or signed and framed match-worn shirt, can re-create that primeval sense of exhilaration.

The flipside is the feeling of redundancy when I couldn't set the example Eddie demanded. I was no longer much use to him. That was a blow to the ego, but I rationalized the reasons. Without wishing to sound like some sort of New Age philosopher, I was at peace with myself, and the world around me. The phone call to Eddie, confirming the reality of my situation, was one of the easiest I've ever made.

I didn't dwell on the swelling in the knee joint, or the severity of my back problems, because I didn't want to sound weak. I stressed I was as lean as I had ever been. In terms of strength, and muscular definition, I was right where I needed to be. I simply fronted up that, as far as running was concerned, I couldn't push on as quickly as he required.

'Look, mate,' I told him. 'I'm just going to take it slow. I need to get my knee right for my future. I pushed too hard and hurt myself. I understand you need to crack on and prepare but just know that I'll be here and I'll be working. When I'm right I'll let you know. If you need good people, if you need a good person around you, I'll be there.'

Compassion and coaching are not mutually exclusive, but they don't coexist comfortably. Players are equally pre-programmed to look after number one. Eddie had other options to assess. I was no longer a hostage to his fortunes, but couldn't get away from the institutionalized brutality of my sport. Better players and bigger men had been down the same pathway.

I looked to a legend like Paul O'Connell, an amazing warrior for Munster, Ireland and the Lions. He had several years' grace at the start of his career, and spent the next decade balancing persistent injury with the responsibility of captaincy. When he spoke about the necessity of isolating stress, and reminding yourself why you play the game, he struck a chord.

Rugby is great for the soul, but terrible for the body. The intensity of the international game is intoxicating, but the hangovers are vicious, metaphorically and occasionally literally. My early years were disrupted by disciplinary issues, and the later stages of my career were interrupted by injury. That's not a happy medium to strike.

I eventually became sick of living on painkillers, of having my life controlled by aspirations to play for England.

Don't get me wrong – I cherished each and every cap – but self-imposed disciplines became wearing, because they eventually bordered on the illogical. They were all I thought about, first thing in the morning and last thing at night.

The moment I opened my eyes, I instinctively gauged how I was feeling. I worried about what I would eat for breakfast. Forget a fry-up – I denied myself a slice of toast, because I knew it would have a knock-on effect. Aware that the horror of my indulgence would be revealed in the weekly skinfold test, I became fixated, to the point of showing symptoms of OCD.

That's probably the way I am wired, and at least part of the reason I survived, at the coalface of the international game, for a decade. The mental pressure I applied on myself, due to the overwhelming importance I placed on maintaining my England place, became self-perpetuating, since it provided a perverse sense of comfort.

Eddie was a constant presence in my life. Like the rest of the squad, I had developed a strange, half-hidden dependency on him, because of the absolute power he wielded. Let's call it Twickenham Syndrome: in dealing with a head coach, players tend to develop a psychological alliance with their captor.

It wasn't unpleasant, since I was at ease with the daily deluge of his texts, and equally content when he periodically left me alone. I treated that respite as a sign of trust and respect; he knew me well enough to realize that I didn't need him standing over me, checking on my progress, to put in the hard yards.

An athlete craves certainty. I knew I needed to purge myself, by training every day. I knew what and when to eat. I knew my way around the gym. I knew what weight to lift, what distances to cover on the ergometer, stationary bike or vertical skier. I didn't know, until it was too late, the limits of his tolerance.

Looking back, I was probably not as politically cute as I could have been during the key phase of my rehabilitation. Eddie monitors England players by proxy. Outside training camps and competition windows, his support staff, principally conditioners, physios and nutritionists, have the remit of visiting us, on our home turf, once a week.

They report their findings to the man dubbed 'The Master' by Jonny May, the speed freak winger named as England's Player of the Year after scoring six tries in the 2019 Six Nations. I had isolated myself from their sphere of influence by doing things my own way, and trusting familiar figures from the Saints support team, like Eamonn.

That denied Eddie his eyes and ears. I probably needed to be more inclusive, less independently minded. Without updates from his men in the all-too-brief off-season, he probably assumed I was on a beach somewhere, like my peers. In fact, I denied myself a family holiday. I shared the bleak rituals of rehab alongside Mike Haywood and Harry Mallinder, teammates who were also recovering from long-term knee injuries.

Mike was twenty-seven, and is an outstanding hooker in the Premiership. Harry was twenty-three, and will play for England. I was thirty-three, hoping against hope that my future wasn't behind me. People who wished me well in the street told me I was still a young man. I didn't feel like one, limping and wincing whenever I stood up with extreme care, just in case my back went again.

I yearned for normality. My body told me it needed rest. I knew my role, and retained the instincts of a competitor. At close quarters I could still chew people up and spit them out, but there were other aspects of the game that scared the shit out of me. I was on the physio table when I blurted out the darkest thought: 'If my knee doesn't get better and I can't play, what are my options?'

There was no easy answer. I looked at the legalities of clauses in contracts covering career-ending injury. I'd paid into an insurance scheme for the entirety of my career, only to be advised that the policy could be contested, because of an operation I'd had on the knee eight years earlier. That's demoralizing when you are about to put your daughter into private school and you have no idea what your future income will be.

Players don't dwell on such realities when they are fit. The game seduces them, with its adrenaline rush. They are caught up in the daily dramas, consumed by the challenges. I'd hope that any player reading this would pause for thought. I'm one of the lucky ones, because I was shrewd enough to find the right people to help me with financial matters, but there are others at panic stations when they finish.

To all intents and purposes, I felt I was finished as an England player when I accepted an invitation to watch Wimbledon from the Royal Box on our first wedding anniversary, Saturday, 6 July, the day after England's official World Cup training squad had been confirmed. Usually I am on my best behaviour on such occasions, when there are games to play and appearances to maintain, but I thought 'Fuck it. I'm not going to the World Cup. We've got a driver. Let's rip into it.'

Traffic problems meant that lunch — lobster and strawberries and cream, washed down with champagne — was underway when Jo and I walked into the dining room. To my horror, the first person I saw was Eddie. Formalities dictated that we had to be seated immediately, but out of respect I first approached him and his wife, Hiroko, with the promise that we'd link up later.

It's a real privilege being in such a situation, but an athlete's animal cunning kicked in. I wasn't about to change my plans for the day, so had a quiet word with a couple of the waiters, and asked that they serve up strong gin and tonics in water glasses. They kept them coming, so by the time we went out to watch the tennis, I was on the way to being pleasantly pissed.

The Royal Box was a sports fan's fantasy scrapbook that day. It contains only seventy-four seats, but with my obvious exception they all were filled by legends. Joe Root, Eoin Morgan, Andrew Strauss, Jimmy Anderson and Stuart Broad represented the England cricket team. Europe's successful Ryder Cup team were alongside the track and field icons Mo Farah and Sebastian Coe. Eddie had Gareth Southgate for company.

He was just down the row from where Jo and I were seated, between the Wales captain Alun Wyn Jones and Maro Itoje. Sure enough, while we were watching Rafa Nadal complete a straight-sets win over Jo-Wilfried Tsonga, my mobile vibrated with the text message: 'Meeting. 3.45 on the balcony.' I slipped out a couple of minutes beforehand, threw down a bombproof cup of coffee, and hoped I'd make sense.

There was a different dynamic to our 45-minute conversation. Eddie obviously enquired about my knee, and I asked for his perception of the biggest challenges facing his team. He spoke about the importance of unity, the difficulties of team bonding, and the need to develop a support structure around his captain, Owen Farrell. I gave him my perspective on the human chemistry of the squad.

I got the impression he appreciated my honesty, which was laced with Dutch courage. Our respect was unspoken, but felt mutual. I was conscious about not promoting myself, falling into the trap of telling him everything I could do for him. We both knew he could have used me in any role he wished. He was the boss. There was no point in false bravado.

I told him: 'I'm not going to waste your time. I'm not going to bullshit you. I'm not going to come in and not be right. I'll text you when I'm ready. If that's a week into the World Cup it'll probably be too late but at least you'll know.' Eddie's reply had an air of inscrutability: 'You need to go and see a guy called Bill Knowles. If you need any help with that, let me know.'

It turned out Bill was a world-renowned American knee specialist, who had worked one on one with the likes of Tiger Woods and Andy Murray. As soon as Eddie returned to Centre Court, to watch Roger Federer, I was on the phone to Phil Pask, a brilliant physio and unbelievable guy who has worked with the Lions and England for approaching thirty years.

He gave me Bill's number, and within minutes, oblivious to the hum of the All England Club spread beneath me, I was explaining my circumstances to him. He called back, as promised, the next day, a Sunday. He would work with me for a fortnight, from the following Friday. Jo, Thea and I flew to Philadelphia on the Tuesday, and stayed close to his Reconditioning and Athletic Development facility in Wayne, to the north of the city.

It's the sort of antiseptic, anonymous suburb that hints at the vastness of the US. It's a cultural cliché: houses are huge and lawns are manicured. You can't walk anywhere. Jo took

Thea to the local playground: it was immaculate, with no litter or dog droppings in sight, but deserted. Where were the kids? To be honest, that wasn't my problem. Hope had come flooding back; my priority was to keep it in check.

I sent a cryptic text to Mike, my collaborator on this book, as we settled in: 'The winds were blowing warmer than I thought,' I typed. 'The story could take another turn, or I could still be fucked.' I'd talked things through with Jo, and come to the conclusion that, although we were blowing our holiday money, it was a win–win situation.

I had to give it a crack, beyond the fact that untimely injury to one of Eddie's three hookers could give me a way back into his squad. I was seeing the best specialist in the world, so it was time well invested, irrespective of whether I got back to playing professional rugby. This was a smart down payment on the family future. I was there on Eddie's recommendation, which showed willing from my point of view. It changed my environment, gave me a fresh stimulus and a different outlook.

Bill's fees for the fortnight were $15,000. Eddie came through for me when I sought support from Phil Riley, the England team doctor. He quietly ensured the RFU provided £10,000 towards my costs; Bill waived the outstanding balance because 'I don't need to make an extra couple of grand out of you.'

I quickly learned that such generosity summed up the spirit of the man. He was a hard taskmaster but a lovely guy, who saw the humanity in high performance. He seemed permanently amused by a previous client, the footballer Mario Balotelli, who had turned up in a previous facility, in Vermont, with only a small backpack, containing his mobile, a charger and a washbag. Bill kitted Balotelli out

in a local sports shop and took him for lunch in his favourite Italian deli.

In technical terms, Bill explains his philosophy like this:
'The best "brace" for any injury is neuromuscular control
and coordinated movement patterns. These can be developed early and often if encouraged to do so. Unfortunately I
find many rehabilitation protocols are more centred on what
an athlete can't do versus what an athlete can do. This is
often designed to protect the healing tissue, but I find the
limitations imparted compromise the short- and long-term
movement qualities of the athlete.'

In layman's terms, he basically told me my knee was
fucked. I needed to have an internal conversation between
my ankle and my arse. My knee was no more than a hinge; it
would be helped by strengthening my backside and quads,
and by developing a greater range of movement in my ankle.
My recovery would be dictated by the principle of what he
called purposeful walking.

It instantly changed how I thought about my injury. He
explained I was limping, because my natural instinct was to
offload the pressure on the knee, to reduce the discomfort. I
had to embrace the pain by pushing down through the floor
as I walked. It hurt like hell, but signalled that I was firing
the requisite muscles.

Obviously, when you walk stiffly, with a peg leg, because
it hurts, your knee doesn't bend as it should. Bill had me
lapping his open-plan gymnasium on a gymnastic sprung
floor. I pushed through my mid-foot, with the heel slightly
raised, so I had to flex the knee. I was making a conscious
movement, whereas in the previous ten years, when the
knee was deteriorating, I was unconsciously trying to protect myself.

I'd developed what he described as a flat tyre run, and lacked the necessary cadence. Bill mimicked the sound of a puncture – 'babum, babum, babum' – and ordered me to 'attack the ground'. I'll never look like a sprinter, but as soon as I pushed through the floor, with a stiff ankle, my running gait became normal.

I've got a natural aversion to the yeeh-ha, high-five, American form of motivation, but it worked. Bill is in his fifties, but fiercely competitive. We worked on what he termed athletic puzzles, playing handball on a trampoline and badminton on the sprung floor. He succeeded in getting me to move naturally, without thinking.

He took me back to my childhood, to relearn what he called micro-skills, like a forward roll, or mounting and dismounting a pommel horse. My body needed to be re-educated to come to terms with the knee twisting in such sequences. He had me free running, jumping over obstacles without worrying about the consequences. Gym rats might giggle at footage of me swinging a large hula-hoop on the end of a broomstick, but it did the job.

An injured athlete devours case studies. Bill delved into his background in skiing, to tell of an Olympic downhiller whose knee range increased by 10–15 per cent when he put her on a playground swing and she repeated the natural movement of pushing and pulling the legs to gather momentum. His feedback, constant, demanding and stimulating, was invaluable.

Rehab is a state of mind, and mine changed. Without discrediting or disrespecting the physios who have treated my knee with massage and constant draining of fluid, I found I didn't need traditional treatment. I just needed to train. The process is ultimately self-driven, but having someone pushing you individually through five hours of intense activity each day liberates the mind as much as the body.

Since coming back from the States, I do the majority of my fitness work in a two-metre-deep pool, at eight o'clock each morning. Running in water provides natural compression and enables your joints to flex. Bill also turned me into a human kayak; he provided me with a floatation bodysuit and an oar, with which I power down the lanes.

His expertise, and professional positivity, highlighted the shortcomings of British sport, which is still in its infancy when it comes to a creative approach to injury. With more money coming into sport, we are entering the era of the guru, who may be expensive but is worth every penny. Bill, for instance, works exclusively with Carson Wentz, the NFL quarterback; his fees are loose change, since the face of the Philadelphia Eagles franchise signed a four-year contract extension worth $144m.

I know of rugby players who are looking outside the sport, to train with sprint coaches. Word of mouth means certain physios are working on a freelance basis with individuals, independently from the club structure. A new type of adviser is driving career progression; ultimately it doesn't matter if they are not offering anything particularly different, because the placebo effect is beneficial.

It makes me wonder how much better I could have become had I met someone like Bill when I was twenty-five. I would have been at my peak, physically, and been ready to reach another level, mentally. As it was, his report, sent to Eddie and the RFU via Phil Pask, described me as a VA, veteran athlete, and a JCA, joint-compromised athlete.

I love America. Over here you just get called an old git.

Bill recommended that I be assigned to an alternative training programme, based on low-impact aerobic work, and aligned to technical drills. I didn't need the percussive nature of the daily grind on the training paddock. If required for a Saturday Test match, I needed only to participate in squad sessions on Tuesday and Friday.

It wasn't me telling Eddie I had to work smarter, rather than harder, but his silence was deafening.

He confirmed I wasn't in the final World Cup squad in a ten-second phone call on the morning of the announcement, 12 August. 'How are you getting on?' he asked. 'Keep working.' I'm a big boy, and realize you are quickly forgotten in this game, but at that moment I felt like a piece of meat, thrown in the bin because it was past its sell-by date.

I would have gone to Japan as kit man, if asked. I felt as if I'd been used, but I'll still have Eddie's back if anyone questions his credentials as a coach. It's my own fault that I missed out on World Cups in 2007 and 2015 because of disciplinary issues and unfair perceptions of unreliability. I regret, bitterly, that I didn't treat the 2011 World Cup with the seriousness it deserved.

An injury, the result of a tackle, and exacerbated on an artificial pitch the following week, wasn't the way I wanted to go out, but the international game waits for no one. It hurts when I hear people refer to me as an ex-England captain, but I can still go back to my roots in New Zealand if I need emotional rescue. Translated from Maori, *Kia kaha* means 'Stay strong'.

I have and I will.

# 2

# Mana

Who are we? Where do we come from? What qualities or faults pass down the generations? Why are we intrigued and inspired by people who exist in old photographs and fragments of memory? Apologies for the Meaning of Life stuff, but even a knockabout rugby player searches for answers to a deceptively complex set of questions.

We're all mongrels, really. My family is no different, though it is scarred by history and shaped by the quiet heroism that flourished in two world wars. I'm hugely proud of my heritage, which features the terror of Nazi Germany, the tolerance of New Zealand and England's tradition of offering refuge to waifs and strays.

The Schwarzschild family first settled in Frankfurt in the sixteenth century. Some 300 years later it was headed up by Moses, a wealthy Jewish businessman who, together with his wife, Henrietta, brought up his children to be open-minded, libertarian thinkers. My great-grandfather Alfred, born in 1874, was the second of their six sons, one of whom died in infancy. He grew up to be a noted artist.

His elder brother, Karl, became a globally renowned physicist and astronomer, who helped Albert Einstein define his theory of relativity while serving as a lieutenant in the German artillery on the Russian front, just before his death from a rare skin disease called pemphigus, in May 1916. They even managed to exchange scholarly letters as the carnage unfolded around him.

Karl wrote: 'As you see, the war treated me kindly enough, in spite of the heavy gunfire, to allow me to get away from it all and take this walk in the land of your ideas.' Einstein replied: 'I have read your paper with the utmost interest. I had not expected that one could formulate the exact solution of the problem in such a simple way. I liked very much your mathematical treatment of the subject.'

That is now known in scientific circles as the Schwarzschild Metric. A childhood prodigy who had written two papers on celestial mechanics before his sixteenth birthday, Karl also made pioneering studies of black holes, electromagnetic fields, the physics of photography and Halley's Comet. An asteroid and a crater on the dark side of the Moon are named after him.

Alfred's art was based upon his study of anatomy. His portraits were scientifically precise, beautifully observed and hugely popular, until the Nazis prevented the sale of his work due to his Jewish heritage. Ironically, he had been awarded the Iron Cross in the First World War, when, as an observer in the German Flying Corps, he held a heavy camera over the side of the aircraft to photograph battlefield terrain before sketching enemy positions.

He married Theodora Lutner in 1924 and had three daughters, Luise, Bettina and Theodora, my grandmother. He twice fled to England from Munich to avoid persecution, in 1936 and 1937. His bank account was seized and stripped before his wife hid their remaining possessions, which were never recovered. She escaped to London in 1938 with her children on a series of dangerous rail journeys. Other Jewish families were forcibly removed from the train in Aachen, and never seen again.

My maternal great-great-grandfather, Herman Lutner, was transported to Dachau and executed in 1941 as a political prisoner. He was a Catholic, not a Jew, but loathed the Nazis and said so very publicly. Alfred fled after being openly defiant towards Hitler, who marched through the hotel where he was having a drink with a friend. His companion, like everyone else, rose, saluted and fawned over the dictator. Alfred sat still, arms folded, and refused to recognize his presence.

Alfred's most treasured possession was a silver tin in which he kept drawing materials. He was briefly interned on the Isle of Man, where he was wrongly accused of spying by an over-zealous policeman who discovered him sketching in the sand dunes. His asthma worsened in the smog of post-war London, and he died of a heart-related problem in 1948.

A small number of his paintings survive, and are hung in galleries in Europe and the Middle East. Others exist only in faded photographs. Postcard-sized sketches and doodles have also been collated, and give a greater indication of family life. They capture my grandmother as a baby, as a young girl singing with her mother beside a piano, and as a teenager tending an allotment while an evacuee in wartime England.

Like most people I'm fascinated by my forebears. So, however far-fetched it seems, it's natural to seek clues to my character from the family tree. I'm no one's idea of a genius, but when I look back I detect the virtues of a successful sportsman, even if circumstances are completely different. My ancestors were disciplined, clear thinkers. They took courageous decisions under immense stress. They were unafraid to be themselves.

My parents developed my work ethic, sense of adventure and loyalty to those around me. My mum, Caroline, was the daughter of Theodora Schwarzschild and Robin Straker, who emigrated to New Zealand when she was ten. They relished the simplicity of rural life, the tightness of small communities and the possibilities of a young country, on the other side of the world. Hard work was a given; the land bred a certain sense of perspective.

My dad, Guy Hartley, is a wiry so-and-so, who would be described in England as a carpenter. The Kiwi version of the job is a bit broader; he can build houses from the foundations up, pouring concrete, lugging bricks and fashioning timber roof joints. I've always carried a photo of him in my wallet; he's my hero, an amazing man. He's been my motivation: all I've ever wanted to do is make him proud.

His parents, originally from Wellington, bought some land in a settlement named Hamurana, near Lake Rotorua, when he was sixteen. They rented Dad a small cottage, attached to a woolshed, when he married Mum, and sold them a two-acre block of the farm when they started a family. Money was tight but my brothers, Blair and Alex, and I played barefoot on gravel roads, without a care.

The lake was 200 metres from our front gate. It was fed by the deepest freshwater spring on the North Island. The water was unbelievably clear; we kayaked and fished with childish clumsiness for brown and rainbow trout, which swam in and out of the reed beds. In summer we would walk a mile to buy ice lollies at the local shop.

Our province, Bay of Plenty, was aptly named by Captain James Cook in 1769. You don't need money to enjoy the redwood forests, thermal pools, beaches and mountains. Whenever I go back to Hamurana, I'm reminded of the Maori concept of Tūrangawaewae, which is literally translated as 'a place to stand'.

I don't care if this sounds naïve, or over-sentimental, but it is a place to which I feel powerfully connected. I joke with my Maori mates that it's my place in the world. It has a distinctive smell of home. I feel emotional, like a soldier returning from combat. I revisit the streams we used to mess about in, and the paddocks where I used to practise my throwing and kicking with a Gilbert rugby ball Dad bought during the 1995 World Cup.

He didn't go shopping very often, but when he did he went big. We never got PlayStations; we were given practical presents, like a hiking kit, goggles, snorkels or flippers. On that particular trip, he bought Blair a basketball, Alex a football and me a pale-blue and green rugby ball, produced for the tournament. It started an obsession.

It went everywhere with me. I'd practise passing with my mates as we waited for the bus, and fantasize about being Jonah Lomu in the playground. When I heard that Rob Powley, the art teacher who coached the middle school's rugby team, was going to be at a barbeque, I'd rampage around the adjoining paddock, convinced he would be impressed by my ball-handling skills.

I kicked that ball until it went smooth and used a mini-rugby ball in pickup games of touch rugby before my grandparents bought me a black and white All Blacks ball for my birthday. On the rare occasions that ball didn't travel with me to school, we would roll up a hoodie in knots to play during morning break.

It's strange, but I don't get the same sense of self in my parents' new 200-acre farm. That's not to say it doesn't provide a release. I spent too much of my time in three-piece suits as England captain; when I go back to see my mum and dad I live in a bush shirt, rugby shorts and gumboots.

We stay in a little cabin, feed the livestock and drive around in a windowless Land Rover. It's just good fun: Thea and Jo love it.

The culture is changing a little, but our generation had a natural affinity with the land. We had tasks to fulfil, and I would often help Dad on the smallholding. I still visualize him in his flannel shirt, dusty from the sawmill at which he worked. He still calls me a 'mucker'. As he explained to me: 'When you've got a kid tagging along what does he do? He picks shit up and mucks in, doesn't he?'

Graham Henry and Richie McCaw have both made the point that the responsibilities and jobs kids have in rural New Zealand form the bedrock of All Black culture. Talent is only one part of the equation; the best players develop a natural grit, a homespun sort of humility, and instinctively never get ahead of themselves. They understand who they are playing for, and why.

The country is raw, but authentic. Kiwis are not materialistic. They don't want a flash SUV, a Chelsea tractor. They prefer a truck because you can put the kids in the back, along with the fishing kit and everything else that assists an outdoor lifestyle. Some of my earliest memories involve climbing in the back of my grandad's battered Land Rover and feeding silage to the cattle.

We did all sorts of good stuff, which would horrify modern health and safety jobsworths. The teachers didn't need to fill in a risk assessment form for our school outings; we hiked for hours and slept under the stars, or in rudimentary log cabins. It might have been politically incorrect, but it was wonderfully innocent.

Dad, and some of the other parents, used to help out. He specialized in setting up zip-wires into local creeks. Standing in the water in a black singlet and shorts, to help us land safely, he had an instinct for the kids who were afraid of getting wet. All it took was a quick downward pull on the wire and they were given a good dunking. Everyone laughed and no one, least of all the victim, was offended.

He's sixty-two now, and suggests he is 'ageing like the finest Cheddar'. He played rugby until he concentrated on his college studies from the age of eighteen, and renewed his interest when he got married. He was a flanker, attracted to the social side of a game that acted as a release for local farmers and sheep station workers. There wasn't a lot left in the kitty after he'd paid for his petrol and a post-match bottle of beer.

He was there for me when I needed him, but he's not the type of parent to live vicariously through the sporting success of his kids. He hates the modern culture of fathers debriefing their sons after games: 'It doesn't matter whether it is positive or negative. It's happened. It's history. There's no bloody point talking about any of it.'

He has a sixth sense about whether or not I'm happy with my performance, which he tends to keep to himself. His critique of my schoolboy efforts was never personal; he offered judgement on the overall standard of the match. Basically, that meant either 'good game' or 'shit game'. Even today, he has to be a bit pissed to talk rugby.

He supports the All Blacks, though he at least admits to split loyalties when I play against them. He tends to take things in his stride. When I was made England captain against South Africa in 2012, he was approached for comment by a breathless reporter from the *Rotorua Review*. 'That's the first I've heard about it,' he told him. 'I've just got in from work. I'm not into this computer shit, and I don't have a cellphone.' Great story, apart from one fact: he had a mobile, but it had been switched off . . .

There's a bit bubbling under the surface. While we were putting this book together I overheard a conversation about what my England career meant to him. 'It's almost beyond profound,' he said. 'I've often been asked that, and told "Oh, you must be so proud." You sort of go "Well, yeah . . ." I can't find the right words to say how much it means, not just to me, but to everyone. It has dawned on me over the last twelve months or so how much people here in Britain respect the young fella. It's amazing. I suppose the quick answer to the question is "It's epic."'

Wow.

Dad gets a lot of good-humoured stick about my career from friends and family, because in such a distant country, with a small population, there are only a couple of degrees of separation between people. Kiwis respect anyone who puts them on the map, however remotely. The local media always referred to me as a 'New Zealand-born' England player, just as they would to someone who has achieved similar status in the NFL or Hollywood.

They are not abashed by aspiration and admire accomplishment. They might want you face-planted into the turf at Eden Park by a marauding All Black forward, but you can still be celebrated as a local boy made good, because of rugby's social status. The game is embedded in the national psyche, though my dad would argue that England football fans are more passionate about their sport.

I'm not sure I agree with him. The key to that emotional link, I've always felt, is the easy access people have to their heroes. All Blacks are not distant figures, although they are associated with myths and legends. They play for their local clubs in small towns, and represent their provinces with pride and ferocity.

An international is a communal experience. The dad gets his mates and the extended family around to watch at home with a few beers, or goes to the clubhouse, where the kids can run free and kick a ball around the paddock. They see their uncles and aunties hooting 'n' hollering when tries are scored, and are drawn in by the passion for winning. A successful team gets kids on board, whether they are following Tottenham Hotspur or Taranaki, Chelsea or Canterbury.

We went through a stage of my international career when my dad's mates were running around in England kits, or spare training gear. Some of the shirts ended up in local clubhouses, but many have been through the wash more than a few times. I call him a weka, after a native New Zealand bird that's also known as a Maori hen. Like magpies, they are notorious for pinching shiny objects, such as spoons or tinfoil, from campsites.

I have a pretty strong English accent, but when I return I pick up a Kiwi twang. The words spill out very quickly, so they form a verbal traffic jam. In terms of acceptance, I will never be seen as one of their own by the All Blacks, who form a very exclusive club. It wasn't as if I was an established player, a mercenary who left New Zealand to seek international rugby elsewhere; I went to England at sixteen to get away from school and experience something different.

The English rugby system moulded me, and I'm proud of how I've gone about it. The southern hemisphere is such a breeding ground for young players that it is surprising more haven't followed my lead, or that of Kelly Haimona, the Italy fly half who first played against me, for Kahukura, in the under-11s.

I played my first organized game of barefoot rugby at the age of nine. The score is lost in the mists of time, but I remember being frozen to the bone. The only way to keep warm was to get hold of the ball, and barrel forward, towards the opposition. Ngongotaha, my club, had heaps of 'cuzzy boys', local slang for Maori lads. Only three players, Shane McGregor, Jason Hahn and myself, were white.

Half of the team consisted of little fat fellas (I preferred to think of myself as big, thanks to Mum's baking) and the other half were skinny and rangy. We were coached by our fathers; everyone chipped in when they could, but training was haphazard because the farm always took precedence, and some of the lads couldn't afford subs. After a season I moved on to the Kahukura club.

It was there I came into contact with one of those extraordinary 'ordinary' people who have the power to shape lives. Jerry Cowley was originally a basketball coach, who played for New Zealand's national team, the Tall Blacks. He was fiercely professional and highly principled, and insisted that, at the age of eleven, we signed a contract, committing ourselves to his team.

He typified the cultural melting pot that makes a modern Kiwi. He was descended from a merchant from the Isle of Man, who married into a Samoan family. His father, a teacher named Oliva, wanted a better life for his ten children, so left on the banana boat *Tofua* for the North Island, where he found a job in a mill town, Tokoroa.

Times were hard. Talaia, his wife, fed the family on fish heads because they were given away at the market. They washed in a copper pot and shared school shoes. What little money they could spare was sent back to the extended family in Samoa. Forced to leave home, so his parents could house newly arrived relatives, Jerry became self-sufficient, and saw sport and education as his means of advancement.

His sport, which included representative rugby, was funded by donations from the local community. He idolized Australia's cricket captain Steve Waugh for his competitiveness, leadership and self-discipline. His accountancy degree was subsidized by after-hours cleaning jobs, paper rounds and a range of menial tasks.

His coaching reflected his character. He was hard as nails, but he cared. He was charismatic, and had great generosity of spirit. He often shared his father's philosophy of life, which he summed up with the saying 'If you give your bread to a stranger, you'll not feel hungry.' More than 3,000 people attended his funeral when he died suddenly, from a heart attack, in 2004.

I was settling in in England at the time, but I'm still in touch with his children. Garrick, his elder son, played rugby for Samoa and the Exeter Chiefs. Ritchie is a doctor and their sister, Sarah, an outstanding netball player, represented New Zealand in the heptathlon in two Commonwealth Games and the 2012 Olympics.

Jerry set me up for the leap into high-school rugby, which was another level entirely. I was a loosehead prop, with no ambitions to make it professionally, but found I loved the incendiary atmosphere of local matches, where the Polynesians got stuck in, verbally and physically, on and off the field. Their culture is spiritually sensitive, but it can be harsh.

You'd hear a shrill voice yelling 'Fucking smash 'em', look around, and notice a mate's mum in full cry on the touchline. Aunties would wander out of the crowd and biff someone with an umbrella if they saw skulduggery in the lineout or scrum. Since our teenage hormones were kicking in, there was always a Mexican standoff or two, usually preceded by a broken-voiced 'Come on then, come on, what you going to do about it?'

I was taught, as a child, never to back down. I had to stand up for myself, and look after my mates. There was a lot of bluff, and something known as 'staunch'. My mum hates the arrogance, bravado and violence associated with the word. It describes a form of intimidation, a sort of hard-man swagger. I became streetwise, worldly enough to have my wits about me.

Rotorua is Maori heartland, and we all understood the significance of *Mana*. This is a powerful, mystical force, which comes from within people, places and even inanimate objects. It symbolizes authority, influence, pride and prestige. Those who possess it are able to perform to their best in any given situation.

The haka might have become part of modern sporting showbiz, but it has sacred intent. It teaches you, as a young man, to stand up to your foes. You look them in the eye and feel the weight of the personal challenge. Never smirk, avert your gaze or turn away, even for a split-second. If you demonstrate weakness by doing so you will be hunted down.

We were taught the school haka from the age of twelve, at Rotorua Boys High School. It didn't matter if you were white, or one of the Chinese exchange students we somehow attracted. You had no option but to learn to harness Mana, and were expected to beat your chest until it was raw. That might sound weird, in cold print, but in the heat of the moment it made you incredibly proud.

I played at least a year up, and would practise the haka in the Marae, a communal meeting place where Maori culture is celebrated. This held family social occasions and religious ceremonies, like tangihanga, in which the group says farewell to the dead. We would do the haka to honour our parents, who watched us in rugby tournaments.

School sport was incredibly competitive, and designed to form the tightest of bonds between teammates. It was the antithesis of the English version, with its wimpy tradition of offering three cheers ('Hip, hip hooray and one for luck') to the opposition. Inter-house competition, which ranged from rugby to public debate, was fierce. When we played a local rival like Western Heights, the school that produced the All Black captain Wayne Shelford, the adrenaline was off the scale.

Our coaches commanded such respect that, to this day, I only refer to one of them as Mr Callaghan. I wasn't worthy of knowing his Christian name. Craig Burrell, who worked with him on the under-15s, was more recognizable, since he had played as flanker for Bay of Plenty in forty-four games between 1983 and 1986. That qualified him as minor royalty.

It is a relatively small province, which consistently punches above its weight in talent discovery and development. It has produced such All Black legends as Grant Batty, the winger who set the tone of the seventies, and current stalwarts like Brodie Retallick and Sam Cane, the vice-captain who fractured his neck in a collision with Springboks loose forward Francois Louw in October 2018.

I played in the same Rotorua Boys High team as Liam Messam, the All Black flanker. We called ourselves Raukura, in deference to the Maori spelling of the name. Liam's brother Sam, a footballer, is one of four former pupils who appeared in the Beijing Olympics. The others were the kayaker Mike Walker, shooter Robbie Eastham and cyclist Sam Bewley, who won bronze medals in 2008 and 2012.

It might not be in the most salubrious setting – someone once counted fourteen car yards in three adjoining blocks – but it is an inspirational place. Mottos in Latin and Maori ('To the stars through hard work' and 'Reach for the mountains') dominate the entrance. It has 950 boys, 60 per cent of whom are Maori. Every pupil spends at least two hours a week studying leadership.

That reflects the influence of Chris Grinter, the school's headmaster since 1991. He was Jonah Lomu's first coach at Wesley College in Auckland, and delivered a eulogy at his funeral, in which he described him as 'a troubled young man' whose 'positive attitude and high expectations of himself' enabled him 'to turn weaknesses and challenges into incredible strength'.

He coached us to one of Rotorua Boys High's four national championships in 2002, when we scored 137 tries in twenty-one matches. It was hard, relentless rugby, against some huge island boys, played with a professional intensity that mirrored a jock culture which owed more to the North American college system than a high school at the end of the world.

To have the headmaster as your head rugby coach was the bollocks. First XV boys were treated as big fish in the tiniest of ponds. We could pretty much do as we pleased. Lessons didn't matter. As long as we committed to pushing ourselves to the limit in our daily training sessions, no one cared if we were caught on manoeuvres outside the gates during school time.

It was all a bit daft. We offered educational opportunities for Fijian and Tongan lads, monsters who would be put up in the school boarding house. It is unlikely they were there in a spirit of amateurism. Our games were shown on national

TV. We had all the benefits of stardom, without the harsher insecurities of playing rugby for a living.

Don't get me wrong. It is a great school, a brilliant advertisement for state education. It incorporates a sports academy for twenty boys, and has a state-of-the-art golf facility, scavenged from a failed local business venture. Chris wasn't best pleased when I became one of the few boys to reject my final year of high-school education, but allowed me to visit during the 2011 World Cup.

It proved to be a productive scouting trip. I recruited Teimana Harrison, the first XV captain at the time, for Northampton Saints, who appointed him and Alex Waller as co-captains for the 2019–20 season when I stepped away from the role. I'm proud of what he has achieved in his seven years at the club. He's a real warrior, good enough to add to the five caps he won in England's back row in 2016.

He's another successful exile who proves that the wheel keeps turning . . .

Kiwis tend to be habitual travellers, with an ingrained sense of adventure. Blair, my elder brother, is back in Rotorua after working around the world. He lived with me in Northampton and played rugby league for the Casuals, who were rebranded as the rather more macho Demons while he was assisting the community department at the Saints.

Blair looked like Tom Hanks in the film *Castaway* when I picked him up from Heathrow. He had travelled through America before becoming a logger in Alaska, where he lived in a shack with husky breeders. There was no electricity or running water; he washed in a lake after spending his days stripping the bark off logs with a double-edged machete. He met his partner, had a daughter, and then headed to Western

Australia, where he worked three-week shifts in an iron ore mine in the outback.

He says he gets bored easily, so he changes everything in roughly three-year cycles. He's now back after travelling the world, and his two children attend the school I once attended. Dad helped him renovate an old schoolhouse, which he bought from a local farmer and transported on the back of a flatbed lorry. When it arrived it still had long blackboards attached to the walls.

Talk about a small world. My best mate, Paul Tupai, was taught in that primary-school building, which was originally erected in the tiny village of Mamaku in 1895. His mum, Mary, still lives in the area, and often visits my parents. He claims to be forty-four, but has had a hard rugby life and looks as if he was in the school's initial intake.

His disciplinary record, for the Bay of Plenty, Northampton and Bedford, makes me look an angel. He has a successful building company and is still affiliated with Bedford, having only retired in the summer of 2018. His son Connor is a young professional who made his senior debut for the Saints against the British Army in the Mobbs Memorial Match in 2019.

I have a mentoring role with him and his sister, Leah, because in terms of age I am halfway between them and Paul and his wife, Nadine. There are no secrets around the family dining table. We've debriefed playing contracts, analysed teams and matches on it. Paul, or Toops as he is universally known, has also dispensed disciplinary advice along the way. If he says you're looking at three months, bare minimum, for a particular offence, you'd better start crafting your defence.

I have a small social circle, by design, and I'm grateful for the life I've been able to carve out for myself in England. I'm not sure I could get my head around Thea leaving home, to travel across the world to work, at the age of sixteen, but I left New Zealand, only two days after playing in torrential rain in that national high-school championship match at Eden Park, with barely a backward glance.

I was ready to attack the world.

# 3

# The Lost Boys

Ah, bless. The poor lambs don't know what's about to hit them. Modern academy players are ripped physically, but unprepared mentally for the wicked wolves of the professional game. Everything possible is done to protect them, but one day they are going to have to step out into the deep, dark forest of men's rugby. Most of them will be eaten alive.

They go into the academy straight from school. Nutritionally balanced meals are cooked for them. They generally don't have to bother about mixing the protein shakes that have replaced a pint or three of Dogbolter. They're good kids, but poor communicators. Somewhere, probably between levels on *Call of Duty*, they lost the ability to relate to people around them.

They lack initiative, that inherent ability to think on their feet. I see it most days at my club, when the old lags turn up for a gnarly weights session in a gym that smells of stale sweat and the by-products of last night's curry. The academy lads are clustered at one end near the noticeboard, scratching their nuts, waiting to be told what to do, and when to do it.

Their guidance comes from whiteboards, in the lecture theatre. My rite of passage was conducted on the hoof in Los Angeles international airport. I was sixteen, alone and straight off the flight from Auckland. Before I climbed on that Jumbo, I had only been on two planes in my life, servicing school trips to Wellington and Christchurch.

I collected my bags, and, in my confusion, needed to check in for the connecting flight to London. There was no transit lounge, no welcoming committee of smiling airline employees, directing me to the appropriate desk or boarding gate. At one point I found myself out on the street, looking up at the 32-foot-high 'LAX' sign above the terminal entrance.

I saw more cars and taxis in five minutes than I had in the previous five weeks at home, and did what came naturally. I stopped a stranger and asked for help. It arrived, though my accent evidently took some unscrambling; it's amazing what a simple question and human kindness can do. I know I'll sound like a dinosaur here, but today's kid would probably text his mum, or thrash blindly around on Google Maps.

Speak to a fellow human being? I don't think so.

There's a lot of guff spoken about the great fellowship of rugby, mostly by those who played around the time of the Boer War, but all sports, at all levels, are about people. It takes all sorts, and you learn to get along with most of them. I was lucky to have four terrific individuals to help me when I turned up in England.

My parents paid for the flights, but I was determined to look after myself. I was there of my own volition; in any case they couldn't afford to underwrite the year-long exchange programme that many Kiwi kids experience, which tends to revolve around drinking snakebite in Walkabout bars and copping off on Contiki tours around Europe. I was taken in by my aunt and uncle, Christine and Phil Straker, in East Sussex.

They're warm, generous and talented people, who run the world's leading saxophone supply company from a 5,000-square-foot showroom in Crowborough, just south of Royal

Tunbridge Wells. Phil, who has played in a succession of bands over thirty years, suggested I attend the local school, Beacon Community College, with my cousins Holly and Jamie, who were a year above and below me respectively. He's a laidback bloke, a casual sports fan, but sealed the deal by revealing that it had a rugby academy. That sounded an ideal progression from Rotorua Boys High, which would repeat its national championship win in 2003 without me.

Academy training was written into my timetable for the first day, when reality hit me with the force of a blindside punch. I'd turned up with a treasured possession, a well-worn pair of rugby boots, to find about seven kids assembled on a patch of grass with a scrum machine in the corner. The coach asked me what position I played – 'prop' – and wondered whether I'd fancy filling in as a lock forward.

It was a great school, academically forward-thinking, and it has subsequently pioneered the development of a successful curling programme, but it wasn't what I was expecting. I'd come from a professional environment where players were climbing over each other to get into the first fifteen. We had four senior teams, and three under-15 teams. It was dog-eat-dog, do-or-die stuff. Getting your first-team tracksuit was a big deal, a symbol of real achievement.

Beacon managed to field a team, most weeks, but I knew my most constructive outlet was the gym, which had a good range of weight machines. I did basic SAQ (Speed, Agility and Quickness) training on the school field, mainly using speed ladders to improve my footwork. It was supposed to be a key component of my development, enabling me to accelerate, decelerate, stabilize and quickly change direction without losing power. It didn't quite work like that, but at least I gave it a go.

I was driven to make the most of any opportunity. I'd pinch a rugby ball, steal into the sports hall, and practise throwing it into a basketball net. I did the same at my aunt's house, aiming at chalk targets on a nearby wall. Chris Grinter, the Rotorua Boys High principal who once urged me to do just that because he sensed I was a hooker in the making, was with me in spirit.

Thankfully, within four days my uncle had introduced me to Dave Pass, who volunteered at the school but was better known as the driving force of the local rugby club, where his son Jon, whom I had played against on a tour of New Zealand, was youth team captain. I paid my subs, got my shorts and socks, and kicked on. As I did so, I was drawn into another tightly knit family.

Crowborough RFC is a proper club, the sort of institution which does so much unheralded work at grassroots level. They run mini-rugby for kids aged between five and eleven, field six age group teams, a vets XV and three senior sides. There's a thriving women's programme, and touch rugby for all ages. I wasn't registered, but before I knew it Dave had got me a trial for the Sussex county team.

They liked what they saw, and I went through the divisional system in London and the South-East. By the end of the season I had made the England under-18 squad. Like Chris, Dave thought I was a natural hooker, though he admitted he winced at the way I barrelled, head first, into contact. He drove Jon and me around the country and simply made things happen.

The best lads from school played for Crowborough. I tried to share my street wisdom by demonstrating the effectiveness of a well-timed sledge; it's remarkable how many fly halves drop a high ball when you whisper sweet nothings in their ear. In return I was introduced to the English tradition of necking a couple of jugs of beer in the changing rooms, immediately after a match.

I hope I'm not throwing anyone under a bus here, but the jugs were supplied by the dads who followed the team. We could drive aged fifteen at home, and drank our fair share in American-style house parties that had no formal invitations, but came up against strict ID rules if we went out on the town. I was accustomed to bars being off limits, so when the team adjourned to the pub I loved it.

I had not long flown home after the end of the school year, during which my academic efforts were minimal, to say the least, when my uncle called. A letter embossed with the RFU logo had arrived, addressed to me, and he sought permission to open it. I was one of thirty-six players invited to an England under-19 training camp in South Africa in July 2003.

The initiative represented a leap of faith by the RFU. It was the first such overseas camp they had organized and Tosh Askew, the coach, was bullish about its ability to produce senior players for the 2007 and 2011 World Cups. As so often in elite development, many in that group meandered into obscurity. Some, like the squad's golden boy, Oli Morgan, a full back from Millfield School who had two games for England in 2007 while playing for Gloucester, found their ceiling.

Others soared. Matthew Tait made his senior international debut at nineteen, was the youngest member of the 2007 World Cup squad, and played thirty-five Tests between 2005 and 2010. Tom Croft went on two Lions tours and made forty appearances for England before he retired due to neck problems. Davey Wilson, the Bath and Newcastle tighthead prop, won the last of his forty-four caps for England against Uruguay in the 2015 World Cup.

We weren't to know it at the time, but he would feature in the incident that caused that fateful knee injury, which prevented me playing in the 2019 version in Japan. It was my 250th home game for Northampton, and he attempted to tackle me a couple of metres out from the Newcastle line. I managed to evade him, but he grabbed my ankle as I was on my feet, wrestling with someone.

I could feel my knee twisting, shouted 'Fuck, Davey, let me go', and, in the maelstrom, the brotherhood of the front row manifested itself. He recognized the alarm in my voice, ignored the fact he could have given away a try, and did what I asked. I was subbed off, barely trained the following week, and exacerbated the damage by playing on the artificial pitch at Worcester, despite my knee ballooning up.

That typifies the way careers are crafted by irony, circumstance and coincidence. Worcester had given me my break when I decided to return to take up that opportunity with the England under-19s. I didn't want to be a financial burden on my folks, needed to make a living, however haphazard, and so asked their assistant academy manager at the time, Graham Smith, if they'd have me.

He'd coached me with the England under-18s, didn't have the budget to offer an immediate contract, but promised to 'sort something out'. He was as good as his word; he organized a couple of hundred quid a month in expenses, and put me in student accommodation while I sorted myself out. I had become a member of the Lost Boys.

Worcester had a deserved reputation for finding diamonds in the dirt. They were national under-19 champions, yet had an underdog's ferocity. I've come to know Graham as a lovely guy; he helped England win the women's World Cup in 2014 and now combines the role of head coach of

Stoke-on-Trent RUFC with being technical director of CN Poblenou in Barcelona. But, at the time, he was as miserable as sin, a hard man the boys feared.

Appropriately enough, he was brought up in the butchery trade. His tales were bloody and brutal. According to him, if you weren't quick enough with your knife on the production line, the guy next to you would slice you across the arm and you'd be gone. I got an inkling of his approach when he called the front-row group together and ordered us to form a semi-circle.

A couple of the regulars knew what was coming, but didn't let on. Graham kicked every one of us in the shin, hard, to illustrate his lecture on the importance of wearing shin pads. By the time I realized they weren't needed, after a couple of games that resembled hand-to-hand combat, I had literally been blooded.

Graham was preparing us for the harshness of the pro game, in a coaching group that also included Gary Meakin, Andrew Stanley and Nigel 'Ollie' Redman, the former Bath and British Lions lock forward who is now Head of Performance Team Development for British Swimming.

They knew the importance of character and understood the value of intimidation. This wasn't the posh version of the game, played on pristine private-school pitches, or in the occasional Premiership palace. This was rugby in the raw, spit and sawdust. My first academy session ended in a fight with the first-team players, whose coaches had ordered us across to maul against them.

Those old boys, seemingly ancient since they were around thirty, waded in, throwing punches. The Lost Boys stuck together, and gave as good as they got. We looked pretty rag-arse, because the academy didn't extend to training kit. We wore odd socks, and Nike England age group training gear, which pissed the senior players off no end, because they thought it flash and disrespectful.

They were good, journeyman players, frustrated because they had never made it at the highest level. We were the young spunkers, cannon fodder, punchbags basically. We'd train with them twice a week and it always ended in a brawl, after either a lineout or a maul. Black eyes and bloody noses were badges of honour.

The philosophy of personal development has changed irrevocably since then. Coaches no longer explore a young player's breaking point from day one. Our Academy coaches glorified and institutionalized our defiance. They knew meekness would be career suicide. They didn't polish the diamond, but roughened the edges.

Technical development, fine-tuning, came later. Although you must practise the basics, like passing, throwing and tackling, rugby isn't a closed skill, learned solely by repetition. Playing matches is the greatest form of education, because it stimulates intuition, improves game understanding. The older I've got, the more sensitive I've become to reading play, and being in the right position on the field. The trade-off for that heightened awareness is, of course, increasing physical fallibility.

As kids, we needed to be tough, ready for anything. We were pushed through surrogate National Service by Phil Taylor, a former Army PTI who, in his more merciful moods, had us in from 5.30am lifting weights. He used to watch us on CCTV. If we slacked off for a moment, slapping a mate on the back or acting the fool, he'd storm in, blow a whistle, and tell us to 'Fuck off out of my gym.'

That was extremely bad news, since it meant we had to endure the torture known as the farmer's walk. The site has since been developed, but at the time we had to trudge towards the bridge that led to an adjoining farm, across the training fields, carrying dumbbells weighing anything between 20 and 40 kilograms in each hand. It was heinous.

Our arms ached, but we were then ordered to push cars around the pitches. On one occasion, in pouring rain, I heard someone shout 'Stop' and pulled the handbrake up. Richard Blaze, who has since developed into one of England's best young coaches, was oblivious, carried on and put his arm through the back window. There was blood everywhere; he must have looked some sight in A&E.

Reverse psychology almost justified such punishment. The shittier it became, the more we relished our resilience. We used to do tractor tyre carries in groups of two or three along the canal. They rubbed our shoulders red raw. The leopard crawl, a military speciality undertaken every Tuesday night, was even worse.

It involved keeping the body as close to the ground as possible, and pushing forward using elbows and knees, along the length of the pitch. We should have paid more attention to the senior players, who turned up in wet-weather trousers. They knew the grit in the ground would flay our skin; since we were wearing shorts we ended up with burns on the inside of the knee, which would weep agonizingly at night. When Richard and I turned up at that South African camp, guys from other clubs were incredulous.

I'm not too bad at coping with pain. Growing up in rural New Zealand, falling out of trees, bred a bit of hardiness. All sport, including rugby and hockey, played on an AstroTurf pitch, was barefooted for my first couple of years in school.

It became second nature, so that I would often forget my shoes, and be forced to walk home without them.

Army types will tell you there is method in their madness. The leopard crawl is essential in combat, since it creates the smallest possible silhouette. It develops hand–eye co-ordination, and stimulates the central nervous system, by instinctively forcing the brain and muscles to work together. There's some logic to that, but they lose me when they extend the argument, to suggest that it decreases stress. Really?

It does create strong people, good sorts who can see through selfishness and superficiality. We found out who's who and what's what in the stretcher carries, another ordeal conducted along the Grand Union towpath. We'd work in teams of six, trying to be cute by carrying the lightest at speed. Suffice to say I never got a free ride. No one skived, because we recognized our responsibility to our mates.

I now know that, when my legs are heavy and my lungs are burning, I have experienced worse. I understand why, in those moments of unconscious thought that define professional sport, I willingly put my body on the line. Not all of the Lost Boys had stellar careers, but we had something more valuable, that glance of recognition that signals mutual trust, respect and admiration.

They will, of course, kill me for such sentimentality.

We were feral kids, who looked after ourselves and were consciously cruel to outsiders. Any new lad who turned up in the Worcester Academy was fair game in a dressing room divided into three sections. The regulars had their own seats, while the players who trained part time while pursuing higher education had their own section.

In this rugby caste system, trialists were fair game. Any one of those lads who inadvertently left his bag on someone's pre-assigned seat, in order to attend an introductory meeting with the coaches, would return to find it thrown across the corridor. He'd be screamed at, and told to change near the toilets.

Many fell victim to a nasty game we called piano fingers. It preyed on the human desire to be liked, and involved a triallist being 'befriended' by one of the lads on his first day. He would give him the lowdown on prospective teammates, and slyly share fictitious secrets. Then, when he was lulled into a false sense of security, the newbie would be advised to ask an established player how his mum's piano lessons were going.

The pantomime that unfolded terrified the uninitiated. The lad being addressed would yell 'What did you say?' and march forward menacingly. Someone would scream in mock horror and hiss 'His mum lost her hands in a car crash.' Richard Blaze was the star turn; he would break down in mock tears, and flee the room in apparent distress. A few others would stalk the new boy, promising retribution for his supposed callousness.

I know of only one triallist who squared up to those coming towards him. Most kids crumbled; those who ran out of the room, babbling apologies, were done, chewed up and spat out. The 'Aagh, fooled you' ritual when the trick was revealed was usually too late. Human nature is strange, though: survivors of the initiation ceremony couldn't wait to be involved in the next one.

I appreciate that, assessed in isolation and out of context, such behaviour looks awful. But dressing rooms are distinctively harsh places. Solidarity is formed in strange ways, by good people. Mark Hopley, one of the Lost Boys, is a hugely respected coach, who runs Northampton's

Academy in a progressive, enlightened manner. Alex Rae is Bedford's player-coach, after a good career with Saints, Saracens, Wasps and Jersey, whom he captained in the Championship.

One of my best mates, Chrissie Hallam, is a goldsmith who runs a successful jewellery business after having played for Worcester, Rotherham and Doncaster. We roomed together in student accommodation for that first formative month. We were skint; it proved impossible to live on travel expenses. I'm not particularly proud that our solution was to pilfer food from fridges, elsewhere in the Uni halls of residence.

Graham came through on his promise, securing a contract of £4,000 a year, just as we moved into the basement room of a five-bedroomed terrace house known locally as the House of Pain. Rent cost us £250 a month, leaving £83 on which to get by. I lived on huge pillowcases of pasta, bought from the local low-cost supermarket, canned tomatoes and poached eggs.

We'd go into the kitchen at the Worcester events centre, and chow our way through as many of the cheesecakes, prepared for that particular day's corporate function, as possible. We helped ourselves to anything we could get our hands on. We stole bottles of milk, steaks and ham off the bone from the fridge, and walked out with backpacks stuffed with toilet rolls. Though the struggle to be self-reliant gave me perspective, it was a turbulent time.

I was brought up to be respectful and mindful of others, but I missed my mum and dad's guidance. I was trying to figure life out by myself, when I was turning from boy to man, and needed someone to put me right. This was before the days of cheap, easy contact through FaceTime or Skype. I was mortally embarrassed when, on one of the rare occasions

I could afford to use the payphone outside the local shops, to inform my parents I was still alive, I had to ask them to send money for a new pair of boots.

My originals fell to pieces, panel by panel, and were held together by duct tape. Ollie Redman gave me a pair of his boots, which were like a clown's shoes, because he was size 13 and I was size 11. I ran like a seal, but had mixed feelings when Mum wired me the necessary cash without a murmur. I so wanted to be seen as my own man.

Looking back, I was caught between contrasting cultures. I'm no psychoanalyst, but I reckon that, subconsciously, I still longed for the certainty of outback life, informed by Maori sensibilities. I'm not particularly religious, though my dad is Catholic, but I liked the spiritual sensitivity of my old school team, where we would say Karakia, incantations and prayers used to invoke spiritual guidance and protection, whenever we boarded the team bus.

I'd moved away from the traditions of the Marae, where we would remove shoes and hats before the official welcome, the night before a match. We'd heard the speech a thousand times before, but treated it reverentially, singing a song as a team and circulating doing the Hongi, the traditional greeting in which we pressed noses and foreheads with the old men and women. We would leave that place spotless in the morning.

We're not talking about angels here. Many of the lads came from the sort of estates where sofas were left to rot in the front garden. There was an undertow of Maori gang culture, which manifested itself in one particular English lesson when the teacher, Mr Hoare, asked us what we wanted most in life. I waffled something inconsequential, but Hemi, a huge Polynesian lad, simply said 'My fucking patch.' We all knew what he meant; he was only twelve, but he yearned for the symbol of gang membership that can only be guaranteed by bad things.

Sam Cameron, who played tighthead prop to my loose-head in high school, took me back to his house when we had an hour to kill after training on Tuesdays and Thursdays. His dad, who was in the Mongrel Mob, would often be there, flicking cigarette ash into a paua shell in the middle of the table. He would greet me with a bright 'Dyly, my boy, how you doing, my mate?' and throw open the fridge. He was a great host.

Hospitality and humility are important. That's why in my first season as England captain I always mentioned the rough arses I played with as a kid in my post-match speeches. They taught me to thank the people in the kitchen, for the food they had provided. They expressed their gratitude to the opposition, their teammates, and the people who had helped them get there. You don't need a fancy education, or a par-ticularly clean conscience, to have good manners.

Everyone in professional rugby, to a lesser or greater degree, is ducking and diving. They're living for the moment, and cut corners. The philosophical tends to trail in a poor second to the financial. I might have needed spiritual heal-ing, but my requirement for more money had greater urgency. Since necessity was the mother of invention, I hit on the wheeze of selling my England kit on eBay.

Special shirts, like my first representative jersey, which is hung in the Crowborough clubhouse, unwashed, mud-caked and spattered with Scottish blood, were off limits. But, at a time when it was impossible to buy player-issued gear through official channels, I would get between £80 and £100 for an unworn pair of socks with the tags on. I'd merely wear the previous week's pair.

If one of the boys left a training top in the changing room, it was going home in my bag. My expenses were limited to a 90p bus fare to the post office, and postage costs. Over the year the scam pretty much doubled my wage. Chrissie and I also turned a profit with a bit of freelance work, undertaken out of the House of Pain.

The rest of the residents were senior players and their mates, who had no intention of slumming it. They paid for a cleaner and for TVs in every room. Everyone from the club piled round to play Halo, one of the original shoot 'em up video games based on an interstellar war between humans and aliens, on the communal Xbox.

Jim Jenner, a number 8 who represented England in the sevens at the 1998 Commonwealth Games, was winding down his playing career after returning to Worcester following a successful spell with Newcastle. His coolness under pressure would save his life in 2018, when he crash-landed his helicopter in a field in Gloucestershire after suffering total engine failure at 1,200 feet.

He lived with his brother Jeff, who had no association with rugby, but was developing a range of successful businesses with him. Today they employ eighty people in a UK-wide property conversion and development company, and own a string of prep schools and nurseries. Back then, they were our guardian angels.

I'd never been afraid of hard work, from the days in which I got the sheep in, or helped Dad de-nail a trailer full of wood. Chrissie and I would go out in the evening, or on days off, and do anything from knocking down stud walls to cleaning out gutters; in return the brothers would feed us, with pizza or a Chinese takeaway, and pay us labourer's rates.

I've never been the rock star – I'm still not – and didn't need to be pampered. I know it has become a middle-management cliché, but I just wanted to get better every day. Failure hurt, and desperation scoured the wounds. I still carry the scar of not making the rugby team at my intermediate school.

I've always felt I've had to prove myself, because I've compensated for my relative lack of athleticism and dynamism by working hard at my skills, and leading from the front. I've always had a stubborn streak, such as when I responded to Mum's refusal to pick me up from rugby training, because I had dropped out of classes, by setting off to walk the twenty kilometres home.

On that day I was rescued by a passer-by, who saw me trudging along the main road out of Rotorua and offered me a ride. But now I was alone, and feeling the force of my ambitions. I resented authority, lacked stability, and, in a sport built upon personal confrontation, was capable of doing some very silly things.

# 4

# Outsider

It was my World Cup final. An under-19 friendly for Worcester against Leicester at Sixways, on a distant pitch that is now a car park, with about a dozen parents and a cabal of coaches on the touchline. It wasn't necessarily about the business of winning, though bragging rights were at stake. It was, to my cluttered mind, an existential crisis.

I didn't merely want to play for England. I needed to do so, to justify an 11,500-mile journey and avoid a taint of failure, as acrid as the sulphur pools of my hometown, Rotorua. I didn't know it at the time, but fate was forming an object lesson in the importance of perspective and the tragic fragility of the human body.

I scrummaged directly against the tighthead prop Matt Hampson, a rising star who, less than two years later, dislocated his neck and severed his spinal cord in a freakish accident in an England under-21 training session at Franklin's Gardens. As a tetraplegic overseeing his charitable foundation, he has become one of rugby's most inspirational characters; as a young man, with his life ahead of him, he simply came across as a good bloke.

My immediate attention was focused on his loosehead prop, Kevin Davies. I'd had very little to do with him, since he had come through the private-schools system, but he represented a threat to the ambition I had decided would define me. Through no fault of his own, to my jaundiced eye, he symbolized ingrained privilege.

Our coach, Dorian West, whose place in front-row legend was assured as the oldest member of England's World Cup-winning squad, had told me, in a training camp at the Broadstreet club in Coventry, that Kevin was ahead of me for selection. It was confirmation of the obvious, since he would be prioritized in training drills, and I would be given the bib that signified a reserve.

I had to make a statement, but my thinking was muddied by a sense of frustration that verged on desperation. A ruck formed, near halfway, about forty metres from their posts; I burrowed forward and found myself over Kevin, who was pinned to the floor. My arms were free; I saw my chance, and unloaded a flurry of punches, UFC-style.

It was an indefensible act, a product of detached logic that I could get away with it. There were no cameras. The referee had players as his touch judges. There was a brief kerfuffle of attempted retribution but I didn't even get a yellow card. Kevin was substituted, with a bloodied lip, and never played for England again.

I have not seen him since. Were I to do so today, I'd apologize without hesitation. My honesty, in admitting to a grievous error of judgement that led to a parent branding me 'a disgrace' immediately after the match, is my only mitigating factor.

The Worcester coaches bundled me away, but I couldn't avoid a reckoning with Dorian. He pulled me outside reception at our next England training camp and got right in my face. 'What are you doing?' he asked, reasonably enough. 'That's one of our players. You can't do that. It's not right. Why? *Why?*'

I had huge respect for him; as a former hooker of great repute he evidently saw something in me, and had been coming to the club to work with me on my throwing. My answer was brief, and probably summarized my immaturity: 'You keep picking him.' The voice in my head was more brutal: 'He was in my way.'

I went on to work closely at senior level at Northampton with Dorian and Jim Mallinder, who called me up as an uncapped replacement for the under-21 World Cup squad in Argentina in 2005. Dorian wielded the greatest influence on my development; his lectures, delivered across the front seat of his Ford Mondeo, would be intense, occasionally fractious but ultimately invaluable.

He understood me intuitively, and knew the job needed a bit of a mongrel. Professional sport is about winning the personal battle, finding a way. I wasn't yet eighteen and was impatient. He saw my issue with authority as a practical problem, whereas the RFU wanted me to see a sports psychologist. I was having none of it, though later in my career I was open to training the brain.

In simple terms, I felt like an outsider, a stranger in a strange land. I'd been different to an extent in New Zealand, as a rural kid hanging out with lads on the rougher side of town, but in England I found myself in the sporting equivalent of a masonic lodge. I didn't know the dodgy secret handshake because I hadn't been to the proper school.

I would learn, eventually, that the game is a great leveller and that someone's cut-glass accent doesn't define his character, but at the time I thought the national team wasn't designed for people like me. Club recruitment reflected a network of tradition, grace and favour. Boys from Oakham School were ushered into Leicester Tigers.

Colston's Collegiate School in Bristol supplied players to Bath. Millfield School had an association with Gloucester.

My first visit to Twickenham prompted a second take from the security guard. 'Excuse me, mate,' I asked. 'Where's the under-19s meeting?' He obviously thought I was a tourist, with good reason, since I had shaggy blond hair, and wore a T-shirt, yellow board shorts and jandals, our version of flip-flops. My worldly possessions were in the Berghaus backpack with which I had travelled, on train and Tube, from my aunt and uncle's place in Crowborough.

I walked everywhere I could, and took a bus when necessary. Many of my teammates were being dropped off from Range Rovers. They wore chinos, loafers and shiny-buttoned blazers, and had bonded over sumptuous post-match teas in their private schools. They were welcoming, when we shook hands and I introduced myself in a Kiwi drawl, but they belonged to a different world.

It might be vulgar to a certain stratum of society, but it didn't take me long to work out the financial pecking order. I was on four grand a year at a Championship club. They were on twenty grand a year, and in one whispered case thirty grand a year, in Premiership academies. Not bad wedge that, for someone straight out of school.

In South Africa I roomed with Laurence Ovens, a prop from Millfield who spent five seasons on the fringes at Bath before spells at Newcastle, Bedford and Rosslyn Park. I caught glandular fever on the last few days of the trip and was dying quietly in bed when he called his parents, who were obviously asking how he had got on, and where he thought he stood, in terms of selection.

He spoke quietly, because he thought I was asleep. I had my eyes closed, but my ears open. I didn't mind his relentless optimism – hell, I'd have said the same in the same situation – but I couldn't believe that he was calling them 'Mummy' and 'Daddy'. He was eighteen, for goodness' sake. Surely that went out of fashion when Nursey waved you off to prep school?

Part of me wanted to be annoyed, but I couldn't help being amused. No one, at our age, had a monopoly on wisdom. We all had our faults and foibles. Being respectful isn't a hanging offence, and we were all prisoners of our upbringing. It helped me to make peace, of sorts, with things. For better or for worse, I was on an adventure.

We lost the third-place play-off, 38–31, to South Africa, in the 2004 under-19 World Cup, where I started every match and began to make the transition from loosehead to hooker. I made my first-team debut for Worcester, an away match against Leeds Tykes in the European shield in 2005, before the call-up to the England under-21 squad in Argentina.

The food in the hotel was shit, but I couldn't afford to go out for coffee and a McDonald's with the other boys, who were two years older and on proper money from senior contracts. My consolation came in the form of a rugby network that was starting to take shape. Ollie Redman was coaching alongside Jim Mallinder. I was forming long-term friendships with guys like Lee Dickson, Ben Foden and James Haskell.

It might be an exaggeration to describe Hask as a shy boy, but, beneath the Archbishop of Banterbury bluster, he has a heart of gold. The sort of energy he brings to a team environment is invaluable, because he is plugged into the mains. All you need to do, to get full value, is to put him in front of a bunch of young players and watch their faces.

An intimidatingly big lad, even before his latest venture into mixed martial arts, he delivers a speech with his entire body. 'None of you young fellas have got any stories,' he tells them, with the assurance of an old trouper. 'You've drunk no piss. You haven't shagged any birds. You haven't done anything. All you've done is rugby, and that's not enough.'

He's a year older than me, and I don't have quite the same dramatic impact when I follow up, by talking about how players are created by the struggle. The young lads concentrate on the status symbols, the Mitsubishi I'm contractually obliged to drive on official duty, and the Range Rover that's pressed into service when I'm ferrying Thea to classes, because they fit their perception of achievement.

They're all vying with each other to see who can get the best lease deal on a Mercedes. I don't mind anyone wanting a nice car, but they have to earn the right to get behind the wheel, and that has nothing to do with the nuances of the Highway Code. They look at me as if I'm from a different planet when I talk about the practicality of getting the bus, and how, as England captain, I used to cycle to training on a Muddyfox mountain bike with a permanently flat back tyre.

That was a hand-me-down from Rob Hunter, a former soldier in the Royal Engineers who ran Northampton's academy before, in 2010, he moved on to coach England under-20s. He's now a key figure with Exeter Chiefs, where he looks after the forwards. He played a big role in signing me, along with James Sinclair, Saints' former Recruitment and Development Director.

Things came to a head when I played at Franklin's Gardens in a Monday night A League fixture. I looked at the facilities, studied a senior squad that included All Blacks and England players of the quality of Steve Thompson and Ben Cohen, and wanted a bit of that. Aware that, as an emerging

England age group player, I was a decent catch, I simply asked 'Would you be interested in me coming here?'

Save me the sermons about loyalty. I was still on four grand a year, though an offer of an annual salary of £18,000 magically materialized from Worcester when news of Northampton's interest emerged. I met Rob and James at Broadstreet after an England training session, when, whatever Mick Hucknall sings as Simply Red's front man, money was too tight not to mention.

I laid it on a bit thick – 'I'm struggling to get by at the moment, like I can't really afford to eat' – and they came up with an immediate payment of £1,500 to tide me over in the three months before their contract offer kicked in. I took the cheque back to the House of Pain in a state of bliss, and went on the lash with Chrissie Hallam and Ned Anderson once it was safely banked.

My Del Boy moment is captured on the WhatsApp group I share with groomsmen at my wedding. I'm in photographs between Ned and Chrissie, and, believe me, my looks have improved with age. We're eighteen, Jack-the-lads out on the town, necking bottles of Moët like they are going out of fashion. That £1,500 was almost five months' pay at Worcester. I bought an iPod and a new pair of boots, and generally behaved like a lottery winner.

Yet money wasn't everything. I accepted £8,000 a year to join Northampton in May 2005 because, unlike Worcester, they guaranteed I would be part of the first-team squad. In fact, they went further. They were going to persevere and play me at hooker. They loved my rawness and intensity. I was going to train with internationals, and be schooled in the ways of professional rugby by the best.

I didn't mind the privations at Worcester, where the offices were in a prefab, the changing rooms were a health hazard and we didn't even have official kit. That helped foster the Lost Boys spirit, but the perception of being second-class citizens, however false, wore thin. Instead of wearing my own stash, I was presented with a well-stuffed kitbag. I was a kid given the keys to the sweet shop.

They told me to pick a pair of boots and trainers, which would be replaced twice a season. I was given a meat pack and a fruit-and-vegetable box each week, and told to help myself from leftovers in the club kitchen. They paid my rent. I had doubled my basic salary, to £666 a month, and had nothing to spend it on. Unbelievable.

Though I was given a taste of the rewards available for the pampered few, the struggle stayed with me. Worcester were prepared to recognize my potential financially, but hedged their bets about meaningful playing time. I wasn't prepared to wait for tomorrow. There would be no more training on pitch number ten, out in the boondocks.

Northampton made a philosophical leap of faith. I was officially an Academy player but they treated me like a man. I was terrified, of course. I started the first four Premiership games of the season, beginning with the little matter of an East Midlands derby against Leicester Tigers at Welford Road. My phone was swamped with messages from my mates, saying 'Fucking hell, Dyls, you're on TV.'

I was on £500 a match, and doubled my wage through appearance bonuses that season. I've never been accused of being serene, but I was like a young swan, assured on the surface and paddling madly beneath the waterline. I dreaded the ball being kicked off the field because, basically, I didn't know how to throw.

It is one thing aiming darts at a chalk line outside your auntie's house, entirely another to remember lineout calls, and concentrate on throwing with pinpoint accuracy while you've got a hostile crowd at your back, speculating about your virginity. I had no real idea about scrummaging; the magnitude of the hit when a first-team scrum engaged turned my spine into hot metal.

Somehow, I managed to avoid being burned to a crisp in a baptism of fire that shaped me for years to come. I never looked back. The team was in transition, but Northampton's director of rugby, Budge Pountney, the former Scotland flanker, was prepared to live with my inexperience because he saw the long-term value of my refusal to be intimidated.

A forwards coach will always have a natural propensity to favour the harder, tougher, flintier character. You don't get too many ballet dancers in the front row, though those guys also have a resistance to pain; it's a workplace that demands a boxer's gluttony for punishment. The fighter's instincts, developed at Worcester, were honed under pressure in those first two years of senior rugby.

I trained ferociously hard, to prove that I belonged. I mainlined the experience of Paul Grayson, who had been Jonny Wilkinson's understudy at the 2003 World Cup and won thirty-two England caps between 1995 and 2004. The old-school influence of Peter Sloane was immeasurable. He won his solitary Test jersey in a 10–9 win against England at Twickenham in 1979 and spent two years on the All Blacks coaching staff, as assistant to John Hart, in the late nineties.

As a hooker, he described himself as 'a thumper'. As a coach, he favoured 'the bark and cuddle afterwards routine'. He took a conscious decision to broaden his horizons after surviving cancer, and loved the process of self-education. He once told the *New Zealand Herald*: 'I saw a lot of guys who never came back. The marble bounced my way. I saw how others battled and you have to back yourself and be the difference.'

He was talking my language, in an accent I recognized.

They called me Big Time in the Academy changing room, because I latched on to the senior players. I didn't mind, especially when my Academy contract was ripped up at the end of my first year, and my promotion was made permanent. I was desperate not to be seen as a little boy, cowering in the corner. I was driven to earn the respect of players I looked up to.

Professional sport offers a rough-and-ready education, but its lessons are timeless. I've tried to pass them on to Connor, Paul Tupai's son, a half back in his first year at the Northampton Academy. Get in there, and get to know the people who matter. Put yourself forward for extra training. Make every spare second count. Don't act like a kid at a new school, because that is how you'll be treated.

I will never forget the debt I owe to his dad, whom I regard as family. Toops was in his prime, a force of nature in his two years at Saints, the formative phase of my career. Budge employed him as an enforcer at loose forward, and it has to be said Toops loved his work. He played more than 1,000 games over twenty-eight years, and could wallpaper Westminster Abbey with his yellow cards.

He emerged in an era when summary justice was employed in rucks. Backs and legs were tattooed by the scars of surgically applied studs. Apart from being forced to undergo a shoulder operation, his only other injury was a broken thumb, caused by an errant punch. Yet he is no cartoon thug; he babysits Thea, as I once babysat Connor, with care and tenderness. He remains rooted to the traditions of his upbringing.

Respect the changing sheds, and the hard-earned cash paid by spectators. Give them your time and appreciation. Respect men of achievement, and the back seat on the team bus. That is a privilege to be earned. Respect life skills, and the eight-hour toil of a working man's day. That will come to you soon enough. You will find yourself in the outside world, and the hangers-on, who told you how great you were, will have vanished.

Academy players who sit and eat together will always have that tag. They will never break the mould. Coaches notice them self-identifying, and come to the conclusion they will eventually be smothered by their comfort blanket. Toops was the mentor I needed, at a time when I couldn't afford the indulgence of hero worship.

All Blacks like Carlos Spencer and Bruce Reihana were my idols, giants who came to life on a TV screen in my adolescence. I was one of the anonymous millions, watching as they played on wet, greasy paddocks, with an entire nation on their shoulders. Now they were flesh and blood, teammates ready to initiate me into their tribe.

In some teams the young bucks literally fight their way to the back of the bus, to sit with the senior players. This was different, almost a sacred ritual of admittance to an inner circle. Growing up so closely attuned to the Maori culture, I knew the importance of the established order. I didn't dare challenge the natural hierarchy of the team; once invited to the back seats, I knew to keep my head down, and speak only when spoken to.

Carlos, who played thirty-five Tests for the All Blacks between 1997 and 2004, called me 'Neph', short for nephew.

He would give me his pickup truck to drive when he was on the piss with the boys. I'd happily not drink, because I listened to their stories, and watched how they handled themselves. I didn't have a car, would take him home and borrow the truck for the weekend. On away trips, he would give me his credit card, order beers and burgers, and tell me to get whatever I wanted for myself.

Bruce, who at forty-three is still fit enough to compete with young players in the sessions he supervises as Bristol's Skills and Performance coach, would produce a salmon, a £50 note, as the team bus drew into a motorway service station, and deliver his instructions. After home matches, he would give me another £50, and quietly say 'Have a good night.' He knew how much that meant, because it had been done to him, on the way up. The wheel keeps turning, although I would only give today's kids £20.

Don't want to spoil 'em. That's my excuse, anyway . . .

Mark 'Sharky' Robinson was another member of the brew crew. He now lives on the Isle of Man and trades off his three Test appearances for the All Blacks, the first of which was in a 64–22 drubbing of England in Dunedin in June 1998. A streetwise scrum half, he came to the Saints after a brief spell in rugby league, where he played one international, as a hooker.

He has not forgotten the injustice of his fourteen-week ban for stamping on Mark Regan, the former Bristol, England and British Lions hooker. Sharky's boot clipped his chin when he was clearing a ruck. Ronnie, as he is known on the after-dinner circuit, admitted to play acting, and was fined £500 for bringing the game into disrepute. But, because it was on TV, Something Had To Be Done. Once Sharky was sent off, suspension was inevitable.

He and Carlos were the half backs in the team, captained by Bruce, which created one of the biggest shocks in European Cup history by reaching the 2007 semi-finals with a 7–6 win in San Sebastián against Biarritz. Robbie Kydd's interception and seventy-yard run for a converted try was decisive. I loved the colour and fervour of a typically Basque occasion, even when Toops conceded a penalty by managing somehow to remove Serge Betsen's shirt in a ruck.

I gravitated towards the Kiwi contingent because I was proud of my heritage, even though I had already represented England, and had been accepted by the senior home-grown players. Matt Lord, who is now a dairy farmer in Owhango, a small North Island settlement on the Whakapapa River that translates as 'the place of wheezy noises', was my other mentor.

I wasn't like other lads of my age, who could send their washing to Mum, and be sure of a special Sunday roast. Lordy and Toops, who lived on the same estate as me, provided the family environment I craved. Their doors were always open, and food was on the table. The kids I once babysat are growing up fast; Matt's son Josh is an academy lock forward with Taranaki, the province that produced the Barrett brothers, Beauden, Jordie and Scott, who made history by playing together for the All Blacks against France in 2018.

The fans, who made Lordy their player of the year, nicknamed him Wookiee, because of his resemblance to Chewbacca in the *Star Wars* movies. He was painfully shy in public, but, as a captain, led by unstinting example. His career effectively ended in a tackle against Bath, when his shoulder was fractured and badly dislocated and he broke four metatarsal bones in his foot.

He retired when a doctor told him to concentrate on walking properly, rather than playing rugby, and the manner of his departure typified his unforced humility. It was announced during a testimonial for Tom Smith, one of Scotland's great loosehead props. We urged him on to the field to take the applause, but he simply rose from the dugout and waved self-consciously before returning to the shadows.

The concept of a team as a family is thrown around a lot, and I've been in some where it was a theatrical illusion. The best teams look after their own, without fanfare and with maximum respect. One of our less celebrated players had two children born with external organs; he wasn't one of the higher earners, so the boys contributed to the medical bills.

There were no grand gestures, merely an envelope, containing donations, passed quietly to a mate. We did something similar, organizing a regular whip-round for the kitchen staff who worked on minimum wage, to feed us each day. It was an act of solidarity, subtle recognition that none of us exist in isolation.

The bonds are stronger when they are personal. You don't just turn up, train with the blinkers on and dash off home. When you know a teammate's wife and kids, and understand their circumstances, you have something substantial to relate to. When you distil the brothers-in-arms stuff, it comes down to interaction between like-minded people. It means more when you have an insight into a teammate's life.

If I see a teammate take a cheap shot, there are only two viable responses. If I don't particularly care about him, I'll have a word with the offender. If I know him as a friend, I'll fly in, to sort out the transgressor. I realize that's probably a clumsy example, but the wider point about standards of behaviour applies to all walks of life.

Team culture is healthy when something gets called out quickly if the group feel it is wrong. That could range from the use of mobile phones in the dressing room, which I hate, to disrespecting the convention that shoes must not be worn on stretching mats. Anyone who is not tuned in is given only one reminder: 'We don't do that sort of thing here.'

On balance, it is probably a good thing that modern initiation rituals have been toned down. In my early days, recruits from the Academy were forced to play Edward Ciderhands while the seniors did their core strengthening session in the gym. They were expected to sit silently in the showers, with two-litre bottles of White Lightning strapped to each arm, and weren't allowed to emerge until they had drunk the lot.

In my solitary season in the Championship, which Northampton won under the new coaching team of Dorian West and Jim Mallinder, we were on the piss every week. It was men's rugby, stripped of the pressure associated with the Premiership. We worked hard, and played even harder. As a captain, I later adopted Jim's mantra that wins were to be enjoyed, but we needed to be smart.

Win and, after some of the seven-hour journeys we had in the second tier, we would pile straight off the bus and into the local nightclubs. Defeat demanded discretion; since Northampton is a tightly knit community, our orders were to behave. Slightly different rules applied in pre-season; I once sustained a black eye in France, in a melee created by having my underpants ripped over my head by Ben Foden.

A few of the boys still habitually streak around Franklin's Gardens when it is deserted, and one particular Premiership team continues to operate a naked-bus policy, returning from away matches. At the risk of identifying them, they need all the distractions they can get on their regular journeys back to base, in Devon.

I'm glad I experienced those excesses, but the professionalism of the game has inevitably diluted drinking cultures. I'm too old to get on it, in any case, but I've learned to listen to sports scientists, who remind us that alcohol increases rates of bleeding. To put that advice into context, if you go on the toot with a dead leg, it will double in size.

Old-school attitudes also once permeated the coaching culture. I worked for twelve years with Jim and Dorian, and developed the sort of love–hate relationship that will resonate with athletes, across all sports. Trust was mutual, but, boy, were attitudes occasionally fickle. When you were injured you were cast out, because you were of no use to them.

That's no criticism, incidentally. It is merely a restatement of the reality that elite coaches are under persistent pressure to deliver results. They are judged by the quality of the teams they send out, and have a vested interest in encouraging supposed selflessness in their players. It formed the basis of a running joke I shared with Dorian.

Ask him about how he handled injury as a player, and he simply recites 'Pills and tape, son, pills and tape.' When I missed a few games with a broken hand, he confided: 'I played with that. I just taped it up.' His generation used to self-medicate with painkillers. 'I did my knee as well, so you'll be all right,' he assured me, waddling away like a seasick version of Popeye on a rolling deck.

It took the patience of a saint not to laugh. Which you will be unsurprised to learn I do not possess.

Dorian remains one of my most significant coaches, because he schooled me in the ways of the world. I craved more than incantations of aggression later in my career, but his private tutorials on a forward's mindset deserve repetition, since they contain non-negotiables that might as well have been written in blood.

Never take a backward step. Don't dare surrender. Never succumb to the force of a tackle, or the damaging intent of someone set on pulling you over in a maul. Take pleasure out of demoralizing the opposition. Do that, my son, and you will be a valued member of the Front-Row Union.

# 5

# Heart of Darkness

You hear people wheezing, as their wind supply gets cut off. They emit a long, low groan as the pressure intensifies. Dribble seeps out, and runs down their chin. Mouth guards drop into the no-man's-land between sets of forwards squeezing maximum force through your neck and spine. You are pinned, naturally looking down to the floor in anticipation of the ball coming in from your left.

You can't move once the packs engage, but attempt to ride the weight being applied. Sometimes you are comfortable with the strain. When it goes bad, and the scrum shifts at an angle, either going backwards or forwards, people are propelled across, over or on top of each other. Everything is compromised, and you are in real trouble.

The memory of one scrum, at Bath, stays with me, like a childhood nightmare. My head went light. I could see stars because I didn't want to exhale, impulsively weaken and lose the advantage of having a chest full of air. The easy way out was to stop binding with my loosehead prop, and allow their big tighthead to exploit the seam between us.

That's against instruction and instinct. We're told to keep holding that tighthead down, and keep him in such pain that he loses the battle of wills. I was holding, holding, holding, in the crystal-clear knowledge that I was on the verge of fainting. It felt as if I was being choked. I'm thinking to myself 'Fuck, I'm gone. I'm going now. I'm going, going . . .'

But I didn't. Their tighthead suddenly succumbed. He had reached his point of no return. To use the brutal, but metaphorical, language of the front row, he had 'died'. We won the penalty, the scrum ended, and my head popped up into the noise. I stood up and, boom, I blacked out. I fell flat on my face, woke up instantly, and got on with the game.

Welcome to my world, the heart of darkness that is rugby's front row.

Professional sport is massively over-exposed these days. Athletes are analysed, patronized, and lionized, but never fully understood. Without wishing to appear condescending, there are certain situations and specific jobs that have to be experienced under duress to be wholly appreciated. My job is probably one of them.

I'll do my best to explain the nuances and rituals of the front row, because it is one of those areas in which the uninitiated have difficulty in reading subtle signs of struggle or success. To give you an example of the daily grind, I woke up this morning with a really sore neck. I was stuck in a training scrum yesterday, with my chin on my chest, and the opposition tighthead, a big strong kid, lifted me. Something had to give so my head popped out.

That's the public signal of distress we all dread.

Scrummaging has changed over the course of my career. When I started we obeyed the sequence of 'Crouch . . . hold . . . engage.' You used to fly into the gap, and the impact was huge. The momentum was scary, and some of the opposing hookers were psychos. They'd read my eyes, recognize my intentions, and simply headbutt me.

I knew the law of the jungle they were seeking to impose. They went for me because I was a young fella, and it would probably put me off. They knew the limits of my comfort zone; I wanted to get my head in there nicely, take the impact on my shoulders. My neck would get a hammering, but that's normal. No one can really teach you how to react when someone sticks the nut on you. It's an introduction to an adventure park in which there's no half-price admission for kids.

Nowadays the gap between the packs, as they line up, isn't so big. The impact is reduced accordingly. We crouch, bind and engage. Calls are a variation on a theme, 'Hit, two three', 'Hit, one two' or 'Hit, two, three, four, squeeze.' Since the sequence is more enclosed and compressed, the process is slightly more intricate. Basically, it becomes an eight-man job.

The front three need to be technically sound, and mentally on it. They must be sharp and streetwise, and try to work the angles. All the back five are doing, bless 'em, is pushing, adding weight. As hooker, I bind very tightly to my loosehead prop. There's a simple rule of thumb to help those unversed in our ways: 'l' for loosehead reminds you that he is on the left of the hooker. His head is free on the side of the scrum.

The tighthead is on the other side, with his head between the opposing loosehead prop and hooker. It's a dirty job, made for a stereotypical rugby player. To paint an unflattering but pretty accurate picture, they tend to be big, fat and dense. It's a horrible position in which to play, and it is not the best platform for natural athletes.

But, boy, are they valuable. Along with rock star fly halves, tighthead props are usually the best-paid players. Why? Essentially, he is working against two people. If he's not up to it, the scrum goes backwards every time. The whole game is built around the strength he represents. The best I played with for England was Julian White. A Leicestershire farmer, he was as hard as nails, and deserved the biggest bucks.

Reading the book *The Blind Side* by Michael Lewis, which explains American football's evolution through the story of the high-school phenomenon Michael Oher, one of thirteen children born to a crack cocaine-addicted mother, it became clear that the most instructive parallel is probably with left guards in the NFL.

They occupy a previously unfashionable position that requires size, speed, agility and durability, but, most of all, a bodyguard's instinct for danger. They earn more than the monsters on the offensive line, or the flashy, fleet-footed running backs, because they protect the blind side of the franchise player, the quarterback. They act as his eyes and his muscle.

You don't want to give an inch in the scrum. The aim is to dominate by putting early weight on the opposition. As soon as the referee says 'engage' we aim to fill the hole as quickly and effectively as possible. It is not about simply hitting and holding; you are under tension all the time, attempting to extend and squeeze your collective weight.

You are strangely sensitive to the efforts of others. I can feel it, even if only one of the guys behind me has one foot off the ground. The tension is eased imperceptibly, and we're at a disadvantage. If the back five aren't pushing their bollocks off, the front row have no chance. You can talk all you like about the complexity of technique in forward play, but we need some oomph behind our backsides.

As hooker, I'm locked in. I don't have any control. The pressure is most acute in my neck. I'm looking for my tighthead to help, making sure his left shoulder is promoted and not tucked away. I don't have the luxuries of the loosehead prop, who can pull his head away, or place his free arm on the ground, in moments of strife. If the scrum is going down, I'm getting a face full of dirt.

We are up close and personal. My face feels like it has been exfoliated after a game in which their tighthead has been constantly rubbing his face on me. I can't grow a beard, but will never, ever, have a fresh shave before a match. I need something there, even a pretty pathetic wispy form of stubble, to protect me.

In the best-case scenario, your face is inflamed by mud, sand and the opponent's bristles. In the worst, the opposing tighthead has scrum pox, or *Herpes rugbiorum* to give it the formality of its full medical name. It's aggravated by repeated abrasion, and involves a *H. simplex* virus type one, or, in a lesser form, bacteria that result in impetigo. A couple of our lads have it; when it flares up they tend to get the plasters out.

Scrummaging is not just a physical process, with occasionally horrid side effects. It has a mental element. Since you get penalized unless you are going forward, you can't just hit and pivot. You need to hit, go forward and then pivot. Influencing the referee, by giving him the impression you are dominant, is a game within the game.

You want to prove that you are the big dogs, so that decisions go your way in other areas, like a lineout or a maul, where scrummaging principles also apply. Everyone gets low, works together, and applies pressure. If your scrum seems solid, and offers the referee a clear picture of being in the ascendancy, he will subconsciously favour you.

When things are going wrong and a front-row forward pops out, a lot of teams try to wheel the scrum. If you are going forward, the ruse is obvious to the ref. You are pumped, because you know you are demoralizing the opposition. You are passing the ultimate test of togetherness. Everyone is ripping in, to help their mates out. No one is taking a momentary respite, because they understand their responsibilities.

Establishing that type of dominance is a gradual process, usually in ten-minute segments over the first half an hour. There's a golden period ten minutes or so before half-time when concentration tends to waver and someone wilts under pressure, but the tipping point often occurs in the last twenty minutes of the match.

There is an element of *mano-a-mano* conflict, but you can't dominate your opposite number unless the guys either side of you, or behind you, are on the same wavelength. Individual lapses of concentration, which impact on collective efficiency, are the most common subject of review when game film is studied on a Monday morning.

Why does, say, one scrum in four fall below expectations, and involve patchy execution of the basics? The answer is usually more nuanced than one guy simply having momentary brain fade. We might have been on the move for the preceding three minutes; someone might have had to make four tackles on the bounce, or hit a couple of rucks.

In that instance, where the legs are a little heavy, a protective form of complacency can set in. Someone might reason that he'll be able to take a breather, and simply lean on in a scrum, because the three previous ones have been perfect. That's when rugby bites you on the arse. Everyone needs to have the same mindset. To drag out that old line, go hard, or go home.

Some players make you want to scream 'Can you please use what you've got?' There's one lad, whom I won't name because there is nothing to be gained by embarrassing him, who could be the best tighthead in the world. He's physically gifted, big, explosive, but mentally weak. He could do it all, earn half a million quid a year for the next seven years as an England regular, but won't because of that fatal flaw. It's no good being remarkable on an irregular basis.

Fitness levels have improved, but you still want your tighthead to be a horrible bastard. You don't want him worrying about his moisturizing, or how he looks in the mirror. You want him snarling, and a little edgy. I've had some prime specimens around me at club level. Soane Tonga'uiha played for Tonga in three World Cups and now, at thirty-seven, is player-coach for Ampthill in the Championship. Brian Mujati played twelve Tests for South Africa, despite being born in Zimbabwe.

Those were the days of big hair and big hits. When the ball was bunged into the scrum those props went to work as if it was a side of raw steak, to be retrieved and devoured. Today's scrum is a lot more technical, because the rule makers have decided to revive a dead art. The ref is looking for me, as a hooker, to make an effort to strike the ball cleanly. If I don't attempt to do so, it's a free kick against me.

I used to try to freak the opposition by making the gap between the front rows even bigger, and then dive at them. It was a macho pretension, a ruse designed to give the impression of being intimidatingly brave, but it worked. More often than not, the other hooker would whinge to the ref about my antics. I'd succeeded in burrowing into his brain.

Old-school scrums were stuffed with guys who weren't outright lunatics, but did enough to suggest that a screw had worked loose down the years. Looking back, I shudder at some of the strokes they tried to pull. If I threw you in there, dear reader, you'd shit yourself, but we got used to the aura of impending violence. It wasn't a new experience, and so we didn't even think about it.

Rugby is hard and attritional, so it is inevitable that it has an element of machismo. That can be a bit of a blunt instrument, but coaches prioritize character and courage. There's a natural balance, since speed and skill are at a premium in certain phases, but softer skills are secondary to brawn. Without physicality you haven't got a game.

Strip it back to basics. You need to be physically resilient when you carry the ball. You seek to dominate, to impose yourself on an individual, irrespective of whether you are attacking or defending. You must be strong in the breakdown to be competitive. If you are not quick enough in the ruck, you will be forced on to the back foot. You will concede ground and, ultimately, a try.

Get them, before they get you.

Those six words summarize the fundamental message in most team talks I made, or have heard. They are put into action in the first scrum, where, in the back of your mind, you don't care about giving away a free kick or penalty. It's a heads-first mentality; you steel yourself to hit, and go over the top of them. It is an eight-man commitment, but as a hooker you are central to how the pack operates.

Sure, you get yourself into situations where a warning sign flashes in your mind – 'This ain't good for my neck' – but the split-second temptation to drop your bind, as a method of escape, is resisted because, as daft as it seems when the heat of the moment cools, you are part of something that seems bigger than yourself. You can't shout 'Stop' and expect everyone to pause.

Both packs are going at it with a desperate intensity. When one of them snaps and surrenders, the consequences are sudden and severe. I've experienced elation and quiet terror when it all unravels. I've been the predator, taking half a metre, driving the opposition backwards in the knowledge I'm about to push them over the cliff. I've also been the prey, when they've rolled over us like a bloody tidal wave.

It's natural to block out the ultimate price paid in such circumstances, but sometimes it is impossible. We train on the patch of grass at Northampton where a scrum collapsed on Matt Hampson, whose life was saved by the prompt actions of the referee, Tony Spreadbury. Hambo regained consciousness in hospital, but was paralysed from the neck down and dependent on breathing through a ventilator.

That patch of grass has bad ju-ju.

We don't talk about the possibility of sustaining such a life-defining injury, but I think about it from time to time. When you pick yourself up from a scrum that goes down, bending bodies out of shape, you think 'Shit, that was close.' That's why you do so much core work on the neck, not just using big weights but repetitive, intricate movements designed to help suppleness and strength.

We call it robustness training. Your body needs to be conditioned to play rugby. There is a nervous edge to things, because you know it doesn't have to be a particularly dramatic incident for something very bad to happen. It doesn't have to be a car crash scenario; a small wheel of the scrum can leave you folded up like a travel map, stuffed into a back pocket of your jeans.

Conversely, when you get a shove on in the scrum it feels good, very good. The crowd get into it, because it is a visible victory. It is rugby in its purest sense, almost primeval in motivation, but it is not just about brute strength. You have to be there in body and mind, responsive to the moods and potency of the group. The best packs are a seamless unit.

The All Blacks have always been smart. They see the scrum as an opportunity to get quick ball, and exploit mismatches in space, across the field. That stands to reason, since they've only got seven players, on their feet, facing them. The other eight are locked in, with their heads up one another's arses. We need to change our culture to reflect that.

Modern analysis institutionalizes innovation, yet, perversely, ensures that new plays have a short shelf life. Paul Gustard, England's defence coach before he became Head of Rugby at Harlequins, set our tone with his far-sightedness. He made us much cleverer in varying when we used the ball. My job was to hook it to the feet of the number 8. The call, to play quickly or keep the ball in the scrum, was dependent on circumstance.

We might be dismissed as 'muddied oafs', but brawn can be compatible with brain.

If we keep it tight, establish forward momentum, we invariably win a penalty; a shot at goal from anywhere up to fifty metres leads to three points and a big moral victory. If we are solid, but going nowhere, the scrum half rips the ball out quickly, and the backs are in play. That puts a premium on athleticism outside the scrum, and also plays on the minds of opposing flankers.

They start what we call 'meerkating'. Instead of having their shoulders down low, pushing and supporting their props, they are preoccupied by the possibility that the ball is about to be played away. They lift their heads, reduce the pressure, and we are effectively scrummaging against six men. Surprise, surprise, we keep the ball at the number 8's feet.

The biggest packs in world rugby, like the Springboks, the Pumas and some of the French units at club or international level, can afford to be macho. They're built like brick shit-houses and get off on pushing everyone around. We're not the biggest, so we have to be smarter, create doubt through variety.

France can be pretty flaky if their assumptions of physical dominance are challenged, but if they get the crowd involved, by advancing two or three metres and forcing the referee to blow up, they grow a couple of inches. They kick to the corner, and bring the ball down in the lineout to set up a maul, which is basically a scrum by another name.

You can see in their eyes that they absolutely love it. It's not really the time or the place to strike up a conversation, but they spit out insults in pidgin English. I've been informed, on countless occasions, that I am 'the son of the bitch'. Yet the beauty of the game is that, after knocking the crap out of one another, we bond through mutual respect and understanding.

It's cool. You are not buddy, buddy, but you bump into guys at the post-match dinner and you realize that 99.9 per cent of rugby players are the same bloke. You learn that perceptions are often inaccurate. Your opponents are pretty good people, who, like you, want to do their bit for club or country and win. They want to make their families proud.

I've never had the sense that anyone has wanted to hurt me deliberately, but I know that if I get smashed carrying the ball, it's a big lift for the opposition because of my status as captain, or 'The Talisman' to use the jokey nickname I've been given by Danny Care, who knows one when he sees one. I will not break the line that often, and I won't inspire the boys to make amazing runs, but if I go quiet I am letting people down.

First and foremost, I'm picked to lead the scrum. It's my job to get the best out of the people around me. I've got to be vocal. I'm on to them all the time about mental complacency. Individuals will screw up, and be pinged on a technicality, but I'm looking for the avoidable disadvantages, meerkating, or other fractional reductions in intensity.

Other than that, my throwing statistics have to be close to impeccable. I've got to be efficient in clearing out rucks. If I get a chance to carry the ball, I must look after it, and try to break the gain line. My highlight reel is not that special. I am a grafter. I understand the attention paid to the speed and subtlety of the backs, but the ball is usually in their hands because people like me get it there.

I'm judged by a number of criteria, most visibly reloads. By that I mean the time it takes me to get off the floor after a tackle. That has been reduced in recent seasons from three seconds, to two. In a defence-oriented game, which usually involves wet, greasy conditions, I make up to fifteen tackles, twenty if I do the full eighty minutes. That's about half the tackle count in rugby league, but it is a different game.

I do a lot of double rucking, where I am one of the forwards following the ball, supporting my backs. I'm the insurance policy, ready to clear someone out if he is inserted with the intention of stealing the ball. That involves getting horizontal, hitting people in the ribs. It's the sort of dog work students of the game don't always appreciate, because it is easier to applaud the obvious, such as a nice clean break at pace.

Forwards win games. Backs decide by how much.

Tight rugby is my rugby. I love that sort of footie. I'm best suited to the old-school up-the-jumper slog, where conditions act as an equalizer. The fast guys don't really want to catch the ball. It's a day for defending, which is the best thing in the world when you're properly organized, and ready for people running lines, and aware of all the moving parts that make up a dangerous attack.

If your legs are heavy, and you've walked into position after picking yourself up from the scrum, you're vulnerable. But if you're working hard, jogging into position and getting your legs pumping, you're set before the ball comes back. You're licking your lips, taking a picture, weighing up the options.

There's the ball. There's the man. Right, I know what's happening here. I'm watching the eyes, the hands. That guy's running out the back. This guy's going to run a dummy line. Always remember the ball is the threat. The best defenders are scanners, constantly assessing ball, man, body shape and space. We used a clip of Frank Lampard to embed the message. He's always looking, looking.

Arsène Wenger spoke to us about top players having radars in their head. The best footballers scan the field between six and eight times in the ten seconds before they receive a pass. With England we CAT scan, using the crossbar and touchline as reference points. It's an early-warning system, in which a glance can give you the information that you are short-handed in certain areas of the pitch. That enables you to fill the space quickly, and defend accordingly.

I love defending in the red zone, five yards from our try line. Space condenses around the ruck, and everyone is attempting to pick and go. It's hard on the head and knees, but the sense of defiance is thrilling. I'm just going to hit you as soon as I can, to take you off your feet. We've moved on from the days when old pros would lie on the ball in rucks, and take their lumps as badges of honour.

During the two seconds in which you are getting off the ground after a high-impact tackle you're generally looking for your lungs. The brain tells you that the ball is in play for thirty-eight of the eighty minutes, on average, but the body is desperate to catch a breath. It's amazing how many players are seized with the urge to tie up their boots, to give themselves a little respite when the opportunity eventually arises.

To reiterate the point, rugby players are conditioned to pain. The nature of the training, the intensity of the fitness work required, establishes discomfort as an inevitable element of the daily routine. It's niggly, as much as anything. You catch your elbows, feet and knees in rucking drills. Your feet get trodden on in mauls. You are piled up, bent out of shape. You simply deal with it.

Watch an injured player. More often than not he will take a knee, or hold his shoulder, but get straight back into the defensive line. He knows, instinctively, that a coach counts those who are on their feet. He is just another body, filling the line. He waits for play to stop before getting treated, because he will be reminded, in the Monday debrief, that unless he's dead he's standing up.

The game makes grown men cry. Morgan Parra, the France half back, wept unashamedly when Courtney Lawes dislocated his shoulder in a tackle. I've done similar damage to myself, charging into a ruck to hit Jamie Gibson, the flanker who is now a Northampton teammate. Instead of bawling, I simply sighed, deeply. I thought 'This ain't right' and knew immediately what I'd done.

My arm was limp, and the pain was delayed. I felt identically when I damaged my medial knee ligaments. It didn't hurt; it was as if my knee was disassociated from my body. Weird. The pain kicks in later, when the fans have gone home. They've had a good day, and probably assume we will have a good night, when, in fact, we're in an absolute state.

It is difficult to sleep on Saturday nights. The adrenaline is still surging, so you feel as if you've had too much caffeine. When I did my shoulder I had to doze, sitting upright on the couch, for about a week, because I couldn't lie down. When I broke my hand, I drifted in and out of consciousness throughout the night, because of the constant hum from the machine pumping iced water around the injury.

Everything stings around your jaw and neck from scrummaging. Dirt and sand scour tiny abrasions. Having a hot shower is agony, because your neck is rubbed raw. One of my little marital rituals is having my wife, Jo, bond my ear with surgical glue, given to her by the team doctor. It's home-based Hobbycraft; I look like Mr Potato Head and reckon I deserve a *Blue Peter* badge, at the very least.

My cauliflower ears bled, blew up to double the size, and turned purple. They were tight, because of the internal pressure, and needed to be drained through a syringe. Guess what? They filled back up. You tape your head up, and go out to train, because the coach isn't impressed by your insistence it hurts like hell. You put your head in scrums and mauls. If you are a lock you put your head between two fat arses. It rubs, and gets banged about again.

It's horrible. When you get the ears drained you can hear the needle piercing the gristle before it finds the little pockets of fluid. You put clips in, pad it out with gauze before taping. I hate needles, but go through it because if I don't the ears will be huge. That's not a good look. It's not funny when I see little kids pointing at me, saying 'Mummy, what's wrong with his ears?'

So much for the glamour of professional sport . . .

I've played when I shouldn't have done, most often when my back goes, once or twice a year. I can feel it coming. I'm tight, too tense, and a little tired. There's a chain reaction, which starts in the hips and groin. It happens when I've not been looking after myself properly, failing to pay sufficient attention to recovery protocols.

As a player, you are always susceptible to the coach who tells you: 'We need you.' It happened early in my Northampton career, when we were playing a Championship game against Cornish Pirates, in Penzance. I was immobile, to say the least. I had almost seized up, since my hips had turned in a self-defensive reflex action because of my back problem.

A six-hour, 300-mile coach journey was the last thing I needed, but Jim and Dorian were adamant my presence was vital. They told me: 'You don't have to warm up, or do anything, apart from play. Just do the scrums and lineouts.' I couldn't sit down on the bus; I simply lay on the floor, with heat packs on my back, for the entire journey. My back issues had almost become a standing joke, but I didn't feel like laughing.

When I go into spasm it is as if the right side of my body collapses. It usually takes a week of intensive treatment, hot baths and anti-inflammatory drugs to work itself loose. On one occasion, when it happened in training, a form of relaxant was injected into the affected area and I couldn't make it home. I was helped to Paul Tupai's house, nearby, and slept on the lounge floor. There was no way I could climb the stairs.

I couldn't believe I was going to play in Penzance, but there I was, on the massage table, in a cloud of Deep Heat, right until the referee knocked on the dressing room door. I couldn't even tie my boots up. The pitch, inevitably, was an absolute quagmire, but they wheeled me out for the kick-off, when we were to receive the ball. No prizes for guessing who it was kicked to; me, of course, on or about our 22-metre line. I caught it and out of defiance leathered it into touch. I lasted until just after half-time, but I was a wreck.

On most occasions, you tend to have an inkling that things are not right, and simply wait to be taken off. The physio is your emissary. When I broke my hand in 2017, I demonstrated that I couldn't close it. He went 'Ooh, yeah.' To make sure he took the right message back to the touch-line, I added 'You probably need to let them know I probably can't throw a lineout or bind in the scrum . . .' As it tran-spired, I survived a couple more phases of play before a lineout prompted the change.

I punctured my lung tackling Richie McCaw during my fiftieth England appearance, in the 30–22 defeat by the All Blacks at Twickenham in November 2013. It was a tasty col-lision. I hit him hard and low, so there was no shame involved on my part. I got up, because I didn't want to be left like roadkill, but was coughing blood and couldn't really breathe.

I spent a surreal night in hospital while my poor wife was waiting for me in the team hotel. She offered to come down to A&E, but I didn't want to make a big deal out of it. I tried to normalize it, by putting it into a rugby context. I rational-ized it was all down to the angle and timing of the hit. The doctors put it in rather more sobering perspective.

They said it was a common injury, sustained in car crashes.

Before you ask, I do wonder whether rugby is worth the potential damage I inflict on myself. I think about it all the time, but I'm driven to maximize opportunity. I put my body on the line to give my family a better future. Living in the bubble of professional sport is a privilege, and one day it is going to burst. I bump into retired teammates all the time, and their message is unanimous.

The real world is not nearly as much fun.

# 6

## Sixty Weeks

'Hey Dylan, just wanted to say that you are my inspiration when it comes to good dirty rugby. I successfully managed this season to eye gouge two players, punch a sizeable Polynesia fella in the mouth and milked two players, getting them yellow carded for something I started without once getting carded myself. Much respect to you and I hope to follow in your footsteps, mate.'

Everyone's a comedian on social media, and I get my fair share of frustrated stand-ups with the IQ of a root vegetable. That example of the art form for idiots is a random choice, the first message I received on Instagram when the wi-fi finally decided to work at home that morning, during my summer of frustration in 2018. It comes with the territory, I suppose.

There's no getting away from preconception or prejudice. I accept, to a degree, it is my fault. I might have played for the Saints for nearly fifteen years, but I'm conditioned to being dismissed as a sinner. People don't want to know that Al Capone bought flowers for his mum. They prefer to be titillated by the gory details of his activities on St Valentine's Day.

It's fair to say I have a distinctive rap sheet. Drop the scroll and it is in danger of unravelling, and rolling out of the door. I have been suspended for a total of sixty weeks, for a variety of misdemeanours, real or imagined. Even Wikipedia, that anodyne summary of someone's life and times, records that 'Hartley has become infamous for acts of indiscipline.'

I'm immensely proud of what I have achieved, in between bouts of perceived mischief and manufactured controversy. We've already established that the front row is no place for the naïve or the non-aggressor, but I wouldn't have had a long and relatively successful career if I was the cartoon ogre some make me out to be.

People I respect trusted me with positions of responsibility. They saw through the stereotype, had faith in my maturity and ability to lead from the front. Being made Northampton's youngest captain, at twenty-three, in 2009, was humbling, since I recognized the symbolic importance of the club to its community. Becoming England captain in 2016 took that sense of pride and accountability to another level.

You have every right to formulate an opinion of me. Many have done so, without due care and attention. It is the way of the modern world. This is my opportunity to put the myths and misconceptions generated by my disciplinary record into context. As in many things in life, it is not a straightforward, black or white, process. There are several shades of grey to consider.

This may sound strange, but there are parallels between long-term injury and disciplinary action. A doctor's diagnosis or an RFU panel's verdict provides an element of certainty, and enables you to make peace with your personal circumstances. It might be a terrible blow, or a tiresomely recognizable test of patience, but it offers the opportunity to plan ahead.

When I arrive at a sudden, unexpected crossroads in my career I sketch out a mind map. This charts new realities, but reminds me the world has not ended. I am still the same person, with unchanged values, abilities and ambitions. The worst has happened. There's no point in letting the imagination run riot. Feeling angry or aggrieved merely encourages vulnerability.

In disciplinary terms, I've already visited the Principal's office. I know the rituals of public punishment. They are consistent, and challenging despite their familiarity. Once a ban is imposed I go through an initial mourning period, in which I grieve, naturally, for lost opportunity. I appreciate I will have to ride out the usual shit storm on social media.

Crucially, I have never lost my inner belief. Whatever external pressure is applied, I'm in control.

That personal perspective is the product of some harsh lessons, and bitter experiences. The biggest black mark against me, the 26-week ban for making illegal contact with the eyes of Jonny O'Connor and James Haskell in a 35–29 defeat to Wasps at Adams Park in April 2007, was the first of seven incidents for which I've been punished.

A charge involving Joe Worsley, which should never have been brought, was thrown out, but that was of little immediate consolation. The week of the tribunal coincided with confirmation of Northampton's relegation to the Championship. I had been spoken of as a live candidate to break into England's 2007 World Cup squad; that dream died the moment the length of the ban became apparent.

Jeff Blackett, chairman of the three-man disciplinary panel, said they had decided thirty weeks was an appropriate punishment but reduced the suspension to twenty-six 'after taking into account his good character, youth and inexperience'. To put that into context, Kyle Sinckler received a seven-week sentence for a similar offence, involving the

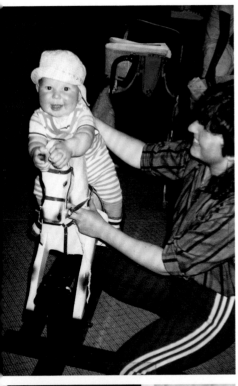

Not sure about my binding technique with the rocking horse, but it's fair to say I was always destined for the front row.

Mutant Ninja Hooker. It's no coincidence that dressed up as Leonardo from *Teenage Mutant Ninja Turtles*. He was the leader of the group.

Rural Kiwi upbringing: we were always outside and barefoot, creating our own fun.

Mum emigrated to New Zealand with her parents at the age of ten. She passed on her love for the simplicity of rural life and the tightness of small communities to her three sons.

My dad is my hero. He always had Landies: when I was about 10 years old I drove at a snail's pace while he picked up hay bales.

Dad loved camping. Holidaying for us meant exploring. You don't need money to enjoy the redwood forests, thermal pools, beaches and mountains.

On one of my first bikes with my big brother Blair. We played on the gravel roads, without care.

Life on Animal Farm. Our smallholding was full of pets.

I'm driving a ride-on lawnmower while towing my younger brother Alex. A health and safety nightmare these days but perfectly normal in the nineties.

We had the freedom of the land. I joke with my Maori mates that it's my place in the world. It has a distinctive smell of home.

Holidaying at Palliser Bay: our 'bach' (a Kiwi beach house) had no water, no electricity and was only reached by crossing a couple of rivers. Some of my best childhood memories were made there fishing and exploring shipwrecks, beached dolphins and seals. We played darts and cards by candlelight in the evenings. Rough waters and rugged terrain.

Me fishing while holidaying at Palliser Bay.

On Pukehina Beach, about 45 minutes from home in Rotorua. Every now and then Dad used to give us a heads-up the night before and take us for sunrise fishing. If you weren't up you missed the trip. I have fond memories of fires on the beach and exploring the dunes.

My first ever club team,
Ngongotaha under-10s,
in 1996.

Kahukura under-12s. Jerry
Cowley (in blue and
yellow) was a great man
and had a huge influence
on me. His son Richie,
our captain, has the ball.
The big kids either side of
him in this team photo,
Kelly Haimona and me,
both went on to play
international rugby.

Rotorua Boys High
under-15s. Coaches Mr
Burrell and Mr Callaghan
set the standards high and
instilled a level of
professionalism even at
14 years old.

Performing the Raukura haka. There are so many emotions involved in performing a haka but for me pride and togetherness stand out.

Me playing barefoot: this is my first ever game of club rugby, playing for Ngongotaha against Rotoiti – I went on to score three tries, a career high.

A rare shot of what looks like a line break! Some will say it's photoshopped.

The happiest day of my life.

Me with my best men and nephew on our wedding day. Left to right: my brother Blair, Connor Tupai, Ned Anderson, Stephen Smith, me, Uncle Si, Paul Tupai, Chris Ashton, Chris Hallam.

Kiwi lock forward Michael Paterson, against Northampton in the autumn of 2017.

Kyle apologized and issued a statement through his club, Harlequins, insisting his actions were accidental. He seemed to be frustrated during the game, and Michael's scrum cap was ripped off in the melee. Kyle might have been trying too hard, and I was happy to move on. He's an interesting guy, a kitchen sink player from a tough background in Tooting who has an amazing capacity to absorb and retain information.

Get him on your pub quiz team, pronto.

He was also bright enough to get the best legal representation, which helped secure a suspension for five weeks fewer than the supposed minimum. He went in with a QC. I was twenty-one, unversed in the ways of the world, and faced the panel without a lawyer. I've subsequently been told that was a budgetary decision by the club; I had to rely on the advocacy of Northampton's CEO at the time, Allan Robson.

For the record, I have never consciously set out to 'do' an opponent, to inflict harm with malice aforethought. Gouging is rightly considered beyond the pale, but if you analyse my conduct, I have erred by reacting impulsively in the heat of the moment, when boundaries are blurred by emotion and competitive instinct.

It is a confrontational game. In the case of Jonny O'Connor I made contact with his face as I was getting up off the floor. It was an act of closed-fist one-upmanship. I wanted to push his head into the ground to remind him of my superiority. That might appear petty, or foolish, in isolation, but professional rugby players will empathize with the intentions.

I think I got a week for that. They threw the book at me for the James Haskell incident, when I went through a ruck, and didn't clear him out very well. Hask is a mate, but at that moment he was an unidentified body. He was slipping past me, and I reacted recklessly. I flailed an arm, reached back, and tried to make contact with anything to stop him.

It could have been his shirt or his hair, but the palm of my hand went across his face. I didn't have the time, and certainly didn't have the inclination, to think consciously about gouging. My fingers weren't stiff when they made contact with the eye area. My palm was open. The only thing closed was the mind of some of my harsher critics.

Hask knew the score. He had played with me, and, though I didn't expect it, gave me a character reference in his evidence to the panel. The problem was the freeze-frame image of the incident. It was deceptive yet decisive because it looked bad. I was judged on the impression of violent intent, rather than the substance of the action.

A picture, in those circumstances, is worth much more than a thousand words in mitigation. One of the most iconic rugby photographs features former Wales captain Garin Jenkins in a World Cup match against Argentina in 1999. A Pumas player appears to be using his head as a bowling ball, with fingers in his eye socket.

It is such an arresting image that opticians use it, in explaining detached retinas. Squaddies at Camp Bastion in Afghanistan showed it to US troops to convince them of rugby's innate hardness, compared to American football. Garin has been told that solitary image has earned the photographic agency £800,000.

An inspirational character, who has worked voluntarily with delinquent youths since his retirement, Garin acknowledges he was lucky to escape serious injury. It must have hurt like hell. Yet the match commissioner decided the photograph made the incident look much worse than it was. The culprit could not be identified.

The Argentinians, asked to reflect on the case, unsurprisingly agreed with Francois Pienaar, South Africa's World Cup-winning captain. He defended the decision to take no action, insisting 'It looks shocking as a photograph but clearly when you see the action sequence it is nothing more than an impatient shove.'

Who really knows what is in a man's heart, and his head?

I was named man of the match before I was cited. Phil Vickery, the Wasps captain, had deliberately stood on my Achilles before giving the referee a running commentary on my supposed iniquity. It was old-school, rough-house footie involving consenting adults. There weren't twenty high-definition cameras focusing on the action in slow motion.

I was in my second season, playing against old lags intent on introducing a new dog to old tricks. I had received the message, loud and clear, in only my second senior game, against Bath. I was a boy, playing a man's game. Danny Grewcock, the England and British Lions lock, slipped his binding and threw three uppercuts at me in the scrum.

Boom. Boom. Boom. As we got up, he simply winked at me, and ran off. I knew, from that moment on, how it was going to be. He was a product of an era when front-row players were not first-team regulars until their mid-twenties. I was nineteen, one of the new breed of academy players coming through, and needed to know my place.

Danny knew he could get away with a cross-generational reminder of the real world. I played in matches in which England teammates would wind each other up for a laugh, squeezing their nuts or fish-hooking when they were in the middle of a maul. If they did that today, they'd be caught on camera. There'd be no getting away with the 'We're mates, it was only banter' defence.

Fish-hooking is rugby slang for inserting your finger in the side of an opponent's mouth, with the intention of pulling him back. That's how, and why, I received an eight-week ban for biting Ireland's flanker Stephen Ferris during our 30–9 Six Nations win over them at Twickenham in March 2012. It's fair to say we have not been bosom buddies since.

It was another case of a missed clearout. He was using a judo technique, of neck rolling, which works on the principle that if your head is moved, the body will follow. It is no longer legal, but by his admission, in his autobiography, his arm was draped over my shoulder as we hit the ground in a ruck. He denies it, but ended up pulling me backwards, by my mouth.

These things happen. I reckon he found a lever and acted on instinct. There was no lasting damage, and the game was generally played in a good spirit. Let's face it, there are phases of play in which we are human missiles. If it was open season, without a moral code in operation, someone could get seriously hurt.

The incident wasn't spotted by Nigel Owens, the referee, to whom he complained. It wasn't highlighted by television coverage, and wasn't mentioned in immediate match reports. Alberto Recaldini, the Italian match commissioner, brought the charge that I'd acted 'contrary to good sportsmanship' but initially got the timing wrong. He said the incident occurred in the twenty-third minute, when it happened five minutes later.

I turned up at the hearing suited and booted. Ferris wore a vest, and gave his version of events over Skype. Asked whether he could have placed his hand in my mouth in attempting to clear me out, he answered 'No chance. There's no doubt Dylan Hartley sourced my finger at the bottom of the ruck and bit it.'

I'd already been honest to the panel, when they watched footage that showed his hand moving across my face, in a pulling motion. I admitted to biting down in a reflex action, since it is natural to do so if you are in discomfort. I couldn't lie. I told Ferris: 'Look, I said I bit you. What else am I supposed to do?'

I was supported by Graham Rowntree, who as England forwards coach understood the nature of the supposed offence, and the frenzied environment in which it unfolded. Jim Mallinder represented me as my director of rugby. The disciplinary panel, drawn from Wales and Scotland, reduced the minimum sentence by four weeks, but I'd inadvertently damned myself. My honesty gave them little wriggle room.

Ferris, who dabbles in TV commentary these days, admitted in 2018 that he still had 'a little bit of a beef with me'. He never played for Ireland again; his Ulster teammate the prop Pedrie Wannenburg had bitten me on the wrist when I had him in a headlock after he came through a maul in a Heineken Cup match at Milton Keynes the previous April. The You-Tube clip leaves no room for doubt, but no action was taken.

Rory Best, his captain for country and province, featured in my next run-in with the authorities, in 2012. I was banned for a fortnight for punching him. I accept I'm open to criticism, but I'm not going to be hypocritical. I didn't, and don't, regard that as a cardinal sin. I saw him coming towards me when a ruck broke down. He didn't seem to be interested in exchanging fraternal greetings as he loomed over me. I thought a knee was coming in my direction so basically got my retaliation in first.

The game has changed irreversibly since that principle became enshrined in Lions legend in South Africa in 1974. Captain Willie John McBride's simple instruction, for everyone to punch the nearest Springbok on hearing the abbreviated emergency call 'ninety-nine', which signalled a teammate in distress, set the tone for an unbeaten three-month tour.

Rugby lore loves high-profile vigilantism. The Battle of Ballymore, the second Lions Test against Australia in Brisbane in 1989, is another classic example of brothers-in-arms at work. The series was in the balance when the Wales scrum half Robert Jones stood on Nick Farr Jones's foot and scraped his studs down the shins of his opposite number while he fed into a first-minute scrum.

Nick went nuts, and as the two smallest men on the pitch rolled around, throwing punches, the enforcers in the Lions pack got stuck in against all-comers. Mike Teague, the England flanker, couldn't quite hide his relish when he called it 'the most violent game of rugby that has ever been played'. His subsequent admission that 'We can't be seen to condone what went on, but needs must' rings true.

I've never experienced that sort of premeditated ferocity. The modern no-backward-step mentality is underpinned by the same philosophy of looking after your mates, but tends to be expressed through handbagging, rather than brawling. There's a lot of chest-puffing and big-boy posing, but it's no longer guerrilla warfare.

Assisting an isolated teammate is, however, non-negotiable. The fracas following the warm-up for the Calcutta Cup match at Murrayfield in February 2018 was a contemporary example of an unwritten code of conduct in operation. I didn't see the incident, as I was already in the dressing room, but the lads were adamant that Ryan Wilson, Scotland's number 8, was in George Ford's face. Brave of him, given his physical superiority.

Owen Farrell saw what was going on, and sprinted down the tunnel, shouting at Wilson to 'Get the fuck out of the way.' Wilson definitely made contact with George; he either threw an arm around him, or pushed and jostled him, depending on your choice of witness. One thing remains clear: you do not lay hands on an opponent before a match. That's shithouse behaviour.

There was a lot of shoving, and a bit of noise, but no punches were thrown in the ensuring scuffle. We subsequently played poorly, but to link that to the premature confrontation was fanciful to say the least. As for Wilson, he escaped a ban for making contact with the eye area of Nathan Hughes during the game, despite the disciplinary panel finding him guilty of an act of foul play.

The game is the game. Rugby is emotive. The reason I'm pretty good at it is that I care enough about it to throw myself into it physically. I need to be simmering to be effective, and occasionally that intensity has worked against me. The Caveman takes over. If someone grabs me, I obey a basic instinct and attack.

The cold, grey fact that I was banned for three weeks in December 2014 for elbowing Leicester's centre Matt Smith in the face gives no hint of the heat of battle, or the tension that defines a traditionally colourful East Midlands derby. Personal rivalries and provocative personalities ensure there is a lot more on the line than in a normal club game.

On this occasion I was in direct competition with Tom Youngs, who wanted my England shirt. I had been serenaded by the Leicester coach, Richard Cockerill, a former England hooker whose shaven-headed, hard-nosed, bulldog-barking approach betrays his self-image as a Big Bad Boss. Even his autobiography was called *In Your Face*.

Though we were only sixteen minutes in, we had reached the first pinch point in the match, a ruck that had formed five metres from their line. Smith cleared me out and pulled me backwards without letting go. It wasn't the time or the place to politely suggest he desist. I thought 'Get the fuck off me' and instinctively lashed out.

The point of my elbow made contact with his nose. He made the most of it, hitting the deck like a shinpad, our shorthand for a footballer, prone to the sort of theatrical behaviour that tends to be disowned in rugby. The referee, J. P. Doyle, was going to give me a yellow card until the television match official, Sean Davey, urged him to review TV replays. They didn't look good.

Events unfold in slow motion when the TMO gets involved. The process seems to take for ever, but, as you feature in more of them, you tend to know what's coming. In my case it was a red card, and another trip to London, for a disciplinary hearing held via a conference call. I was thrown into limbo, wondering, once again, about the longevity of my England career.

The immediate priority, though, had been the team Christmas party, held that night in a private pub at the Carlsberg Brewery. We ripped into it, continually chanting 'Fuck Leicester' in recognition of a 23–19 win, earned by fourteen men and confirmed by Jamie Elliott's 77th-minute try, converted from the touchline by our fly half, Stephen Myler.

Those are the nights when all the motivational prattle about team bonding makes perfect sense. The reality, that club loyalties are inevitably tempered by international ambition and commitments, blends temporarily into the background. My seventh and hopefully final suspension, for six weeks two years later, was partially down to the difficulty of squaring that particular circle.

I was tired and distracted following my first sequence of autumn internationals as England captain, though initially grateful for the respite of being on the substitutes' bench for my reintegration game, Northampton's Champions Cup tie against Leinster. I am not a great watcher at the best of times, and my mood darkened as we were on the wrong end of a caning.

We were losing the psychological battle, and failing to break the gain line. We had a soft, self-satisfied air that intensified my frustration at the reduction in the resolution I had taken for granted with England, under Eddie Jones. When I came on as replacement, I wanted to make a statement, set a new tone.

I wanted to do damage, but not in the way it transpired, through a straight-arm tackle on Sean O'Brien, their Lions flanker. I didn't intend to take anyone's head off; I wanted to be positive, dominant. The intention was good, but execution was very poor. The TV cameras inevitably zoomed in on Eddie, sitting in the stands with his head in his hands.

He read me my fortune in an interview, soon after the match: 'If he has his arms in close he does not hit a bloke like that. We are consistently reinforcing good technique. We have spoken to Dylan and he has done numerous skill-sessions to pick it up. He is not the only one with that flaw.' That meant only one thing, at least an extra half an hour to my working day.

Alignment between club and country wasn't as good as it could have been at the time, so I was caught in the middle, and trying to please two masters. I had a leadership role at Northampton, and drove to Pennyhill Park, England's training base in Surrey, on my day off. I was doing additional fitness sessions, and intensive technical work on my tackling, despite a bad back.

There was no option. I was a rookie international captain, still carving out a niche. Eddie liked to see me put more in than the rest. I had to play the political game, prove my work ethic, and remind him I could be of use. The shaggy-haired roughneck had to be pushed further back, into the convenient mists of time.

Though I have become a little more malleable down the years, I'd still probably get a mention as a player vulnerable to incitement, but the modern game is too fast to make it worthwhile targeting individuals for a concerted wind-up. If you are set on following that path, the obvious candidate would be the scrum half, because he tends to have a small man's chippy nature, and controls the tempo of the team.

Everything goes through him because he's the one who moves the ball. If someone slyly holds him on the floor, he is going to start struggling and swinging, because he knows he has to be at the base of the next ruck, to maintain the supply line. That happened to Danny Care in a recent club match; he lashed out, and won us a penalty.

At international level, in particular, Big Brother is always watching. That's why we need our own witness. Richard Smith, the QC, is seated among England coaches and analysts during matches, plugged into the live TV feed. I can testify to the accuracy of the independent Chambers UK Guide, which describes him as an advocate who 'achieves incredible results from seemingly impossible situations'.

A criminal and sports law barrister with more than thirty years' experience, Richard has been England's legal counsel since the 2003 World Cup, when Clive Woodward recruited him following disciplinary problems on tours to the southern hemisphere, with which management failed to deal effectively. The RFU baulked at the cost, so Woodward simply sourced sponsorship from a rice company.

Our QC is fully integrated into the squad, attending training camps, and has helped a series of players in successive World Cups, from Mike Tindall in 2007, through Courtney Lawes in 2011, to Piers Francis in 2019. He is a direct conduit to the authorities in citing cases; my most recent cause for gratitude came in the aftermath of England's 12–6 win over Wales at Twickenham in February 2018.

It was a tense match, in which we protected two first-half tries by Jonny May. The crowd were in full cry when, following the award of a penalty against us seven minutes before half-time, Owen Farrell and Aaron Shingler, the Wales back row, went at it on the floor. In an instant we had an old-school punch-up, in which Maro Itoje introduced himself to Alun Wyn Jones.

I did not stand idly by, and once the scuffle had subsided, with the referee warning us that 'You must calm down', I cleared my throat and spat on the ground. It's not a terribly delicate process, but I do not wear a gumshield, and often find that one of my nasal passages becomes blocked during a match.

I was oblivious to the witch hunt being simultaneously launched on social media by Welsh fans, who used a YouTube clip taken from the live TV coverage to accuse me of spitting at an opponent. The so-called 'story' gained traction on Twitter and Facebook, and before long I was being condemned as a 'dirty fucking bastard', guilty of 'disgusting behaviour'.

Eddie Jones came up to me afterwards and asked 'Did you spit at anyone?' I denied it categorically, and he attempted to reassure me by insisting 'The QC is on to it.' The Welsh team management didn't complain, but because of the unfounded rantings in cyberspace the independent citing commissioner, Eugene Ryan from Ireland, felt duty-bound to investigate.

Citing is a very formal process, and charges need to be levelled within forty-eight hours. As captain, I would always check in with Richard, to ask, quietly and confidentially, whether he anticipated any problems. On this occasion he said he was 'dealing with a couple of things', including defending Owen from potential bother over a high tackle.

Rumours of the nonsense on social media reached me at the post-match dinner, just before the QC pulled me out-side, to warn me that, on one particular foreshortened camera angle, it appeared as if I had spat on an unidentified Wales player, lying on the ground. Dave Guyan, who liaises with the citing commissioner for the RFU, was in the con-trol room of a broadcasters' truck, seeking alternative images.

The TV guys were, by then, shutting up for the night, having completed their highlight packages. I returned to the dinner, sick to the stomach, and forced myself to mentally rehearse my speech. I'm normally comfortable with the cere-monial requirements, but the thought of standing up to speak, believing everyone had leapt to the conclusion I was some sort of animal, was uniquely disturbing.

About forty minutes later, just as I was about to get to my feet, Richard Smith came up, murmured 'It's dealt with' and showed me a freeze-frame photograph that proved my inno-cence. The outstretched leg of the Wales player was at least four feet away from where I had spat. To his great credit, the citing commissioner made a point of seeking me out later to apologize 'for putting you through that'.

He had not allowed the situation to worsen, by using his prerogative to wait to make his judgement call. The episode is now seen, in Six Nations administrative circles, as an object lesson in the responsibility of the authorities to the players, in consciously seeking evidence to support not making a charge, where doubt exists. It might not be as obvious as some of the wounds we suffer on the pitch (blood streamed down my face during that particular match) but we fret off it.

On a personal level, it brought home the importance of respect among my peers, and the cumulative stress of dealing with the threat of disciplinary action, immediately after the draining experience of a high-profile international. I knew I hadn't done anything wrong, but seriously considered retirement that night because of the threat of a miscarriage of justice.

I couldn't face the prospect of dealing with the usual suspects, media critics who could be relied upon to form a hanging jury. I didn't want to go through the demeaning process of wearing my Sunday best, and turning up at yet another tribunal that would decide the authenticity of my character. I just wanted to turn up for work, the following week, as a rugby player.

That, of course, is not as simple as it seems. I don't expect sympathy, because I accept the unforgiving nature of modern sport and it is right that I should be held responsible for my actions, which I have had cause to regret down the years. My disciplinary issues cost me a place on the 2013 Lions tour of Australia, and resulted in my exclusion from the World Cup, two years later.

More of that later, but, in hindsight, my six-month ban in 2007 captured the mood of the times. It was the first major citing case. Rugby was becoming more corporately aware, increasingly responsive socially and commercially. Big brands didn't want to be associated, overtly, with the dark arts and ruffians rolling around in the mud. They wanted to ride on the shoulders of shiny new heroes.

Rugby needed to clean up its act. I had been on a steep upward curve until that fateful match against Wasps. I had made my England Saxons debut as a replacement a couple of months earlier, in a 34–5 win against Italy A in Exeter, and scored three tries in as many games. Brian Ashton, the senior coach, had not been in touch directly, but the word on the street was that he was impressed.

I was a bolter for his World Cup squad, but written out of the script the moment the newspapers hit the desk at Rugby House, opposite Twickenham stadium. Blaring headlines about the imposition of the biggest ban in recent history meant I would be seeking redemption while England were losing the final, and their title, to South Africa in Paris in October.

Northampton's relegation was a blessing in disguise, since it allowed me to recalibrate my career, below the radar. I was away from the Premiership, and the spotlight of Sky TV, playing every week with my mates. I made lifelong friends, like Chris Ashton, in that period. We won every game, and I found a degree of serenity through my simplicity of purpose.

Despite the relative poverty of my surroundings, people who mattered were watching. I was taken by temporary England coach Rob Andrew on a two-Test tour of New Zealand in June 2008, as third-choice hooker behind Lee Mears and

David Paice. I didn't play in either match – we lost 37–20 and 44–14 in Auckland and Christchurch respectively – but it proved to be a formative experience.

I had left New Zealand as a rugby nobody, six years previously. The schoolboy from Rotorua Boys High was living the dream, flying business class around the world, staying at the best hotels, and being mentioned in the same breath as the All Blacks. Sure, I had doubts, but I felt I belonged.

I was on my way.

# 7

## Stone Age to Space Age

I was in the right place, at the wrong time. It didn't take a genius to work out why the England senior squad, scoured by narrow loyalties and personal insecurities, was in decline. The atmosphere was unwelcoming, almost sour. No one introduced themselves. No senior pro was prepared to give a new kid an even break by offering a friendly word of advice.

When I walked into the dining room for the first time, the team dynamics were clear. The Leicester players, clustered around one table, didn't even lift their heads in recognition. They had every right to ignore me, since they were the swinging dicks of Premiership rugby, at the start of a three-season run of first-place finishes, but their insularity was double-edged.

Club teams are clans. They mistrust outsiders, develop distinctive rituals and establish their own hierarchies. Successful sides at international level are driven similarly by individual agendas, but cemented by a collective spirit that is sometimes difficult to define. Tribal priorities are placed into perspective by a bigger goal, which strengthens and unifies the group.

That's tricky when the majority of the coaching team is also closely identified with one particular club, in this case the Tigers. This England team would be moulded, if not made, in Welford Road. Martin Johnson, the Leicester legend and World Cup-winning captain, had taken over from Brian Ashton as head coach in the summer of 2008.

The two coaches with whom I had most contact had obvious and understandable allegiances to him. John Wells, the former Leicester captain, looked after the forwards. Graham Rowntree, a pillar of the Leicester front row for seventeen years, focused on our scrum. It wasn't exactly a Mafia, but I felt like an outsider, at risk of offending the family code.

I might have been raw, but I understood what was going on, and why. At that time, club held greater sway than country. Leicester was in its pomp, and took pride in its reputation as a blue-collar, working-man's club. Players made a point of driving unspectacular cars, into which they would pile unannounced on a day off, on some sort of Secret Squirrel mission. Anyone who turned up in anything remotely shiny was dismissed as soft.

When the club is the one constant in a player's life, the bonds made there are exponentially tighter. As we saw in English football at that time, when the so-called Golden Generation under-performed because of the mutual suspicion created by cliques formed around Chelsea, Liverpool and Manchester United, that doesn't help to build a successful national team.

Faced with what I took to be internal resistance, my instincts kicked in. So what if there was no one to fling a protective arm around my shoulder, and show me the way to the physio room? I wouldn't be intimidated. I would make my mark through my competitive edge. That wouldn't involve triggering fights in training, but it did mean I wasn't fazed by physical contact.

I was determined to show willing, to prove I had what it took to survive. I didn't waste reps in the gym. I just got stuck in. My lifestyle wasn't the best, but in terms of my training ethic, I'd pitch myself against any hard-nosed veteran. I was subconsciously laying the foundations of a long career, in demonstrating my determination on a habitual basis.

I earn my chance at the weekend by the way I work from Monday to Friday.

We slipped to eighth in the world rankings, soon after I won my first cap, for a five-minute cameo at the end of a 39–13 win over the Pacific Islanders at Twickenham in November 2008. Four other debutants – Delon Armitage, Riki Flutey, Ugo Monye and Nick Kennedy – had started, but I'm pretty sure I made the biggest impact.

For non-rugby reasons, sadly.

I embraced the prevailing post-match tradition that any new cap had to have a drink with any England player, past or present, who bought him one. The drawback was that it had to be downed in one, and you had no control over its content. Jason Leonard, former England prop and full-time Fun Bus driver, set the tone with a glass that conservatively contained a bottle of white wine.

He's a lovely bloke, but dangerous. By the time I was introduced to weapons-grade versions of a Rusty Nail, a cocktail that combines Drambuie and Scotch whisky, I was levelled. I don't remember too much after that, but the image of me tackling Martin Johnson into the side of the team bus lingered through the subsequent retching and remorse.

I was supposed to perform my initiation song on the way back to Pennyhill Park from Twickenham, but they couldn't wake me. I somehow reached my hotel room and, in my last moments of consciousness for the night, suffered a predictable calamity attempting to take my shirt off. Remember, kids, cufflinks are a drunk's mortal enemy.

I have quite large hands, and couldn't get them out of my shirt sleeves, once I had thrown off my jacket. I contorted myself and managed to free one arm before dragging the shirt over my head so that it hung from the other arm, where the cufflink was evidently attached with superglue. In my befuddled state, I stood on the shirt and yanked it.

Big mistake. The sleeve ripped, from wrist almost to the shoulder. Peering through the fog of the following day's hangover, I knew one thing. I couldn't afford to reveal my stupidity to anyone, including the kit manager. He needed my England suit, so that it could be dry-cleaned, but I wasn't about to give him a shirt that should really have been recycled as a dishcloth.

I went through that autumn's internationals wearing the shredded shirt, which I'd quickly remove in the changing room so no one could see its distressed state. After games, I'd put my jacket on with indecent haste, and keep it on for the rest of the evening. Dressing rooms tend to be chaotic after matches, but it still seems incredible that no one noticed.

I loved Jonno, despite the complications of his Leicester affiliations. I had never played against him, but obviously respected his achievements and his back story, as a young forward who hardened himself in King Country in New Zealand, where he arrived as a quiet 'Pretty Boy' and was mourned as an All Black who got away when he returned to the UK.

At the time I had little to compare myself to, but I identified with someone whose apprenticeship began at Tihoi, a small settlement where the rugby team consisted of farmers, bush workers and pig hunters. The pitch had to be cleared of assorted animals, and branches protruded from the goalposts; by all accounts it is now a field on which swedes are grown.

Jonno was firm, and fiercely committed. He coached as if he was still captain. It wasn't a question of transmitting tactical strategy or sharing technical excellence. In retrospect, I recognize a little of Eddie Jones in the way he lived the game. He wasn't bothered with coaching orthodoxy, pursuing the latest training fashion or following a fleeting New Age motivational programme.

His strength was in tapping into the game's fundamentals, the raw material of a winner's mentality. He spoke from a deeply personal perspective, of formative experiences under the pressure of big-match rugby. Maybe he wasn't best suited to the breadth and formality of a head coach's job, but he was a brilliant person to have in a competitive environment.

Did we let him down? To be brutally honest, given the implosion that occurred at the 2011 World Cup, we did, to varying degrees. Even in those early days, there was an element of indiscipline, on and off the pitch. The generation who played with him were probably a little too familiar. It is easy to forget that the transition from amateurism had lingering after-effects.

I was introduced gently to the team, and spared the harsher judgements of those autumn internationals. I had a ten-minute run-out in a 28–14 loss to Australia, was given twenty-two minutes in a record 42–6 defeat by South Africa that Jonno rightly described as 'brutal', and played thirteen minutes in a 32–6 loss to the All Blacks, in which we conceded fifteen penalties.

I continued as understudy to Bath's Lee Mears in the 2009 Six Nations Championship, in which wins over Italy, France and Scotland partially compensated for a tonking in Wales and a gutting 14–13 defeat to Ireland at Croke Park in Dublin. I started in another loss, against the Barbarians, before being first choice in home-and-away Tests against Argentina, in which we won 37–15 at Old Trafford a week before losing 24–22 in Salta.

Lee was in the 37-strong Lions touring squad in South Africa, where he started the first Test, a 26–21 defeat, before slipping down the hookers' pecking order, behind Matthew Rees of Wales and Scotland's Ross Ford, who replaced an original selection, Jerry Flannery of Ireland. I had no realistic chance of selection, and figured my time would come.

That worked out well, didn't it?

You never feel established as an England player, but I gradually felt more comfortable in international rugby, where I gravitated towards younger guys like Ugo Monye and James Haskell. Lee helped enormously in that process. He understood the nurturing aspects of his role, as the older guy proactively supporting the team's succession planning. He gave me his time and his trust, and taught me how to conduct yourself, on a personal level, in the twilight of your career.

Steve Thompson saw things differently. He regarded me as a threat, following the reversal of his decision to retire, due to a severe neck injury sustained in a Heineken Cup pool match against Biarritz at Franklin's Gardens in January 2007. He didn't even pretend otherwise. It was business, not personal. There was no real relationship, beyond the practicalities of our respective jobs.

We were, in our own ways, defined by personal history. His view of me had been established when I was an emerging player during his time at Northampton, which ended when he joined Brive, initially as 'recruitment and technique adviser'. He, of course, had a World Cup-winner's medal, and a place in the pantheon of contemporary rugby heroes.

Human nature being what it is, the intimacy of his link, as a celebrated teammate of Jonno, Jonny Wilkinson & co., gave him a natural advantage when he was restored to the England squad. To be fair, I was given a fair crack of the whip. With the exception of an 18–9 defeat to Australia in November 2009, I remained first choice, up to and through the subsequent Six Nations.

I still had a lot to learn, though. I trained hard, but wasn't fully focused. That's partly my fault, but also down to the environment in which I was operating at club level. We were professional, in terms of being paid, but had an unprofessional approach to our trade. We didn't talk about being the best. We wouldn't analyse what it would take to win things, consistently.

Now everything is geared to the following day's training, which is, in turn, designed to maximize my opportunity to perform at the weekend. I stretch assiduously, and use the paraphernalia of recovery sessions – ice machines and compression equipment – at home. In my downtime, I can be found in the pool, rather than the pub.

It is the difference between the Space Age and the Stone Age. Looking back, I wasted several years, just bumbling along. We merely maintained the rhythm of playing a few games. My lifestyle choices were terrible. I was distracted by the prevailing drinking culture, and did some stupid things, none more so than on a Wednesday night in Cambridge before an East Midlands derby against Leicester.

We hit the student bars, hard, and ended up trying to steal a bicycle. A police patrol spotted us, chased us successfully, and threw us in a paddy wagon. Since we were in fancy dress, we were hardly inconspicuous. That saved us, since the desk sergeant was a Saints fan, and managed to facilitate our release, with an appropriately stern bollocking.

The sacred law of *omertà* was obeyed, we won 7–6 at Welford Road as if nothing untoward had happened, and went back on the lash. Any thought of potential arrest, negative headlines, public shame and a media car crash was swept away by the first Saturday night pint. What were we thinking? Not much, to be frank. We kidded ourselves that we would be purified by the intensity of our training.

Sure, we worked hard, but to what end? No one stopped to consider whether our training was relevant. Today's England team is governed and galvanized by a modern mindset. At the risk of sounding like some sort of PowerPoint puppet, that means doing everything possible to lead the world in personal and collective progression through innovation and intelligent preparation.

Under Jonno the prevailing view was that an England player was, to all intents and purposes, the finished article. In my case, that could not have been further from the truth. I needed to hone the micro-skills that contribute to the continual evolution of a world-class sportsman. Instead, work on small but essential elements of technique was sacrificed to the game plan.

That's diametrically opposed to the coaching philosophy of Eddie Jones, and such effective lieutenants as Steve Borthwick, Paul Gustard and Neal Hatley. They ensure players practise to the highest possible standard. Of course, match preparation has its place, but the concentration is on the individual, rather than a loose view of running a pre-planned move that involves twenty-five guys to a greater or lesser degree.

I need a sounding board, whether I am nineteen or thirty-four. I'm screaming for a coach who knows my position, understands my personality, and appreciates the value of both new techniques and old certainties. It took time, too much time, for me to gain greater recognition of the process of improvement. That involves instilling good habits, without stripping the player of responsibility for his performance.

Lineout throwing is one of my fundamentals, and I benefit from rehearsing my routine. It is pretty basic: if the ball lies straight in your hands, and your hands go to the target, you will be accurate. It's a bit like throwing a dart, or a tennis ball. I played badminton and the same principle applies: point at the shuttlecock before a shot and you won't miss it. It is amazing how kids improve when I tell them simply to point to where they want to throw the ball.

Repetition helps, but nothing beats in-game experience. That's where you learn to control your breathing, to compose yourself so you can see things in sharp focus. There's so much going on in front of you at a lineout. You're thinking about the pace, positioning and shape of the throw. You have five different calls, and must be ready to hit any one of them.

The locks tend to make the calls. With England that means the likes of Courtney Lawes, Maro Itoje, George Kruis and Joe Launchbury working with the lineout professor, the forwards coach Steve Borthwick. Boy, do they do their homework. The plan, to exploit known strengths or to identify and target specific weaknesses, is renewed on a match-by-match basis.

I don't need to be bogged down by the search for the options; I just need to know what they are. It's a complicated process, but preparation is relatively simple. I trust the guys to make the right calls at the right time. As they're walking into the line, they're assessing the angles, anticipating where space can be created. Signals are usually verbal, but can be physical.

The non-verbal ones are usually picked up on quickly in this age of obsessive analysis, and so are changed regularly. The Irish, for instance, gave the game away when certain players put their hands on their hips. That was the trigger for the ball to be thrown, suddenly, to the back of the lineout. When I'm preparing to throw I know what the first option is, but I'm also reading my teammates' eyes, to see if anything has changed.

Verbal calls are pretty straightforward, and feature letters, colours or numbers. To give a simple example, black means throw to the front, green signifies a throw to the middle, and gold tells me to bung it to the back. The options are preset, and loaded, but they can change, if the caller has spotted an opportunity. He might just say 'No.' That's his message to me that we're going to the second option.

The caller is looking at the opposition pods, the guys who lift the jumper. He might sense space at the front, and yell 'Black.' Boom. You've got to be ready to go. If the composition of the line suddenly changes, you've got to stay on the caller's wavelength, and respond accordingly. It can be complex; there are double-bump moves, and triple movement where you're suddenly hearing 'Gold' and aiming at the tail, from which the backs can be given quick ball.

Preparation has become multifaceted in recent years. At England level there are pre-meetings involving specialist coaches and associated players. Plans are drawn up and stress-tested through presentation to the wider group. To take kick-offs as an example, I would propose a certain strategy to the squad, but be open to change, through constructive debate.

For too long, people went out to play for England without clarity. There was too much confusion, and ideas fell through the gaps. You just can't rock up on a Saturday, and assume everything will work itself out. There will be moments when it all falls apart – when a lineout disintegrates it is sometimes best to hurl the ball in flat, and hope it hits someone on the head – but you can't blag it.

Time is limited during the frenzy of an international, so players need help to be able to think for themselves. The delivery of the best messages, and their enforcement when your brain is on overload and your body is screaming for respite, is critical. They need to be policed, as part of a process that involves practising with a purpose.

Unopposed training sessions, without the reality check of anyone competing on the ball, have limited worth. If you carry the ball without a defence attempting to frustrate you, and then simulate being tackled, only for two guys to come over the top, mimicking the action of a ruck, it achieves little, apart from stimulating a false sense of security.

During a match, I'm relying on trigger thoughts or movements. So, for example, I touch the floor momentarily, to check I am maintaining the correct body height at a ruck. That's a product of Eddie's training methods. If he sees someone higher than he should be, he blows his whistle and asks the self-perpetuating question: 'Why are we stopping?'

He wants us to see the session with a coach's eye. A top team continually feeds back to itself. As captain, I try to set the tempo on the pitch by pointing out a potential failing before it becomes costly, but in an ideal situation every player is sufficiently switched on to think quickly, on behalf of his teammates.

In Eddie's world there is no point in doing something unless it is done properly. He walks around with a ball loaded in his hand, ready to be tossed into play if he spots a fault. That could involve poor supporting play for a player running into contact, the wayward delivery of a slow, sloppy pass, or failure to kill the ball in the event of a knock-on.

Turning the ball over is a cardinal sin. Something like 80 per cent of tries in international rugby are scored within the first three phases of play following a change in possession. The defending team needs to organize quickly and effectively to keep its line intact. That's why I'm shouting 'React' in moments of danger. All it takes is for a couple of lazy props to be a bit dim-witted, and wander back into shape. The next thing they know the opposition have broken through, and are on their way to score.

Rugby will always be about brawn, but if you are smart you make it so much easier for yourself. One of my greatest frustrations is one-dimensional thinking. Let's say we're facing Billy Vunipola, one of the best ball carriers in the world, in a Premiership game against Saracens. I've played for coaches who insisted on doing what we had always done, a so-called A+ kick-off, straight to him in the deep.

We were basically giving him a clean catch, doing what his team wanted and expected. They had a psychological lift, and Billy was ready to rumble, knowing he had between ten and fifteen metres to establish his momentum before contact. Why wouldn't we want to make them think by hitting a different area of the pitch, away from his sphere of influence?

Spare me the prattling of wannabe Rambos, who demand a physical manifestation of desire from the safe side of the fence. This is not about manning up. It's not a case of being intimidated by the prospect of putting yourself in harm's way. I'll tackle Billy all day, chop him round the ankles to halt his progress, but cleverness is as integral to rugby as courage.

If you play as you train, and augment the benefits of training well with the emotional spike of excelling under pressure, you get at least an eight-out-of-ten performance. It's hard to get up for every match, because of the relentless nature of what we do, but if everyone falls back on familiar habits and does their job when they are feeling flat, you can retrieve a seven-out-of-ten performance.

Self-awareness is so important. The England team stepped up a level because we recognized that, for certain Six Nations matches, we were in danger of peaking too early, physically and emotionally. We amended the intensity of training, balanced our physiological approach, and completed our mental preparation by adding the magic powder of game day.

The numbers don't lie. On average, the ball is in play for thirty-eight minutes, during an eighty-odd-minute match. The ball is turned over thirty-eight times; you can either design training to replicate the game, with a turnover each minute, or intensify it, so that possession changes every twenty seconds. That helps to create unstructured, instinctive play, which is an All Blacks speciality.

The best teams, in all sports, have training drills designed to stretch skill and imagination. To use football as a reference point, look at Barcelona: their so-called *rondos*, in which a group of players protect possession from pre-assigned 'hunters' in a small space through passing the ball with mesmerizing speed and accuracy, are hugely influential.

The drill re-creates match situations, apart from shooting at goal. It improves teamwork, decision making, fitness, coordination, creativity and competitiveness. Contrast that to old-school, structured play that's still prevalent in some areas of English rugby. Everything is predictable, black and white. Players are treated as chesspieces, to be manipulated rather than given freedom of expression.

The best coaches are facilitators. They test their players ruthlessly, but trust them. They create an environment that encourages repeated excellence. The mindset shifts. It's not a case of standing there and pushing, or battering tackle bags. I appreciate the question seems simplistic, but what do we need to practise to get better?

We need to be able to think quickly, and react quicker still. To do that, we need to be physically fitter, mentally sharper. We must get off the floor faster, and realign quicker, whether we are attacking or defending in event of a turnover. We can do our weights, slog through our aerobic programmes, take out the insurance of prehab work, but the mind is the next area of advancement.

How can you measure someone's mental state of preparedness? There are a lot of people out there who'd be happy to pay top dollar for a reliable answer to that particular question. I find when we drift into a game, or, conversely, strut around as if we know it all, we have paid lip service to key messages, which underpin preparation.

I've learned to sense a looseness of thought before matches. I've become better at identifying the individual who is too relaxed. Some weeks, for example, he might stretch diligently; on other occasions he might just be sitting there, with very little going on behind the eyes. Dullness of thought leads to fractional failure to react: will he be first to a ball on the floor?

I get twitchy when I see players on their phone in the dressing room. Why do you need to be on social media, or checking your Snapchat, before a game? Where's your head at? What are you thinking about? Why are you connecting with the outside world when the only people you should be connecting with are the people around you, in that room?

I believe in the sanctity of the changing shed. A team can feed off its inherent energy. Messages delivered in the moment, in that environment, can be powerful. At Northampton, after one bonus point win, early in the season, I noticed that three players didn't come in and shake hands with their mates. I waited until we were together on Monday morning before making my point, without mentioning names:

'Boys. It's too easy to get the phone out straight after a game, to check your social media and the texts from your mum or your missus. You can be too quick to get the suit on, get out of here, and get on it on a Saturday night. What's the point of fucking yourself physically in training during the week, going out and executing our plans, and not celebrating everything we have strived for?

'You work hard all week to get the result, so enjoy it. That doesn't mean staying in the changing room until one in the morning, bingeing. It might mean just having one beer, or even sticking with your protein shake. Just acknowledge that you've grafted with your mate either side of you. This is a special place.'

The upshot of that at club level is the man of the match now gets a box of Carlsberg, which is dropped in the middle of the changing room. We have a beer, and hang about. After a week spent with the forwards, I might make a point of sharing a drink with the half backs. The ressies take the shirts, remove the GPS monitors, and then muck in with the rest of us. We sweep the sheds before filtering out, to meet friends and family.

I tried to introduce something similar with England, where we have a calming fifteen-minute spell immediately after a match. Measured on a digital clock in the dressing room, that's our 'whoa' time, to acknowledge what we have just experienced. We have a beer and a song, usually a libellous number dreamed up by Jonny May, the evil lyrical genius. You have to enjoy it; otherwise international rugby is just a blur.

When I first broke into the England team, senior players couldn't wait to get their suits on and make a few quid through personal appearances in the sponsors' lounges. They were crawling over each other for the extra bunce, and a strict hierarchy was in place. If you had fewer than twenty-five caps you weren't even allowed in the queue.

Some of the boys did very well. Payment was usually in cash, a couple of grand in an envelope. As a young fella I bit my lip, but eventually started to complain that I was not being cut in on the deal. With the benefit of hindsight I'm annoyed at myself, in allowing the conduct of players I saw as role models to influence my own behaviour.

Our match fee at the time was £9,000, if memory serves, but there was always a chance to make a few extra bob in the hospitality suites. The match fee is now £23,000, which can be bumped up a little by commercial appearances. The boys give value for money, since a sold-out Twickenham generates around £8m. I'd love to see fees double in the next decade.

The obsession with ducking and diving has been replaced by an emphasis on recovery and resilience. The game is more punishing, physically, but the current generation of players is better conditioned than its predecessors. They are bigger and stronger, but there is always room for the smaller, skilful guy. It's about playing to your natural attributes, thoughtfully and relentlessly.

It is still possible to have the occasional, brilliantly enjoyable night out with your mates, but I shudder when I think back to our final days of preparation before flying out to the 2011 World Cup, in Australia and New Zealand. We went on the booze, big time. I fell asleep outside a nightclub in Kingston after one session, and only got back to the team hotel because a passer-by recognized me, and poured me into a cab.

Given what went on in that tournament, the Good Samaritan might have regretted his charitable gesture.

# 8

# Dwarves, Drinks and Destiny

We left Heathrow as the pride of English rugby, the best of the best, at the start of a World Cup adventure. By the time we landed in Auckland, twenty-four hours later, we had assumed the renegade mentality of a club Extra B team determined to do damage on an end-of-season stag trip to Magaluf.

Dawn was breaking as we checked into our hotel, SkyCity. The sensible approach to jet lag involved avoiding caffeine and alcohol, enjoying a little light exercise on a stroll around the harbour, and maybe sweating away the strains of the journey in the Cardio Room. We were told a few drinks wouldn't do any harm.

By 7am we were in the neon-lit netherland of the hotel's casino, with its 2,100 gaming machines and card tables, on which 150 games were available to lighten the wallet. By the end of the day a couple of senior players were informing team management that they had to pay a £2,000 bar bill, run up by a few of the lads in a nightclub.

That was the good news. The bad news was that one of the players had shoulder-charged a bedroom door off its hinges, searching for the teammate he suspected had taken a dump in his bathroom sink. The dumper had, apparently, taken action because someone had stolen his shoe collection, to which he had a weirdly emotional sense of attachment.

I know what you're thinking. I wasn't involved in that sticky situation, though I did capture the aftermath on a video camera, and will admit to doing more than my bit to run up the bar tab. I was in awe of the way the veterans took charge of the situation, in telling the RFU's liaison officer to sort payment out of the social kitty.

Can you imagine the media firestorm that would be created by a similar charade, involving Gareth Southgate and the England football team at a World Cup? Questions would be asked in Parliament, and sponsors approached to explain how such behaviour could be reconciled with their corporate social-responsibility programmes.

Incredibly, not a whisper of the carnage was picked up by the press pack. They had enough time, and due cause, to up their game in a mad month or so after that, when the pretence of professional credibility was shredded by a series of controversies that, combined with a quarter-final defeat to France, did for Martin Johnson.

The thought of such chaos, on day one, will be mind-boggling to any rational observer, brought up on the honour of representing your country at the highest level. But professional sport tends to follow a perverse logic; viewed through a jaundiced eye, it should not come as any great surprise. We were far too loose, even before leaving England.

Jonno was a fantastic leader, through the force of his example, but in such a climate his trust was too often counter-productive. He had old-school faith in his players, and was determined to treat us like adults. He refused to impose a curfew, left drinking to our discretion, and expected us to make what he called 'sensible decisions'. He deserved much better.

No one around him helped, by reading the warning signs. I was young and irresponsible, and needed a tighter leash, as did a few others in the squad. I look back with remorse at the way things unfolded, but they were a reflection of the times, rather than an outright condemnation of a group of players who, to be fair, worked as hard in training as they played out of hours.

I look back, having experienced the intensity of a marginal-gains culture, with a sense of sadness and lost opportunity. I now understand how far removed we were from an elite high-performance unit. But would things have turned out differently had I recognized the error of my immature ways and emulated the über-professionalism of Jonny Wilkinson?

I honestly doubt it, though I have often regretted not gravitating more towards him in my formative years. I love talking with him now, listening to his insights, as one of the greatest players of all time. I milk each minute with him, hang on his every word. As a mentor, he's unsurpassable, but my role models had different priorities.

The scales had tipped too far, up to and including that World Cup, towards social slackness. Jonny was way ahead of his time, with his obsessive approach and habitual self-criticism, but too few of us had the self-discipline to join him in giving the extracurricular activity a wide swerve. A lads-on-tour mentality is simply incompatible with such a big event.

What were we doing? It's a fair question.

The undercurrent of mutual suspicion between players and the RFU had its roots in the messy transition from amateurism to professionalism. In 2000 Jonno, as England captain, staged an impromptu press conference in the car park of the team hotel, alongside his predecessor, Lawrence Dallaglio, and scrum half Matt Dawson, and threatened to strike.

Frustrated by negotiations with the RFU, whom he accused of being 'old-fashioned, patronizing and arrogant', Jonno explained at the time: 'It's not just an issue about money. It's the principle, the way the RFU have handled the situation. They are affecting the guys' livelihoods on a matter of principle.' A deal was reached, yet a fundamental issue festered.

Most of the manoeuvring passed over my head, but the background noise of Twickenham politics was impossible to ignore. A faction within the RFU, and their allies in the media, agitated for Clive Woodward to replace Rob Andrew as England's elite rugby director in the build-up to the 2011 World Cup.

Andrew had been given the responsibility of approaching Jonno, who had done no formal coaching since retiring following the 2003 World Cup win, in 2008. England's incumbent coach, Brian Ashton, had no idea his job was being offered to someone else. Andrew's time at the RFU, in a variety of roles, spanned three World Cups and four coaches, Andy Robinson and Stuart Lancaster in addition to Brian and Jonno.

Trust was hardly helped by the leaking of three supposedly confidential reports, to which we had contributed honestly but anonymously, in a post-tournament review. In one of them Andrew criticized Lewis Moody, our captain, for leading a delegation of senior players to complain about World Cup payments in the weeks prior to our departure for New Zealand.

Our protests were staged with tongues firmly in cheek, but had a serious intent. We took a stand when expected to attend a farewell dinner at Twickenham, organized commercially by the RFU, after a hard day's training. We had been in pre-season mode in camp for a couple of months. The senior players weren't impressed that we would be unpaid, when the authorities, by selling tables, were making money out of us.

That reflected the prevailing climate of financial entitlement, and I went along with it. Suited and booted, we didn't budge when the team bus arrived at the function. We were always going to get off and go in, but sat there for at least five minutes to make our point. Just as the alickadoos were starting to panic at such a public demonstration of our displeasure, we filed in.

Did reputations count against us? Possibly so.

Jonno would be criticized, with the benefit of hindsight, for remaining too loyal to those with whom he shared the 2003 triumph. Lewis Moody was retained as captain despite missing the 2011 Six Nations, in which Tom Wood excelled at flanker, through injury. Toby Flood did very well as first-choice fly half in that tournament, but lost his place to Jonny Wilkinson at the World Cup.

I was in the same boat. First-choice hooker in the Six Nations, which we won despite a solitary defeat by Ireland, I started only one game in New Zealand, the 41–10 win against Georgia, in which I was sin-binned after being penalized at the breakdown. Steve Thompson, another 2003 veteran, took preference in what was a last hurrah before he retired for a second time, due to another neck injury, sustained in training at his new club, Wasps, on our return from New Zealand.

We won all three of our group games in Dunedin, before moving to Auckland, and the 16–12 victory over Scotland that clinched qualification for the knockout phase. Dunedin is a lovely place, with a harbour and hills formed by an extinct volcano, but we were bored, and took Jonno's advice, to get out into the community and sample local culture, a little too literally.

My head was all over the place. Looking back, I behaved like a tourist. It was outrageous, given what I would become accustomed to in Test weeks under Eddie Jones. One afternoon, out for a walk, I saw a guy in the street and, on impulse, offered him $1,000 for his car, a crappy old Vauxhall Victor. He accepted, so Chris Ashton, Ben Foden, James Haskell and I had our wheels.

I can't speak for others, but I was so unfocused I couldn't wait to get out and about, and have fun after training. It all got very messy, very quickly. The RFU, bless them, didn't exactly help by setting up a free bar after we had beaten Argentina 13–9 in our opening match. A night out in Queenstown, the adventure lifestyle capital of the South Island, was never going to end well.

We had reached the point where everyone either goes home or gets a kebab to cure the munchies, when we spotted a bright-pink neon sign that screamed 'Midget Madness'. I'll ask you the key question: You're ten pints deep at the time. What are you going to do? Well, we did the same, and trooped in behind Mike Tindall, who had captained us in Lewis's absence through injury.

It seems faintly absurd re-reading these words, more than eight years on, but I would like to point out that no dwarves were thrown at the Altitude bar that night. Did we have a laugh and a dance that turned into a drunken wrestle with the little people? Sure, but no offence was taken. Irish and Welsh players had got up to something similar in the same bar over the previous week; Brian O'Driscoll was supposedly among those carried out, blind drunk.

We awoke the next morning with stonking hangovers, but were determined to make the most of our day off. Queenstown, a natural playground in which the cold clear waters of Lake Wakatipu are overlooked by a dramatic alpine range, is the sort of place where bucket lists come to life. The squad had three options, the first of which involved a quiet coffee after a recovery session with the physio.

These days, I might join the mild boys. Back then, I was a fully accredited member of the wild boys. The second option, a sheep-shearing experience followed by a bit of gold prospecting, didn't really appeal; I was in a group of seven players who got media knickers in a twist by choosing to take on the Awesome Foursome.

When in Rome and all that . . .

We were in the heartland of extreme sport, and the RFU were paying. We took a helicopter ride through a canyon, white-water rafted down a freezing river, and then yee-haahed our way out, between sheer rock walls, on a jet boat. Fair play to old guys like Simon Shaw, Nick Easter and Tom Palmer, who joined the Vauxhall Victor mob of Foden, Ashton and Haskell on the trip.

The *pièce de résistance* was a bungee jump into the Nevis gorge, a rite of passage for any self-respecting adrenaline junkie. You take an open-air cable car to a cabin, swinging in the wind 134 metres above the gorge's stony floor, and leap. The eight and a half seconds spent in freefall are simultaneously terrifying and addictive.

Judging by some of the more hysterical media reaction, we might as well have been playing Russian Roulette with a loaded gun, given to us by the All Blacks. Jonno, in the increasingly familiar role of lightning conductor, argued our case publicly and forcefully. Other problems, bubbling up behind the scenes, were not so easy to dismiss.

We had barely returned to our rooms at the Scenic Hotel Southern Cross in Dunedin, when Ashton, Haskell and I were summoned to the team office. They'd received allegations of misconduct involving ourselves and a chambermaid, the day before our opening game. A Sunday tabloid was working up a story with supposed sexual connotations.

Your world comes crashing down when you hear those horrible words. You can't get them out of your head, even though you know you can prove your innocence, which will not prevent your name being dragged through the mud. You are criticized in front of your teammates, who are told confidentially what's going on during a team meeting. You wonder whether they think you're dickheads for causing such distraction.

For the next fortnight we trained and played in a limbo, not knowing what would emerge, and when. We were drawn into a secretive world of lawyers and lines of enquiry, of crisis management strategies and impending controversy. I had never felt so low, and thought deeply about the direction I was taking. I wasn't giving myself a chance to play well. I had to change my outlook, and curb my drinking.

The first fire that needed to be fought began to rage forty-eight hours before the Georgia game, when the guys at the Altitude bar helpfully released CCTV footage of their self-styled 'Mad Midget Weekender'. Mike Tindall, who had recently married the Queen's granddaughter, Zara Phillips, was shown chatting to an unnamed girl.

I felt for Mike, a great guy and an outstanding teammate. The fact the mystery woman was a close friend of Zara was initially lost in a welter of manufactured outrage and innuendo. To be clear, we hadn't helped ourselves, but, as England rugby players, we were tasty prey for the sensationalists. They were looking for any angle to take us down.

Problems began to multiply. Dave Alred, the kicking coach whose unorthodox methods had won the trust and admiration of Jonny Wilkinson, and Paul Stridgeon, a former wrestler who now oversees strength and conditioning programmes for Wales and the Lions, were banned for the final group game for switching the ball in the 67–3 win over Romania without asking the permission of the referee, Romain Poite.

The turbulence was unrelenting. A sponsor's day for Land Rover, when we had settled in Auckland, was another fiasco. It was sold to the players as a relaxing break, in which we would go surfing and sea fishing, drive off road in the sand dunes, and have a barbecue on the beach. I was preoccupied, and didn't fancy it, but ten players signed up.

It went downhill, fast, when they discovered that the beach had essentially been turned into a film set. There were cameras everywhere, and they were expected to drive in formation at thirty miles an hour in a shoot scheduled to last for four hours. I bet it sounded brilliant when the creative boys ran it up the flagpole, back at base. At that time, in our prevailing mood, it was an open invitation for chaos.

Manu Tuilagi and Tom Wood had no intention of obeying their hosts' speed limit, and the rest followed suit. Land Rovers are brilliant vehicles, really responsive in such conditions, and the lads had no inclination to act as extras in a glossy commercial. They simply laughed at guys knocking on their windows after the first run, pleading for them to keep some sort of shape.

I've seen the subsequent footage, which was surreal. Dashboard cameras captured the boys laughing and honking. All communication channels were open, so they could hear cameramen in the helicopters shouting 'This is shit.' On one subsequent swoop, to try and get some usable footage, they focused on Ben Foden, who was hanging out of the window, with someone holding his legs.

Everyone's tempers were short. There was no surfing, fishing or barbie. The only refreshment was a few sandwiches and bottles of water. Land Rover complained officially to the RFU, who they blamed for miscommunication. It was a shambles, a real shame, since they are thoughtful and proactive sponsors, who do an awful lot of good work at the grassroots of the game.

Ironically, video evidence proved decisive in our defence of the allegations involving the hotel employee, Annabel Newton. We were messing around with a camera throughout the tournament, with the intention of providing social-media content, and it was running when she came into my room, 510, looking for her walkie-talkie, which had been pinched. Hask, Chris and I had just returned from training.

The door was on the latch, because there was an easy-access policy on the team floor. She asked for her radio back, and what we thought was a playful exchange ended with Hask asking for her to kill Dave Barton, one of the RFU press officers, in return. I said nothing, because I was filming, apart from to confirm that the 'V Bangers', which Hask described as 'our gang', referred to my Vauxhall.

It was silly schoolboy humour, and she left the room in good spirits, with her radio. Her subsequent allegations of sexual misconduct were nonsensical. At no point did anyone touch her. It was an excruciating experience, but I made a point of playing the video of the incident to my mother, and asking whether she saw anything wrong with it. She was bemused when I told her it was going to be a tabloid splash.

It's a bewildering process. We were staggered two days before the Scotland game, when we were advised to pay her $30,000 to make the problem go away. To his great credit, and with the full support of Chris and myself, Hask refused, because 'as soon as we pay hush money we're saying we're guilty, which we are not'.

The situation was bizarre, to the point of unreality. We were given a bouquet of flowers for her and expected to apologize for something that never happened. Farcically, given the circumstances, the England team management and the hotel manager then left the three of us alone with her in the hotel manager's office.

We were convinced it was a set-up, and searched for a hidden camera. Annabel was clearly as confused and uneasy as we were; that gave us all pause for thought. She readily accepted our instinctive apology for any misunderstanding. The reality, it seemed to us, was that she had been swept along by a no-win, no-fee lawyer with a vested interest in escalating the situation.

When it became clear we had a complete video record of the original incident, and a full transcript of the conversation, he didn't have a leg to stand on. The tabloid newspaper, which had sent the RFU a draft outline of the piece it intended to publish, suddenly went similarly quiet. I was genuinely shocked how close they came to publishing damaging fantasy in a sensationalized 'world exclusive'.

A formal police investigation in Dunedin concluded we had no case to answer, and I was exonerated in the subsequent RFU enquiry, but we still spent forty-eight hours in the eye of a headline-driven hurricane once the watered-down non-story was published. There was a lot of flak about 'rich boys' who needed to prove they were not 'drooling fools'.

If the build-up to the quarter-final, which also involved the suspension of Delon Armitage for a high tackle and the fining of Manu Tuilagi for wearing a sponsored gum shield, was fractious, elimination didn't stop the bleeding. The day after a poor first-half performance allowed France to build an unassailable lead at Eden Park, Manu was formally warned by police after jumping off a ferry into Auckland harbour.

I wasn't involved, though I had seen him and a few of the lads in a vineyard on Waiheke Island. The second-biggest island in the Hauraki Gulf, it is a beautiful place, a sanctuary of white sandy beaches, nature trails and olive groves, a forty-minute ferry ride from downtown. The boys, who didn't have families with them, were going for it, so subsequent events weren't entirely shocking.

I was decompressing with my parents and Jo. I knew I had reached a crossroads. I needed time to understand what I wanted to be, and what I needed to do. That could only come from within. It was the start of a five-year process of personal realignment, which was completed by Eddie's gesture of faith, in asking me to be England captain.

I had been a little boy lost, walking into that England dressing room for the first time. I am not about to throw anyone under the bus, because I got to know some great guys, but when you are in that position you are influenced by what you see and hear. It was the end of an era. I was smart enough to realize that I could no longer behave like an idiot.

It always sounds a little hackneyed when life is spoken of as a journey, but we all need help along the way. My path wasn't smooth, even after I acquired greater maturity and experience, but I valued the calmness and context given to me by Stuart Lancaster, when he replaced Jonno as England's head coach, initially on an interim basis for the 2012 Six Nations.

His teaching background obviously informed our first meeting. I was the difficult pupil, the boy at the back of the class who had to be told he could no longer get away with flicking blotting paper at his mates during lessons. 'I'm not sure about you, Dylan,' he said. 'I've heard good things and bad things, so I am going to give you a chance.'

Lanny had been working with England Saxons, and was obviously aware of the potential of the group excelling at under-20 level, which included the likes of Owen Farrell, George Ford, Mako Vunipola and Joe Launchbury. He was the new broom, sweeping away the old guard, though he stressed that attitude was just as important as age.

I was one of the younger players, like Ashton, Haskell, Tuilagi and Foden, who survived the cull. I had to convince him I had the diligence and self-discipline to change my ways, because, as a proud Englishman, he did not want the national team sullied by selfishness or stupidity. He was the bridge between Jonno's old-school tolerance and Eddie's new-era severity.

I really liked him, though I found him too task-focused, to use the jargon of modern performance sport. At his best he's an inspirational coach, as he proved by winning the Champions Cup and the PRO14 title with Leinster in 2018, but, for all the right reasons, he allowed himself to be preoccupied by the restoration of our reputation.

He was an intriguing study in contrasts. A naturally precise and demanding clipboard coach, with a beanie stuffed over his forehead and a whistle hanging around his neck, he was as on-message as a backwoods missionary when it came to the public aspects of the job. He wanted people to share his emotional commitment to English rugby.

We all had a vested interest in rebuilding the game, but, in my view, you shouldn't ram a philosophy down someone's throat. I'm proud to be English, even though I wasn't born here. I've not met a player who is indifferent to the honour of representing his country, even though there were occasions on which the privilege was taken too lightly.

But a team culture is built intimately, from the inside. It cannot be imposed externally. You should not need to be told to talk about it; your commitment should be expressed naturally, through the intensity and integrity of your performance. Become too vanilla, too pre-programmed, and you are in danger of losing your authenticity.

We went through a phase of media training, in which we were encouraged to express the importance of our national identity. All very well intentioned, but when you get a list of bullet points on the subject, to stress during interviews, it is all a little cringeworthy. There comes a time when the priority, winning matches and titles, seems somehow secondary.

In one sense Eddie had an advantage over Lanny, in that he was a foreign coach, hired to win things. He had been around the block, and wanted us to amplify his self-assurance. Did we want to be the best in the world? Hell, yeah. Did we want to impose ourselves, and win every game? You bet. That was the reason why we were there.

It seemed, in that transitional period under Lanny, that we were trying to please all the people, all of the time. Jonno never hid his loathing of the media. The famous brow would furrow, and he would tell them: 'I'm going to talk to you like this, so deal with it.' Lanny tried so hard to be welcoming, inviting them to watch training and eat with us.

We were expected to cosy up to them, to rebuild the brand and restore our Brownie points. That's understandable, up to a point, because rugby, like all major sports, is obliged to self-promote in a competitive marketplace. But our humility was supposed to be extended, so as not to offend our opponents. We were too worried about headlines condemning the 'arrogant English'.

Let's get real, here. There's nothing intrinsically wrong with saying, in a polite manner before a game, 'Fuck you. We're going to win.' Any self-respecting international athlete wants to do so. They prepare well, and believe in their teammates. As captain, I didn't particularly care about spouting platitudes about the opposition. I just wanted to talk about how good my team were, and how much they had put in.

That's not to imply Stuart wasn't a winner. He is a good-hearted man who invested so much of himself in the job that failure hit him very hard. That's an instinctive reaction, which will be recognized by players the world over. The depth of your disappointment will drag you and your family down if you allow it to do so.

But, under him, we were bridesmaids who never managed to catch the wedding bouquet. The biggest games led to our biggest disappointments; the tone was set in the 2012 Six Nations, when a team containing seven Twickenham debutants failed to prevent a Wales Grand Slam, because the TMO disallowed a potentially equalizing try by David Strettle in added time.

Lanny was confirmed as head coach, despite interest from Nick Mallett, the former Springbok and Italy coach, and Wayne Smith, the so-called 'Professor' who has been central to the All Black coaching team for seventeen years. I quickly benefited from the surprising subtlety of his man management.

I was not the most obvious candidate to captain England when Chris Robshaw was sent home before the last Test on the summer tour of South Africa with a cracked thumb. The end to my domestic season had been disrupted by the ban for the Stephen Ferris incident; my promotion was clearly designed as an early examination of my leadership qualities.

The 14–14 draw, following two narrow defeats, provided a platform for the autumn, when near misses against Australia and South Africa were richly compensated for by a fantastically intense 38–21 win over New Zealand. Stop me if you've heard this before, but I missed those three games because of a knee injury. It was beyond gutting.

Tom Youngs seized his opportunity, and, despite my recovery, started four of the five matches in the subsequent Six Nations. Again, we faltered within sight of the summit, losing the chance of a Grand Slam when we were blown away, 30–3, in the madhouse of Cardiff's Millennium Stadium. I came on twelve minutes into the second half; we conceded two tries to the winger Alex Cuthbert, and had to stomach 70,000 Welshmen screaming 'Easy, easy, easy' at us long before a merciful end.

It wasn't all bad, although it felt like it at the time. At club level, our culture was thriving. We were flying in the Premiership, and players were starting to push persistently for international recognition. The chemistry of the season seemed perfect; a special buzz, created in the sanctuary of the dressing room at Franklin's Gardens, extended across the town.

Northampton's history of failure in five previous Premiership semi-finals hung like a toxic cloud over Saracens' new artificial pitch, at the bottom of the M1. They had finished top of the table in the regular 22-match season, twelve points ahead of us, and were prohibitive favourites. They were the self-styled wolf pack; we made them look like pussy cats.

Reaching our first Twickenham final, in a ferocious performance that blended pace and precision under pressure meant everything on a personal and professional level. My two muckers in the front row, Brian Mujati and Soane Tonga'uiha, were immense in a 27–13 win that was, in effect, their leaving present.

The team were brothers-in-arms. The fans were ecstatic. The symmetry of renewing traditional tribal rivalry with Leicester in the final merely added to a sense of destiny, on the verge of fulfilment. What could possibly go wrong?

As it turned out, an awful lot . . .

# 9

# Respect

I was not in a good place. I withdrew into myself, and had no interest in engaging with the outside world. I blamed myself for the hurt I had inflicted on people I would never really know, beyond chance encounters in the local laundromat or in the aisle of my nearest supermarket. I had betrayed their trust, and sacrificed their innocence.

They had self-consciously offered their best as I walked to training, or wobbled along on the bike with a permanently flat tyre. They had invested in me emotionally as leader of the history boys, the first group of players to give a small town the chance of basking in the glory of national supremacy. It was meant to be Northampton's year, our title. It was a big, big deal.

So much for folk heroes and fairy tales; Disney's scriptwriting team evidently took the day off on Saturday, 25 May 2013. The magnitude of our 37–17 defeat to Leicester in the Premiership final at Twickenham, and the manner of my sending off, for supposedly abusing the referee just before half-time, tainted everything.

Engulfed by controversy, and haunted by the assumption I had let down my teammates, as well as the supporters who had travelled in record numbers, I had also to come to terms with its cost. I would never wear the contents of the British Lions kit bag, stored with due expectation in a bedroom at home. The handmade suit for that summer's tour of Australia would remain in the wardrobe.

I treated my phone as toxic, but felt obliged to reply to one of the many voicemails left in the twenty-four hours after the game. It was from Leon Barwell, who had stepped down as Northampton chairman earlier that month on medical advice. His voice was faltering but his humanity was deeply affecting: he had rung to check that I was OK.

The son of Keith Barwell, our owner, Leon passed away little more than a fortnight later, aged forty-six, following an eighteen-month battle against bowel cancer. He knew death was near; the trip to Twickenham, designed as one last occasion to be shared with his family, visibly took a lot out of him, but he remained on the pitch afterwards, consoling the team.

As players, we often get carried away by the minutiae of performance and the exaggerated emotions of our trade, but this was a moment to pause, and reflect on the game's deepest, and most painful, lessons. Rugby is an evocative sport, because of its rawness, and its worth cannot be adequately measured by caps, medals and trophies.

As I have got older, I have come to realize that its lasting significance lies in the quality of the friendships that are formed, often under fire. I've already spoken of my affinity with Paul Tupai, my brother by another mother. My relationship with Leon, although not as close, was another indication of the ties that bind, through sport.

He became a Saints director in 1999, and succeeded his father as chairman in 2011. He was a successful businessman and in true family tradition called a spade a bloody shovel. He was approachable, far-sighted and fair-minded. He believed in the ethos of rugby, as a game for all with well-defined values, and actively involved season ticket holders in the decision-making process.

The club game is built upon the generosity, perseverance and wisdom of such men.

I got to know him through his attendance, every Friday, at the Captain's Run, a distinctive pre-match ritual that is one of the milestones of our working week. His physical deterioration over the last year of his life was obvious, yet his spiritual commitment to club and team seemed to grow in intensity. He loved to talk about the game, and its immense possibilities.

His legacy is a charitable foundation, established in his name. It provides emotional and financial support to families of cancer sufferers, by funding special days out and a unique range of personalized events that help to provide everlasting memories. It is too easy to overlook the fact that one in three families struggle to pay utility bills after a loved one's diagnosis with the disease.

Leon's final act of understated, unrecognized kindness, in being sufficiently concerned to seek me out, was typical, but uniquely inspirational. How could I obsess about the unfairness of my situation? What right did I have to bemoan my fate and ignore my blessings? Without knowing it, he helped me hold it together. His example forced me to push my shoulders back, and front up to the world.

His funeral, at All Saints in the town centre, was attended by more than 900 mourners. It featured a brilliantly funny and moving eulogy by Jim Mallinder, our director of rugby. I led my team, and former players like Chris Ashton, into the church as a mark of enduring respect for who Leon was and what he represented.

Respect: a seven-letter word with significance and implications.

Like all rugby players, from wheezing, hungover veterans on a muddy park pitch to frighteningly honed international athletes on manicured fields of dreams, I was brought up to respect referees. I obeyed the convention of calling them 'sir' to acknowledge their authority, and generally minded my *p*s and *q*s in their presence.

It would be churlish of me, in the extreme, not to respect the achievements of Wayne Barnes, the official who dismissed me at Twickenham on that fateful afternoon. He retired, to deserved accolades, after the 2019 World Cup, to devote more time to his alternative career as a barrister, operating from chambers in the Shard, in London.

His experience, in refereeing more Premiership matches than anyone since the RFU offered to employ him in 2005, should perfectly complement his courtroom skills, as an advocate or prosecutor. They involve attention to detail, empathy for the individual and an awareness of the limits of laws. Those skills were noticeable by their absence during the incident that still scars my career.

Before we go into the whys and wherefores of the red card I was shown for supposedly calling him a 'fucking cheat', I'd like to put the game into further context. Victory would have been a huge personal and collective achievement, but it was not without its frustrations, even before we arrived at Twickenham.

I had poured myself into that season, with the additional incentive of winning the starting shirt for the Lions. That ambition, annotated on a list posted on the wall of a small upstairs room that acted as my office, was tantalizingly close to fulfilment when I received a letter, confirming my selection for the summer tour.

I had grafted as never before, for club, country and the brotherhood of the home nations. I slogged through extra training, went for long bike rides on two evenings during the week, and signed up for CrossFit sessions in a local gym. I was fit and strong, leaner and lighter than I had ever been. My captaincy hit a sweet spot, with team and town. The Premiership final seemed to signal that everything had come together perfectly.

Imagine, then, my irritation with the avoidable distraction of being called into a meeting with Nick Johnson, our Head of Performance at the time, on the Friday afternoon before the final. He wanted to complete the formalities of an end-of-season review with the coaches that somehow couldn't be postponed until the Monday. Crazy, but I was given no option.

My mood darkened when it became clear I would have a maximum break of two and a half weeks, following the Lions tour, less than half the downtime given to the other lads at the club. I was already tired, physically and mentally, and faced another seven high-profile, highly pressurized matches.

I know this sounds needy, but rugby players are no different to any other working man. They accept they will miss birthdays, weddings, christenings, high days and bank holidays, but they like their personal circumstances to be at least taken into account. The edict meant that I had to cancel a long-planned family holiday, which involved seeing my newborn nephew for the first time.

The intended reunion was facilitated by a close friend, John Spence, whose Karma group owned a hotel in Bali. I hadn't seen my parents in more than a year; it emerged that Dad had been ill, but didn't want to burden me with worry. A lot had been invested psychologically in what was a once-in-a-lifetime trip. I had a proper barney with the Northampton management, and left the room blazing.

Did I go into the final in the best frame of mind? Probably not. Did their intransigence contribute to the way things turned sour in the final? It might have done, though I cannot be certain. The row definitely created an air of tension, and an undercurrent of aggravation created by what I considered to be an injustice. It felt like unnecessary thoughtlessness that bordered on contempt.

Local rivalry threw firecrackers on to the bonfire. Reaching the final was old hat to Leicester; it was their ninth in a row. They knew the territory better than us, and had taken the precaution of factoring the referee's person-ality into the occasion. Richard Cockerill, their director of rugby, admitted afterwards he had warned his players that Barnes was the sort of official who 'likes to be treated with respect'.

In their eyes we were the country cousins, getting carried away by a rare outing with the big boys. Since they finished ahead of us in the regular season, they were given the Eng-land dressing room, and allowed to unveil and wear their 'home' kit for the following season. We were in second-string light blue.

A lot was on the line, so it was unsurprising the first half was tumultuous. A Stephen Myler try reduced an early ten-point deficit, and the TMO denied us the chance to draw within a single point in the thirty-fourth minute by disallow-ing what looked, through our admittedly biased eyes, to be a legitimate try by Ben Foden.

Scrums were messy, and not helped by the referee. The ball emerged from only two of twelve set pieces, from which we were penalized six times. We were being jumped by the Leicester pack, hit and rolled without punishment, and when a penalty was given against us in the thirty-ninth minute I exclaimed 'We are up against it here, boys.' Barnes obviously regarded that as a reflection on his performance.

'This isn't how you behave as a captain,' he told me. 'Please keep your comments to yourself or I may well have to deal with it by way of a penalty.' I replied 'Sorry, sir. I am talking to my players' but he cut in. 'Listen to me, please. If you talk to me like that and I think it is to me I will have to deal with it. Do you understand?'

I said 'Fine' but the game was bubbling. When we were awarded a dropout with time up on the clock at the end of the half, Myler misunderstood instructions that he could not kick the ball on the full into touch to complete the formalities. 'You can't do that,' Barnes exclaimed to him, when he did so. 'I just told you that.'

It was chaos. He awarded Leicester a centrally positioned attacking scrum on the 22, just as a group of yellow-shirted children stampeded up the touchline, to take part in a dance sequence scheduled for the interval. Some made it as far as the pitch before they were called back; both coaches had flicked off their stopwatches and were turning to head to the dressing room.

I approached the referee for confirmation, and he insisted 'The scrum must take place' because 'it is the player's responsibility' to obey instructions. There was an edge to his voice that suggested he was flapping, losing control, and failing to think rationally. In retrospect I had prodded him to that point, which was the wrong thing to do.

Just how wrong became clear in the aftermath of the scrum, from which they were wrongly rewarded for pushing early by the award of yet another penalty. I was on my knees, and was staring down Tom Youngs, their hooker, who was on the ground as I rose to my feet. When I was upright, I mouthed the words 'Fucking cheat.' It was the product of simmering personal rivalry since we were competing for an England shirt and I felt I was being shown up on the big stage.

No match, especially one as important as the season's grand occasion, is played in a vacuum. My comment was, in truth, also directed at Dan Cole, Tom's best friend and our tighthead prop at international level, who was also in the mix. He had never really opened up to me; his loyalty to Tom was obvious and understandable, since he was in his sixth season at Leicester and followed clan code.

Those niceties were lost on the referee. I was staggered when he flourished a red card in his left hand, and stood there, nonplussed, as he explained, to no one in particular, 'This man has just come up to call me a fucking cheat. He leaves the field.' That was the longest walk of my life; I instinctively covered my face with my hand as my mind raced through the consequences.

I wasn't to know it at the time but, with a wonderfully ironic sense of timing, this was exactly the moment my wife, Jo, was walking up the concrete staircase, to reach her seat. She had turned up late after mistiming the motorway traffic, and couldn't work out what was happening, and why the Leicester fans were joyfully jeering me.

Jim Mallinder, perplexed, mentally rewrote his half-time team talk and ushered me down the tunnel as I tried to rationalize what had just happened. I had no history with

Barnes. He was a familiar figure at England training sessions, knowledgeable and engaged. Why would I go against everything I had been brought up to believe, and question his honesty and even-handedness? It was the dumbest thing I could do.

I have been guilty of many things in my career, doing the sort of grunt work that often involves conflict, but that is not in my repertoire. My parents drummed into me the importance of good character. They demanded I respect my elders, and address figures of authority with due deference. They taught me that those considerations, how I carry myself in daily interactions, would define who I was.

As I sat in the dressing room at half-time, a detached, almost ghostly figure, I slowly took off my boots and came to terms with the realization that I was being doubted in the most pertinent and personal manner by thousands of timid souls who would never understand how sport is so tied into an athlete's self-worth.

There were no tears, no self-indulgent displays of anger, just a numbing sense of disbelief. I was stumbling through an anxiety dream, made flesh. The obvious temptation, to call a cab and slink away in a coward's retreat, had to be resisted. In order to live with myself I had no alternative but to take it on the chin, face up to the consequences.

I knew what was coming when I pulled on a training top and walked back out, to sit on the bench. I was the prize exhibit in a fairground freak show. The photographers didn't need to be alerted by the crowd's murmur of recognition; they immediately got up close and impersonal. Hand-held TV cameras bored into my face.

It was unpleasant and embarrassing, because my team-mates were responding brilliantly to adversity. Foden and

Lee Dickson scored tries in a second-half fightback, but such defiance was unable to prevent Leicester winning a record tenth title. I kept a private promise, went up to receive my loser's medal, and prepared for the moment of reckoning on our return to the dressing room.

What would the group think of me? They had followed me, as captain, as a mark of respect for my resolution. They knew me as someone who played close to the edge, but I had never shared the guilt I felt whenever I received a card, and placed additional pressure on them. It was irrelevant that I hadn't done what I was sent off for; I had fucked it up for everyone.

I tried to read the room. Any one of those players would have been forgiven for blowing their top at me. My apology to them was not a long one; my emotions were in such a state of flux I couldn't find the right words. I knew that, in such a situation, they were just that, words. I took a front seat on the bus out of Twickenham, dialled the lawyers, and attempted to sort my life out.

It was a whirlwind. I felt sick and struggled to sleep. The Lions were gathering the following day, and travelling to Hong Kong on the first leg of the tour, a game against the Barbarians, on the Monday. My hearing was set for Tuesday, so it made sense for them to call up Rory Best as cover in any eventuality. I phoned Warren Gatland, the head coach, and told him to forget about me. I didn't want to turn up as a spare part when the tour was already underway.

I reasoned I was going to get a ban, irrespective of the merits of my defence. The only time I left my house before I travelled to Newmarket to face the disciplinary panel was to see Toops. He was as honest as ever: 'Mate, this is how it will pan out. You're a shabby kid with a bad record. They'll support the ref.'

I had a problem with perception, but was determined to plead not guilty, even if it resulted in a longer suspension. I argued that Barnes was not looking at me when I said those fateful words: he could only have acted on hearing them, without full context. I was in his world of legal representation, though he wasn't present; his marriage that summer coincided with the third Lions Test in Australia, so he called in from his stag do.

I wasn't questioning his ability to do his job. I knew how much preparation went into his refereeing, especially in familiarizing himself with the complexities of the front row. I also knew that, as an RFU employee, he could not afford the blowback of admitting he had made an honest mistake. There was no personal animosity, since he has referred to me as 'a superb leader' in subsequent interviews, but he has never deviated from his insistence that I acted in a moment of frustration.

The three-man panel ruled I was guilty of a mid-range offence, and banned me for eleven weeks. Judge Jeff Blackett said 'We cannot get around the fact that Wayne Barnes was certain that Mr Hartley's comments were directed at him. Wayne Barnes said that if he had had any doubt in his mind, then he would have given the player the benefit of the doubt. In terms of sanction, calling a referee a cheat is an attack on his integrity and contrary to the core values of rugby and therefore we have taken a serious view and provided a serious sanction.'

Experience told me there was no point in appealing. Jo pulled the car around the back of the Holiday Inn, which it has to be said lacked the gravity and grandeur of the Old

Bailey, and I left via a fire escape to avoid reporters. 'At least I know now,' I said, as I settled into the passenger seat and pulled off my tie. 'Shit happens.'

The trolls on social media would lighten their sad little lives by having a go. I would worry, once again, about the impact on my international career, and even contemplate retirement. I was tainted goods, and people would not want to be around me. Sponsors would drop me, because they don't want to be associated with trouble. I understood that, and simply got on with it.

Missing the Lions tour was a big blow, because I had trained so hard for it, but I had never fully bought into the legend, best articulated by the famous Ian McGeechan speech in South Africa in 1997: 'You'll meet each other in the street in thirty years' time, and there'll just be a look, and you'll know just how special some days in your life are.'

I understand the power of the emotion he was expressing. I appreciate the honour of selection, and the special nature of friendships formed across national boundaries, but my affiliation is more tenuous. The Lions are unique, but have never been central to my rugby life, because of my Kiwi background.

Would I have enjoyed returning to New Zealand as a Lion in 2017? Obviously, though non-selection was leavened by my status within the England squad, and made easier to handle by a thoughtful telephone call from a friend within the media, the night before the Lions touring party was announced. 'Don't get your hopes up,' he warned. 'I've just talked to the team manager and I don't think it is looking too good for you.'

He didn't need to make that call to me. He wasn't looking for a cheap quote; I respected his professionalism, because it cannot have been easy. It was quickly justified, since a variety of media platforms began to report that I hadn't been picked. This wasn't a lone journo, taking a punt. It can only have been briefed, as an obvious storyline. I was big enough and ugly enough to accept it. Plenty of other things will define me as a player.

I put out a message on the England players' WhatsApp that night: 'Boys. I know there will be disappointment tomorrow, because I've had a heads-up on mine. Just remember this tour doesn't define you. Those of us who go, learn from it, and come back better players. Those of us who don't, have an opportunity to grow this team even further.'

Eddie Jones's message was complementary, and characteristically blunt: 'Learn how to beat the All Blacks because that will benefit our team.'

I was comfortable with my fate. Fitness problems that would conspire against me before the 2019 World Cup were hidden below the horizon, and at least I didn't have to deal with the sort of uncertainty about my future generated by the setback in 2013. That was eased by another one-on-one meeting with Stuart Lancaster, in which, psychologically, he again went back to the classroom.

He gave me time to get my head together before asking to meet, a couple of weeks before he was due to name a 33-man squad for the autumn internationals against Australia, Argentina and the All Blacks. He was direct, and to the point. I had to understand where to draw the line. His definition of discipline was clear and concise: whatever the rights and wrongs of any given situation it was non-negotiable.

I came off the bench in the 20–13 win over Australia, was named man of the match against Argentina, and ended up in A&E after our 30–22 defeat by the All Blacks. Tom Youngs might have played in all three Lions Tests that summer, but I had won back the England shirt. I started every Six Nations game the following spring, when we won the Triple Crown but lost out to Ireland for the title on points' difference.

That England scrum had a nucleus of three Northampton players, with the rapidly developing Tom Wood and Courtney Lawes packing down alongside me. Luther Burrell, who would leave the Saints to sample rugby league with Warrington Wolves in the summer of 2019, was the regular outside centre and Lee Dickson added to our strength in depth at scrum half.

That season, at club level, had elements of a crusade. I do not wish to appear trite, but Leon was never far from our thoughts. His loss was a reminder, a rallying point for a restart. The best teams are a product of an evolutionary cycle, and we were given additional offensive focus by George North, the Wales and Lions winger.

I had two new props. Alex Corbisiero, the England loosehead who played in two Lions Tests in Australia, had injury problems but was already morphing into the media star he has become with NBC in the United States. Salesi Ma'afu, who joined us from Western Force, had made history by playing directly against his brother Campese for the Wallabies against Fiji in Canberra in 2010. They had both been making their debuts for their respective rugby nations.

Salesi has a pretty gnarly family tree; he named his son after his brother, who in turn was named after David Campese, the Wallaby winger who was in his pomp when Salesi was born in 1984. They were brought up in the western suburbs of Sydney; a third brother, the youngest, 'Apakuki, plays for Tonga as a result of his dad's heritage. Their mum hails from the Fijian island of Kadavu.

Salesi seemed to adapt to East Midlands tribal custom pretty effectively, and was sent off for levelling Tom Youngs with a looping left hook in the 2014 Premiership semi-final at Franklin's Gardens, our first victory against Leicester in ten matches. Tom accepted his apology with good grace. I missed the game, having fractured my shoulder in a league match against them six weeks previously.

I'm not the greatest spectator, despite reluctant practice, and this was an exhilarating performance, but an excruciating watch. We trailed by eleven points at half-time, played the last twenty-four minutes with fourteen men, and won, 21–20, when Tom Wood barrelled over in the corner with less than two minutes remaining.

The place went nuts. The whiff of cordite, created by ill-feeling, muscular endeavour and raw drama, took time to clear. This was turning into a saga, driven by a sense of destiny. We faced two major finals in a fortnight; was an unseen hand guiding us towards a spectacular form of salvation? Who knew, but we weren't short of believers.

I'm not exaggerating here, but literally a day had not gone by, since that defeat at Twickenham the previous May, without me dwelling on a redemptive return. This was the culmination of a ten-year journey, along a path that contained several sinkholes that could have swallowed my career. Every incident, each injury, had led me to what seemed like the point of no going back.

I had to think smartly, and rationalize risk. Though it killed me to do so, I sat out our first final, in the European Challenge Cup against Bath at Cardiff Arms Park. Once again, we trailed at half-time, this time by seven points.

Stephen Myler, whose consistency at fly half had forced him into England contention, was the rock on which our 30–16 win was built.

He kicked twenty points, to add to tries by Phil Dowson and Ben Foden. It was our first trophy for four years, but celebrations were tempered by the looming shadow of Saracens, who lost the Heineken Cup final to Toulon on the same weekend. They finished top of the table during the regular season, nine points ahead of us, and had their own unfinished business to attend to, following our win at their place in the previous season's Premiership semi-final.

Rivalry was intense, though perhaps not as poisonous as it had become against the Tigers. I had unqualified respect for Steve Borthwick, who would go on to play such an important coaching role with England under Eddie. The final was his 448th, and last, appearance in a sixteen-year playing career, in which he had captained his country, and two clubs, Bath and Saracens, with distinction.

I defied medical advice and made my comeback, replacing Mike Haywood fifty-four minutes into a typically tight and tense contest. This was a performance hewn from the heart, rather than one reproduced from a bloodless training ground game plan. It was decided by perseverance, diligence, willpower and a thought-provoking element of good fortune.

We entered extra time only because Charlie Hodgson's attempted conversion of Marcelo Bosch's equalizing try rebounded off the upright in the seventy-fourth minute. Myler and Hodgson traded penalties in extra time, before Hodgson gave them a three-point lead and triggered a Northampton siege. We would not be denied.

I was directly behind him, so I saw instantly that Alex Waller, our replacement prop, had burrowed over in the final seconds after Luther Burrell had been brought down fractionally short of the line. It could never be that simple, of course, since we had to wait for four minutes before Graham Hughes, the TMO, sanctioned the award of the try.

Everyone, including the referee, J. P. Doyle, forgot the formality of the conversion, which Myler kicked despite the distraction of hundreds of people running on to the pitch. The bedlam, lubricated by tears and punctuated by fist pumps, featured some of the worst dad-dancing known to man. The feeling when I lifted the trophy, in conjunction with Tom Wood and Phil Dowson, was the ultimate natural high.

It took time to recognize the role fate had played. The referee had awarded Owen Farrell a second-half try, and Alex Goode was lining up a conversion attempt before the TMO prompted him to review the decision. Goode's pass to Chris Wyles in the build-up was found to have been forward; a similar offence, by Burrell, which led to our second try by George Pisi, was missed.

I had barely slept for a week, and though I wasn't intending to change that before flying to New Zealand on the Monday to join the England touring party, personal priorities were placed into perspective by the joy expressed by Keith Barwell and his family. We knew that, somewhere celestial, Leon was raising a glass to us.

Keith joined the players in dedicating the win to his late son and to our mascot Luis Ghaut, a promising full back who had been diagnosed with a rare bone cancer, osteosarcoma, the previous year. Luis posed with the trophy, on the pitch with us. When he died, aged thirteen, little more than three months later, Lee Dickson spoke in terms to which I, as a father, can relate: 'I've got three young boys, and it really hits home when you look across the table.'

Rugby is a compelling game, which reveals character, unites strangers, and reminds you to count your blessings.

# 10

# Rocky Road, Beautiful Destination

Customs control at Auckland airport is a strangely serene place, unless you have something dodgy in the backpack. The sound of native birds, played over the public-address system, soothes the soul and sends me back to the Kiwi bush. On this occasion, hungover and tired coming off a two-day bender and an extended 27-hour flight, I needed all the respite I could get.

Lee Dickson, who had thrown himself into celebration of Northampton's Premiership win with similar gusto, wasn't so fortunate. Jet lag protocols and nutritional strategies, established following our shambolic arrival at the 2011 World Cup, were quietly and conveniently ignored because of an injury crisis at scrum half.

Lee, dealing with a niggle of his own, was plonked on the bench, and barely knew what planet he was on when he played the last eleven minutes of a 20–15 defeat by the All Blacks at Eden Park as a replacement for Ben Youngs. England's tour to the land of my father didn't get much better for a bloated 48-man squad that was never allowed to breathe.

We moved on to Dunedin, where we were billeted in the type of motel that usually puts up school teams, as part of a policy designed to stress our humility. Nothing wrong with that, but a large group of professional athletes, looking forward to a holiday at the end of a long hard season, is easily bored and prone to distraction.

Stuart Lancaster's insistence on a dry tour, without the safety valve of a social, came to a head after we lost the second Test more comprehensively than a 28–27 scoreline, eased by late tries by Mike Brown and Chris Ashton, suggested. Tom Wood, my roommate at the Bates Motel, was intent on seeing some of his North Otago teammates from a Jonno-style gap year in New Zealand rugby.

He had started the Test; I replaced Rob Webber seven minutes into the second half. We'd shared an exacting season with Northampton, and I understood why he wanted to have a couple of drinks, shoot the shit, and debrief that day's game with his mates. 'I'm going out,' he announced. 'I am twenty-eight years old. I've got a couple of mortgages and three kids. He's saying we're not allowed? That's bullshit. It's petty.'

Tom's a big lad, with physical presence. He drives a camouflaged Monster Truck, and is the sort to survive the Apocalypse. He's also a man of principle. He was determined to put on his civvies, and walk out into the night through the lobby so that his defiance was noted. I agreed to join him, but persuaded him to take the more diplomatic option of leaving down one of the many fire escapes. We had three quiet pints, talked about rugby with old friends, and stole back to our room.

No one was any the wiser. Our recovery session the following day was unaffected. No petrol was poured on the fires that were inevitably beginning to break out within the squad, which was expanded because so many of us were involved in the Premiership final. Lanny was well intentioned, but he underestimated the timing of the tour, and the dynamics of having so many players simply waiting for the season to end.

There's a natural delineation in touring parties between the twenty-five guys in the match day squad, which includes two additional reserves, and those on the outside, looking in. The chosen ones' mental energy is focused on the game, their individual roles and responsibilities, so it is natural they are blinkered, to the frustration of those implicitly forgotten. Wearing a suit to a Test match, rather than a tracksuit, is the mark of Cain.

In this case we had twenty-three guys trying to come to terms with the fact that their tour was over before the final Test, in Hamilton. That, in its way, is a bigger test of character than facing the world's best team in their backyard. Non-playing members of the squad are the best barometer of your internal energy; if they start moaning, and visibly view training as a chore, you're in trouble. The intensity of preparation inevitably declines.

We took over a local restaurant for our team meal and, at around ten o' clock, the playing party stood up to leave. The other lads were given a pass out until midnight, an empathetic gesture designed to ease tensions, which flared when Dave Ward, our fifth-choice hooker, auditioned as a smart-arse. 'Standard,' he said. 'Woody's leaving early.'

Tom fixed him with a neutron bomb stare, which hollowed out his insides. There's a bit of Del Boy in Wardy; he misread the mood by trying to laugh it off, and sagged into his seat, with his eyes lowered, as Woody shouted 'Stand up, come outside, and let's sort it.' Tumbleweed blew through the room; it was like that classic Western scene, where the saloon door swings and everyone's eyes dart about, wondering who will go for their gun.

Wardy folded. If there was a hole in the floor he'd have dived into it. 'I thought so . . .' Woody said, before we headed for the bus, having been named as starters. His contempt wasn't the best precursor to a dominant All Blacks performance. We were blown away in the first half, and trailed 29–6 before the moral victory of exchanging converted tries after the interval.

That was the All Blacks' seventeenth consecutive win. They didn't need bullet point protestations of pride in their predecessors, and the value of their heritage. Their debt and desire were a given. They lived the culture, quietly and with devastating effect. I didn't attend their university of rugby life because I made a personal choice, in moving to England, that I have never regretted, but I knew their syllabus.

I'm not talking about sweeping the sheds, or enforcing the No Dickheads rule. The All Blacks may have made such concepts trendy, but they're not unique to them. I give greater credence to the power of a playing philosophy that central- izes individual character, moulds it to the collective will, and demands unquestioning self-reliance.

Kiwi coaching has elements of the Johan Cruyff approach in football; development is skill-related, rather than gov- erned by a player's size. Players appreciate that everything must be earned. I'm not saying there are free passes in the English game, but once a young player forces a foot in the dressing room door it is easier to enter, and stay there.

Too easy? When I examine the example set by the Franks brothers, Ben and Owen, I begin to wonder. They are among a select group of twenty men to have two World Cup win- ner's medals. They know their places in the All Black bloodline, since they are registered as numbers 1084 and 1094 respectively. Those victories in 2011 and 2015 earned them respect, but denied them respite.

Central contracts in New Zealand rugby are awarded annually. No one has the sinecure of a multi-year deal. This creates a constant need for a player to prove himself under the most intense competitive pressure. Falter, or demonstrate the merest hint of self-satisfaction, and the response is ruthless. Reputations are deemed to be like today's newspaper headlines: tomorrow's kitty litter.

Owen is hailed by the former head coach Steve Hansen as 'one of the great All Blacks'. He won 108 caps over a decade as a prototypical modern prop forward, strong, quick and mobile. Yet, at thirty-one, the sword that hangs over the head of every Kiwi player fell. Hansen and his fellow selectors, Ian Foster and Grant Fox, controversially left him out of their 31-strong squad for Japan.

Their reasoning was unsentimental. Owen passed the test of being human granite, but failed to match the ball-carrying qualities of younger men, such as Nepo Laulala, Ofa Tu'ungafasi and Angus Ta'avao. He accepted his fate with a warrior's stoicism, explaining 'I'm well aware as a professional athlete, and especially an All Black, that your time in the jersey isn't owed.'

It was an honourable retirement. He joined his elder brother at Northampton for the 2019 season. Ben, another tighthead, who played forty-seven Tests for New Zealand between 2008 and 2015, had joined us from London Irish a year earlier. He is not a man to be messed with, having squatted 300 kilograms at the family gym in Christchurch, but he combines hardness with unforced humility.

He is as much a product of the salmon fishery as the All Black production line. As a young player he would train early in the morning, chop and fillet unimaginable quantities of fish over an eight-hour shift, and then go out and butcher himself on the paddock. He didn't do so with any great pretensions of self-sacrifice: it was how it was.

That's why he gets in two hours before training, and brings his own food, stored in a coolbag containing Tupperware boxes. It is a product of his diligence in everything he does, and force of habit. As he explains: 'When I started, we didn't get food. You took your lunch to work, and I've just continued doing it.' I hope against hope that our young players, who are spoon-fed chicken breasts and fresh fish, understand the importance of the gesture.

Hunger need not be literal, but it is essential if they are to have half the career that guy has had. We're growing out of the idea of a professional sportsman as a working-class hero, but that is what an All Black still represents. They're grounded, and take nothing for granted, because they have had to reaffirm their credentials at every level of the game. Today's academy kids might have had weight programmes since the age of fifteen, but they need to be toughened.

One of Eddie Jones's tenets of faith is the importance of self-reliance, which he endorsed in his study of two Tour de France cycling teams. It underpins the ruthlessness of his approach not just to his players and coaches, but to his support staff, who are expected to go above and beyond the traditional boundaries of their roles within rugby.

In cycling, for instance, the physio makes the athlete's bed and helps prepare the food on the road, so that when the cyclist gets off his bike he can eat quickly and efficiently, before washing up his own plate and utensils. The same 360-degree view is demanded of kit men and doctors; they see a need, and muck in. There's a pride in contributing in other areas; they operate outside professional silos.

Independent-minded people make better athletes and I suspect rugby is too keen to wipe a player's backside. The modern player has a protein shake thrust in his hands after a gym session, drinks it, and looks at the empty container with a 'What do I do now?' sense of helplessness. We all have to be accountable for our own mess: that's the broader message of sweeping the sheds.

You don't take your strapping off and chuck it on the floor. Would you walk into the living room at home, and toss dirty scraps of bandages across the new carpet? Of course not, if you value domestic harmony and have a shred of self-respect. So why, then, would you not bother to clean up after yourself at work?

Players at club or international level are expected to pack their bag carefully after a game, and look around to check whether their individual space is clean. Only then can they leave. That's not creating a legacy, the buzzword written on countless whiteboards. It's common courtesy, common sense. Thinking of others encourages a broader view: such an attitude is transferable into other areas of team development.

I'm not denying for a second that professional sport is inherently selfish, since personal rivalries, which can sour if they are allowed to go unchecked, tend to flourish like woodland mushrooms in a wet, warm autumn. But while I've never shirked a challenge, and have always had a keen sense of my place in the pecking order, I've never allowed it to become personal.

I like to think I played like it wasn't a day job. Entirety of commitment has been one of my greatest strengths, but also a recurring weakness. In the case of my rivalry with Jamie George, it was the spark that created the inferno which ended my hopes of playing for England in the 2015 World Cup.

Northampton topped the table in the regular season, and consequently had a home Premiership semi-final against Saracens, who had finished fourth, with eight points less. It was a bitty, frustrating game, and I spoke, in the immediate aftermath, of our 29–24 defeat being 'a hollow feeling, a season's worth of work down the toilet in eighty minutes'.

My mood didn't improve. I was cited for an incident in the fifty-eighth minute which, true to form for me, was a product of rugby's basic instinct. We had just scored a try, taking Tom Wood over the line in a driving maul, the most vivid and satisfying indication of collective domination. It's a Caveman moment, when the hunter-gatherers return with a freshly killed Tyrannosaurus for tea.

I screamed 'Fuck, yeah' as I got to my feet, turned, and took two paces forward, to find Jamie in my path, entering his in-goal area. I wasn't about to miss a chance to rub it in and he, to his credit, wasn't going to get out of my way. I leaned forward on the walk and, to emphasize my superiority, put my head on his temple, beside his right ear.

My celebration was over-zealous, and, as a veteran of sixty-six Tests, I should have been more aware of the dangers of one-upmanship, which had got me into trouble previously. But there was no momentum and no malicious intent. Jamie didn't even blink; he merely spread his arms wide, in a gesture of bewilderment. This wasn't a Glasgow kiss, delivered after ten pints of heavy and two fried Mars Bars. If you don't believe me, look at the YouTube video, and reach your own conclusions.

The RFU disciplinary tribunal, convened in Coventry on the Wednesday evening, accepted my guilty plea for what even they termed 'a low-level offence' in which, according to Sean Enright, the chairman of the panel, 'There was no significant injury to the other party, the opposition player was not removed from the field of play and the incident did not affect the game.'

I still got a four-week ban, applicable from the start of the new domestic season, which ruled me out of England's three World Cup warm-up games, two of which were against France and the other against Ireland. It also meant I was unavailable for the tournament opener against Fiji. I didn't begrudge Jamie his subsequent promotion to the World Cup squad at my expense.

He's a smart boy who, over the following four years, has shown maturity and increasing levels of leadership. His running game is eye-catching, because of his ability to break the lines. He knows what he needs to improve, and applies himself impressively. He has a natural appetite for work, and, despite assumptions of aggravation, I've never had an issue with him.

People who leap to easy conclusions should remember that I've been around for a long time. I'm used to the theatrics of selection, the debate about which hooker should start. It is more highly focused, since I play in a solitary position. Unlike, say, a flanker who has three options when number 8 is taken into account, in my job you are in direct competition.

Competition is healthy, and as far as I am concerned it goes no further than that. I have not forgotten the hostility I encountered from more experienced hookers at Northampton in my early days, and won't treat a young fella as if he has threatened my grandma. I've lived with critics who preferred Jamie George, Tom Youngs, Steve Thompson or

Lee Mears, and got many more England number 2 shirts than number 16s.

Jamie was twenty-four at the time of that incident, so wasn't an unfamiliar figure. He was uncapped, in the process of paying his dues, and I could see that he was a good character. I've got no issue with anyone who makes it work for himself. We all deal with the paradox: selection is in our hands, because it is down to us to play well, but out of our hands, because we are reliant on the perception of a coach, or a selection panel. We can't pick ourselves, much as we would like to.

I knew what I brought to the party, irrespective of the inconvenience of my suspension. I had the experience of sixty-six Tests, compared to the thirty-four caps shared between the four other relevant hookers, Youngs, George, Rob Webber and Luke Cowan-Dickie. I had started eight of the previous nine internationals, immeasurably improving the accuracy of my throwing, so my lineout success rate was consistently above 90 per cent.

Unfortunately I also had something else the other lads lacked: a sheaf of disapproving headlines a metre thick. They were weighing Stuart Lancaster down when he called to arrange a meeting, at the Hilton beside junction 15 on the M1. It was there, in one of those soulless conference rooms with bowls of mints, overpriced mineral water, notepads and freshly sharpened pencils that he got down to basics.

'Look, I can't afford to take you,' he said, as an opening gambit. He cited three reasons, including the prospect of my questionable match fitness for the two decisive group games, against Wales and Australia. He also attempted to argue he was not allowed, by World Cup regulations, to take the risk of effectively entering the first game with only one hooker, in the event of untimely injury.

I wasn't having that; even if someone broke a leg in the build-up to the Fiji match, England would still have been able to utilize Kieran Brookes, one of the reserve props, as an emergency hooker. Australia turned up at the tournament with only two hookers, in any case. It quickly became clear that Lanny's decision was dictated by image, rather than the principles of performance.

He had already cited a code of conduct in excluding Manu Tuilagi from his World Cup squad following his conviction for assaulting a taxi driver and two police officers. Once he knew I was not going to appeal the verdict, or even the severity of the suspension, I was toast. He went public on a loss of trust, and my need to control my emotions.

He spoke, reasonably enough, about the predictability of problems with any group of players over a four-year World Cup cycle, and the need to minimize them by responding 'proportionately and effectively'. But I couldn't help but notice that he referred mainly to me in the past tense. There was no point responding, since his mind was made up; I simply swallowed my medicine.

Looking back, it makes me realize how dependent a player is on his coach's faith in his basic qualities. Eddie was unwavering, once he nailed his colours to my mast. When controversy erupted periodically, he would invariably say 'Look, mate, you fucked up, but I still like what you give us.' Stuart didn't have sufficient confidence in me, or himself, to deal with media disapproval.

It doesn't take long to become a non-person, officially at least. I was removed from all the England WhatsApp groups, and made a point of keeping my distance, but was inevitably contacted by my mates within the squad, fifty-strong when they entered camp on 22 June. They did not play their opening World Cup game until 18 September, an eternity.

The work was hard and relentless, by common consent the most physically demanding the boys had experienced. The situation was complicated by insecurity, created by intermittent culls. Players have a sixth sense for vulnerability, irrespective of whether it is their own, or that of others. The final process, of trimming the squad to thirty-one players from forty, was brutal because of the proximity of the prize.

Lanny preferred Roundheads over Cavaliers, despite his imaginative decision to facilitate and accelerate the introduction of Sam Burgess, who made twenty-four appearances for Bath, and won five Test caps for England, in ten months before returning to rugby league. It was an ill-starred experiment that I had no problem with, since Sam was a good player and a good guy. He deserved respect for leaving his comfort zone.

Did he come into rugby union on a promise? Lanny was obviously a fan. If anything he should have been bolder in his advocacy of someone who stirred cross-code politics. I appreciate that, as a coach, he had a difficult balancing act to pull off, since guarantees are an open invitation to complacency and resentment, yet he fell off the high wire.

It was obvious to everyone that Luther Burrell was under direct threat from Sam's arrival. In effect, Lanny turned a training game into a personal duel between them. When I heard of the circumstances, I felt instinctively for Luther, an ever-present in the previous Six Nations. How can you convince a coach you deserve selection in such an artificial environment?

The players knew what was going on. True to form, Tom Wood and James Haskell played to the gallery, walking out to training in full game day warm-up kit, complete with presentational jacket and the team's Beats by Dre headphones. All that was missing was the *Rocky* theme tune. Needless to say, both were pulled into the office afterwards for a bollocking.

That typified the joylessness of preparations. I wasn't there, of course, but friends within the squad complained of a stuffy environment in which people felt unable to be themselves. You have to enjoy turning up for work, whatever you do to make a living, and the consensus was that all colour had been drained out of the team.

Eddie's approach was diametrically opposed to that of Stuart. He was content to allow Hask to be the entertainer, because he recognized that he made the group happier when he was bouncing around in Archbishop of Banterbury mode. In return he expected Hask to play with consistent ferocity. There was nothing complicated about his contribution; he simply went in hard and smashed people.

The fallout from failure to emerge from Pool A was pretty toxic. The pressure of being the home team proved to be overwhelming; anyone who peddled the 'It's Coming Home' line clearly hadn't been paying attention. If you looked objectively at England's record under Stuart we hadn't won anything substantial. We had underperformed in critical matches, against Wales and Ireland.

We lacked the ruthlessness and self-belief of world champions. We didn't have the momentum of a form team. The squad's dedication was undoubtable, given the grind of such unstinting preparation, but they were too often told what to think, and how to behave. Psychologically, they were unable to respond when big matches, against Wales and Australia, turned against them.

I appreciate the significance of traditional rugby virtues, of humility and fair-mindedness, but international sport tends to reward the ruthless and the bloody-minded. Teams with a win-at-all-costs attitude tend to be a self-fulfilling prophecy. The weight of the shirt, and the nation, proved too much in that World Cup.

I was in a familiar limbo. Part of me was grateful to have the break, but the impact of isolation is consistent. Every time I received a suspension I went through an impulsive phase of not wanting anything to do with the game. I didn't want to listen to the manufactured hopes around the England team, the constant conversations based on ifs, buts and maybes. It's just noise.

That reticence is partially a result of the lingering strain of attending the usual kangaroo court, where the outcome seems pre-determined. The subsequent stress of enduring the casual ignorance of no-mark strangers doesn't seem worth it. Yet, as a wise man once said, rocky roads can lead to beautiful destinations.

That August, while my old teammates were punishing themselves at Pennyhill Park, my life was suddenly enriched by Thea's birth. Parents will recognize the contradictions: euphoria mingled with terror, and peace was somehow created by hyperactivity. Crucially, love conquered all. I have never been more focused on my good fortune, despite having lost out financially because of my ill-timed fall from grace.

Perspective isn't always acquired so painlessly. A couple of years earlier, Chris Ashton and I had been given permission by Stuart Lancaster during the Six Nations Championship to visit a mutual friend, Jeremy Paxton, at his futuristic home beside the Thames in Caversham. He was an amazing man, a water-skiing champion, helicopter pilot and publishing genius who became one of the original eco-warriors.

We were preparing to leave, after a typically engaging evening, when Jeremy suffered a cardiac arrest, caused by undetected heart disease, and died. Our sense of helplessness was indescribable. We stayed until 2am, giving statements, before returning to the England camp. Sporting priorities we had accepted as perfectly normal hours earlier seemed trite in the shadow of such tragedy.

Jeremy lives on, through his 550-acre nature reserve in the heart of the Cotswolds. Few people outside the squad and my immediate family realized the significance of an acutely personal tribute I paid to him in my next match, in Ireland. I inscribed the initials JP in felt tip pen, beside the cap number on my shirt as a mark of respect.

Without wishing to be too profound, we are all products of our experience, good and bad. I've occasionally had to reassure myself that having a few chinks in the armour is an advantage. My career has never been plain sailing. There's always been a rogue wave, waiting to bring the mast crashing down. That has prepared me, tested my resilience.

Look forward. The view over your shoulder is largely irrelevant. When Lanny resigned as head coach that November, I did what every player does, and focused on his replacement. Eddie Jones, who had led Japan to a historic win over South Africa in the World Cup, was appointed as England's first foreign coach later in the month.

Soon after, I received a random text message. 'Work on leg strength, mate. Work on it.' It was unsigned and I didn't recognize the number. I asked around, discovered it was from Eddie, and decided politeness was good politics, because at the time, having been excluded from Stuart's squad, I was out in the bush. I simply replied 'Yes, OK, thanks.'

I didn't know him, but the week before he was due to name his first elite development squad, I took the initiative and phoned him. I explained I had fractured my hand, but I so badly wanted to prove I was worthy of making his team that I was prepared to play, even though scrummaging would have been close to impossible, since I couldn't bind, or throw properly.

'Mate,' he replied. 'Don't even fucking try. You're the best set-piece hooker in the country. Train right, and get your hand ready.' I was still working through the permutations of that instruction when his follow-up call, inviting me to breakfast at Pennyhill Park, gave my head another wobble. I'd have been stupid to refuse, but had to prepare for any eventuality.

The options were pretty clear, even if the meeting was shrouded in an air of mystery. I could be travelling down for that final, formal, handshake, the icy courtesy used by a new coach who wants to clear out old faces, and introduce new names. He might be paying his respects to me as an experienced player, in order to pick my brains about the state of an inherited squad. He might even be dangling the carrot that I wasn't entirely out of the reckoning.

Captaincy? The thought didn't enter my mind.

I reasoned that if he was going to invest in me, as a fellow hooker, I might as well look the part. For some weird reason, I went for the full Jarhead effect, and shaved my head. I don't know what came over me, but the thought of having hair didn't seem that businesslike. I essentially had one question for him: 'What do you want from me?'

It was like any first meeting, when you are both circling, trying to assess one another. Eddie came across as sharp, witty and spiky. He was obviously not a conformist. He wasn't afraid of disagreement, and used silence well during our conversation. He had a small man's belligerence and a big-picture view of life.

It is easy to nitpick with someone who is happy to be known as an iconoclast. Some will argue there are negative connotations to aspects of his coaching, but he is a lovely guy. He takes pride in developing continually as a coach, and as an individual, but the spine of his approach, the core of what he does, hasn't changed that much since day one.

He spoke about his experience of coaching Saracens for a season, and told me: 'I always liked you when we played against you because you were aggressive.' He acknowledged that England had good players, who needed a rougher edge. He was speaking my language, because although I'm not the most skilful, I have a competitive intensity which can be transmitted to the rest of the team.

His vision was of a streetwise team, playing with raw intelligence and an awareness of their strengths. He wanted to build it around the best set piece in the world, excellence in the three traditional elements of scrum, lineout and maul. He spoke of me being central to that ambition, as the best hooker in the league.

He talked in general terms about leadership, and the responsibilities of captaincy. Rugby was a chaotic game that required cold-blooded, clear-minded leadership on the field, in the heat of battle. Then, straight out of the blue, he asked

'Do you want to do the job?' I didn't give him time to change his mind.

Having taken on board his first test of my character, a promise to maintain secrecy, I walked out into a new day, and a new world.

# 11

# Slam Dunk

'Every morning in Africa a gazelle wakes up. It knows it must outrun the fastest lion or it will be killed. Every morning in Africa a lion wakes up and knows it must run faster than the slowest gazelle or it will starve. It doesn't matter whether you are a lion or a gazelle, when the sun comes up you'd better be running.'

'The rhino is up and running, boss.'

'Good. Keep running.'

Life with Eddie would never be dull. His texts were the timeline of my new life. I didn't tell Mum and Dad about my promotion until the eve of the announcement, out of respect to him, though I did share the news of the captaincy with Jo and Toops. The media barely got a sniff of it, and I figured it was likely to be a brief, wild ride, for a transitional Six Nations Championship.

When I stood back and thought about it, in the calm before the storm triggered by my unveiling, I understood the logic of Eddie's faith. There were no guarantees, since it is the sort of job that tends to be relatively short term in nature. Six seasons captaining my club had at least given me an appreciation of the mechanics of the role.

Everything with England is on a different scale, of course. It's bigger, bolder, adversarial and defining. Predictably, my selection got under some hot, starchy collars. Eddie knew what was coming when he explained that 'the biggest risk was not to take a risk' at the press conference which preceded the ritual round of photos and set-piece interviews.

A shout-out is due to the postman who had the misfortune to have Rugby House, the RFU's HQ, on his round in Twickenham's semi-detached suburbs. Eddie's first bulging mailbag contained several letters branding his first major decision as 'disgusting'; one headmaster of a minor public school even threatened to remove rugby from his curriculum.

I say, old chap, steady on . . .

Eddie saw through the distractions. I quickly got to know his modus operandi. He demands as much from you as he demands from himself. He's tireless, since he doesn't appear to sleep much beyond two or three hours a night. I've occasionally caught him napping on a flight, or nodding off in a taxi, but wasn't brave enough to take a sly photo, and post it on the players' WhatsApp group.

His message was consistent, and reinforced on a daily basis. Don't just float through a session. I want you better today than you were yesterday. The critical difference between his approach and that of previous England regimes was the relentlessness of contact. His emails, voicemails and links to performance-related articles arrived on cue, irrespective of whether we were in camp or back at our clubs.

I would often wake at 4.30am, thinking about training plans or sequences. I didn't have the nerve to text Eddie with ideas that formed as I lay there in the pre-dawn darkness. I knew he would be awake, and would probably have a wry smile to himself at my susceptibility to his yearning for improvement if I did make contact, but I waited until a decent hour as a matter of courtesy.

He was in our heads because he realized the potential of releasing the latent energy of a group of players who had been simmering for a couple of years. By the end of the Six Nations, the senior lads were coming to me privately, raving about the sense of liberation they felt. Sure, there were a few barbed words, but they were regarded as another sign of his investment in us as people.

I received a crash course in high performance, from one of its best exponents, in the ten days or so before we started the Six Nations against Scotland at Murrayfield. I knew, on a basic level, how a team ran, but Eddie put the parameters in place. He was looking for a bit of attitude, and had chosen, in me, someone with the roughest edge. Rugby priorities were non-negotiable.

Off the field, he left it to me to frame our own rules. He empowered us as grown men, to think for ourselves. He removed managerial mundanities without sacrificing authority. His rationale was straightforward: 'Do what you want' he told me. 'If you want to drink beer, drink beer. If you want to have a social, or do fun things, just talk to me and book it in. Just don't fuck it up.'

He warned us we were not fit enough. We had to be open to change. Everything we had ever known about training would be shaken up. There were different expectations, and a different philosophy would lead to the expansion of our work ethic. He intended to make us uncomfortable, but gave us clarity about how we were going to play.

There would be a new level to our working day. There would be scenario meetings, classroom sessions. They would essentially be coach-led, but designed to create debate and decision making among players. Questions investigated our initiative: if we were fifteen points behind, how would we respond? Are we going to go long or short from the kick-off? How are we going to regain the ball?

Everything was designed to put us on the spot: 'Dylan, you get a penalty in this area of the pitch with five minutes left, what are you going to do? . . . . Senior players, is that the right answer?' It was challenging, refreshing and unifying. Eddie's illustrative clips, for analysis and retention, were taken from rugby league, in Australia's NRL, rather than the usual All Blacks showreel.

He acknowledged the breadth of attacking options within the squad, but we were going to begin by playing identifiably English rugby. We would squeeze teams in the set piece. We would incorporate the best structure and organization in our defence. We would be physical, intimidating, strong and resilient. We would find that extra 2 or 3 per cent, to be the best.

My biggest challenge, in dealing with the concertina effect of the build-up to the opening game, was getting to know the group. There had been a couple of bolters introduced during the World Cup, younger players like Jamie George with whom I had not worked previously. One of my first jobs was to break down barriers, get the squad connected and aligned.

Eddie introduced me to the group on my appointment, when I stressed I would do my best for them. There was no pomp and circumstance; Eddie thanked Chris Robshaw for his work as captain under Lanny and I tried to humanize the challenge that awaited us. If they threw themselves into it, as I intended to do, we could create the comradeship that creates successful club teams.

I might not be the most polished speaker, especially in front of my peers, but I was prepared to make myself consciously uneasy in making my mark. It is rather like speaking to 1,000 people at an end-of-season dinner; you don't particularly want to do it, but you prepare, you care, and you reach another level as a person through the experience. To use the corporate jargon, you upskill.

In a sense, I acted out of character in my first team talk, the night before the Scotland game. I have never been a flipchart captain, but there I was, felt tip at the ready, turning over a page of size A1 paper containing a list of the ten top-ranked teams in world rugby. England were number eight, pretty much as low as we could go. The Scots were seventh.

'It literally can't get any worse,' I said, gesturing towards the table. 'Let's climb this ladder, starting tomorrow. Long term we want to be here, number one in the world. We want to be number two at least, because then we will be contenders with a chance to be number one. We have an opportunity to write our own history, and to do that we have to be accountable to each other. Every match in this tournament is a stepping stone.'

The performance against Scotland was pretty poor, but we won, 15–9. Chips were down and victory was all that mattered. Leading the team out, into the usual swirl of pipes, was a strange experience, but leaving it, when I was replaced by Jamie in the seventy-sixth minute, was even stranger. We could still have lost to a converted try at the time; it was the equivalent of being forced to stand back, and watch a child take its first faltering steps without being able to dive to the rescue.

I didn't care about convention. I wasn't about to sit down and sink into my quilted substitute's coat. I was up, as close to the touchline as possible, shouting instructions which were a stream of consciousness, and probably obliterated by the tribal din of a Murrayfield crowd. I knew how important it was to hang on. Defeat early in the Six Nations can quickly crush confidence and momentum. Don't win that first game, and it can be a long two months.

I didn't care how we played. All that counted was the result. If you win, Saturday night is good, Sunday is great, the Monday morning debrief is fine, and you just roll into the next game. If you lose, Saturday night is full of self-reproach. Sunday is a time to brood, and look for answers. The Monday morning debrief can be a minefield of personal agendas and aimless finger pointing.

Eddie had the knack of making you feel like you had learned something from his meetings. He got me thinking in a different way. He unlocked my mind. As captain, the tenor of my messages to the group had to match those of the head coach. I had to speak like him, think like him, so we could prepare as he wished.

On first impression, he was informal, charismatic. He would pace the room, hold it with humour while not necessarily engaging. He had a habit of looking down at the floor, and going off at a tangent, before suddenly switching back, on message. He reminded me of a psychologist, because of his ability to suddenly engage and strike.

He doesn't stop. You wouldn't want any other example from the man at the top. Imagine turning up for work before the boss. He rolls in at ten o' clock, scratches his arse, and gets himself a cup of tea before he wanders over to ask how things are going. Not a great look, is it? But if you get to work, and the boss's car is already there, you know your future is linked to a guy who wants to put the hours in, so he can be as successful as possible.

Occasionally, the principles of performance are perverse. Victories were critical, in terms of the provision of stability and the re-establishment of competitive credibility, but the matches themselves almost seemed secondary to the broader task, of shaping a culture that could sustain us in a new four-year cycle.

Recovery was sacrosanct, instead of an optional extra. Under Stuart, the boys would walk straight to their cars, in their kit, from the training paddock on a Tuesday afternoon, eager to get the most out of Wednesday's day off. Under Eddie, people were reluctant to go home. There were ice baths to endure, carefully coached stretching sessions to undertake.

No one was allowed to go through the motions. Everything was measured to the minute. This was partner-assisted torture, designed to teach us to stretch through pain. We needed to increase mobility, to be lower at the breakdown and the scrum. By stretching the hip capsule, a ligament that connects the top of the leg to the pelvis, we would become more flexible and mobile.

These daily classes, conducted in blocks of ten players at a time, were brutal. I would often become light-headed through the effort, but, as captain, I was expected to set the best example. My wake-up call from Eddie duly arrived when a media session overran. I could have dived into the stretching class for ten minutes, but decided to go straight to another strategy meeting.

His intelligence system was scarily efficient. 'Not a good enough excuse, mate,' he snapped, when I explained the reason for my abbreviated schedule. 'You could have gone to the stretch session, or rearranged it for later. I like you as a bloke but I can't carry you. You can fuck off home. You're telling me you don't want to be here.'

I protested otherwise, knowing I would pay for every minute's respite I had grabbed, in order to sit down for a bit of peace. His tone was different. He was making an example of me, to prove that in his squad there are no exceptions. When he says that everything has to be earned it is not a scare tactic. It is real. I wouldn't expect it any other way.

That was a lightbulb moment. I couldn't afford even to give the impression of paying lip service to the notion of perpetual progress. Looking back, I think he saw a little bit of himself in me. We didn't hang out together, beyond the formalities of coach–captain promotional or administrative activity, but hookers are a distinctive breed. We do our best work in a dark and dangerous place.

I found it fascinating that both he and Gareth Southgate, his football equivalent, made a point, publicly, that they were forced to pick players who weren't good enough. That's not aimed at a specific individual, but it is the sort of comment that's read and regurgitated by wives, parents and friends. It soon gets back, and can create resentment.

Eddie saw things differently. It was an invitation to excel, rather than outright condemnation. Talent is merely part of the equation; for all the lofty talk of a growth mindset, as if it is something mystical, a player must have the simple motivation of wanting to be better at his trade. Eddie was saying, in so many words, that if you are not working constantly, seeking integral improvement, you're gone.

It's progression through a form of emotional, even intellectual, osmosis. Eddie quickly had me watching matches more analytically, studying the themes and textures of a performance. He soaked me with his curiosity: how could England benefit from a tactical nuance I had spotted? I would immediately text him and compare notes.

Italy, in front of a 70,000 crowd at the Stadio Olimpico on a Sunday afternoon in Rome, were the next challenge. They were a team still trying to find a way to win, and had yet to impose themselves on the Six Nations, beyond an occasional upset. Getting close, and always losing, must make patronizing praise for pluckiness difficult to bear.

We have never lost to them and every time I face them I struggle to supress the nagging thought that I don't want to be in the England team that does so. This game followed a familiar pattern. It was competitive for sixty or so minutes. There were a couple of flashpoints, which we profited from. All of sudden Jonathan Joseph ran in three tries, and the scoreboard was telling us we had scored forty points.

The squad was in its initial stage of evolution. Paul Hill and Maro Itoje made their debuts as replacements, coming on for Dan Cole and James Haskell respectively. Paul, a tighthead prop who had joined Northampton from Yorkshire Carnegie the previous summer, was only twenty, a baby in front-row terms. He won his five caps in 2016 before losing momentum at club level, and has time to come again.

Maro, the same age as Paul, rapidly blossomed into a poster boy for the new regime. His potential had been spoken of in whispers for a while. He was the sort of player loved by both the media and the talent development specialists, an articulate lad shaped by the sort of multi-sport background that defines many successful athletes.

He represented England as a junior in the shot putt, played football to a good standard at centre half, and knew his way around a basketball court. The privileged nature of his education at Harrow School disguised the street smarts he showed, in recognizing Steve Borthwick as his ideal rugby tutor. Having siphoned off Steve's experience and wisdom, in the art of lineout and lock forward play, he shrugged aside the stick he took for media profiles that characterized him as 'a thinking man's enforcer'.

His speed and agility were obvious assets, but there was something less tangible about him. He was respectful, but dared to be different. The clue to his character was contained in an incisive ESPN article about him by Tom Hamilton, when he led England in a successful retention of the junior world championship in New Zealand in 2014.

Most forwards find their literary level in picture books like *The Very Hungry Caterpillar,* or *Where's Wally?* Maro found solace in poetry, written on away trips in his formative phase at Saracens, when he travelled as a non-playing reserve. I was struck by the maturity and thoughtfulness of one of his poems, reproduced in the piece by Tom Hamilton. It captures the inner thoughts of a young player, embarked on a rite of passage:

> There comes a time
> There comes a time
> When a boy must become a man
> When fear must turn to bravery
> When thoughts must turn to belief
> When this belief must turn to action
> When one must love and one must hope
> When preparation turns to performance
> When strangers turn to friends
> When friends turn to foes
> When joy fulfils your mind
> When anger fills your heart
> When one must stand up and lead
> When one must sit back and listen
> There comes a time, when the time must be taken

If such words were impressive, his numbers added up in training. Eddie saw our third win, 21–10 over Ireland at Twickenham, as 'a pretty decent step up' but ramped up the intensity of our preparation. It was a two-way process: we put the work in, and he provided constant feedback through the use of such tools as GPS tracking.

He used statistics from our first week of training under him as a basic gauge of progress. 'Look at how shit you were,' he would say, flaunting our relative weakness. We were judged on the number of accelerations per minute, either carrying or supporting into contact, rucking or chasing a kick. We were expected to be back in the game, off the floor, quicker.

When GPS reports were downloaded into our inbox, we logged on impulsively, eager to see our names associated with green numbers, which signified acceptable progress. Anything less than 85 per cent efficiency meant extra conditioning sessions. Eddie had quietly reminded me of my obligation to work harder than the rest; I set myself a target of being in the top three in reloads and accelerations on a daily basis.

The numbers were not necessarily cold, or one-dimensional. They were a position-relevant barometer of effort. I was nowhere near the quickest, for example, but had to prove I could still accelerate, for my size and natural pace. The challenge seeps into the subconscious, and becomes a state of mind. You don't amble after a high kick, you sprint head down for five metres. Only then do you look up, and see where the ball has gone.

Personal pride was tweaked consistently and not too subtly. Statistics were pinned up everywhere; players would linger in front of the lists, locked in private contemplation and comparison. There was a pressure to perform. You would look at your opposite number's statistics and think 'Fuck. He got ahead of me yesterday. I need to do him today.' It created a competitive edge which took our training to another level.

We worked hard, and smart. Eddie's speciality was in spotting global trends and tailoring them to our requirements. He recognized there would be occasions on which to play unstructured, instinctive, southern-hemisphere rugby, but balanced that with an understanding of how, and when, to play a structured game, based on the set piece.

This wasn't an academic exercise; I had never played for such a naturally communicative coach. In effect Eddie was confirming continually that our strategy was correct. When we started winning, it became a self-fulfilling prophecy. We knew what we were doing. We were ahead of the curve. We were concentrating on being original and distinctive. We had stopped asking 'Why?' and were wondering 'Why not?'

When you're on it, you're on it.

As the championship developed, we began to appreciate the impact of attention to detail. Our analysis suggested we should attack the short side against Wales, the only other unbeaten team, and bypass their midfield defence. That, aligned to the accuracy of Owen Farrell's kicking, enabled us to build leads of 19–0 and 25–7, sufficient insurance against a late comeback.

The Triple Crown was not won without turbulence. Joe Marler escaped punishment for calling Samson Lee, the Wales tighthead prop, a 'gypsy boy' because of the promptness of his personal apology at half-time, and his genuine contrition. He was also cleared of striking Rob Evans, the

Welsh loosehead, with his forearm. Dan Cole was gouged by a third Welsh prop, replacement Tomas Francis, who was cited and banned for eight weeks.

The lurid headlines tended to overshadow other indications of advancement. Maro had quickly formed a pivotal second-row partnership with George Kruis, a World Cup fringe player whose phenomenal work ethic and increased carrying capacity were transferred straight from the training pitch. Billy Vunipola credited Eddie for making him rediscover enjoyment of the game. Man of the match in three of the five matches, he was fitter and more thoughtful in his play than ever.

The irony was that, internally, we were being conditioned to ease the emphasis away from the individual. Even now, certain sections of the media struggle to get their heads around one of Eddie's central beliefs, that modern rugby is a 23-man game. He helped us cut through the habitual misapprehension that substitutes are second-class citizens. Being on the bench does not signify inferiority.

That was why he changed the terminology of selection, in recasting replacements as finishers. It wasn't a shallow PR move, or an underestimation of the significance of the starters, who set the tone for the performance. It was a meticulous reflection of an unconsidered truth, that sometimes you need your most effective team on the field at the end of a game, when the result is in the balance.

That might not say much for me, since I rarely lasted for a full eighty minutes, but I would leave the pitch having worn down my opposite number, who might not have the luxury of a quality understudy. Forced to stay out there for the duration, he would then be vulnerable to the energy and strength of young thrusters like Jamie or Luke Cowan-Dickie.

We operated on expectations, rather than rules. I had a thing about the cohesion created by mutual respect. I wanted us to eat as a group, because I had come from a club culture in which the squad splintered on the evening before an away game. It got to me that some players would pile into a cab for a cheeky Nando's, followed by a film, while others would be in a half-empty team room with a couple of coaches, slurping soup and toying with lasagne.

What's that all about? You are either a team, or you are a disparate collection of individuals. You will be expected to watch one another's backs, in the heat of battle the following day. I wanted players to relate to one another on a human level, be curious about their teammates' lives outside the game. It was a time to talk, to share. It was a straight ten press-ups for anyone caught contemplating their phone.

The work was bearing fruit. England's first Grand Slam since 2003 was on the line in Paris that March. It would be a pressurized situation, neutralized by Eddie allowing us to consider how far we had come, in such a short space of time. Instead of concentrating on the emotional constriction of the moment, he posed the question: 'How good does this feel?'

It invited us to recall the hurt of previous narrow misses, and to draw confidence from our preparation, which, if anything, was more intense than ever. The irony was that, in one of our pre-match scenario meetings, 'How will we respond if Dylan is off the field?' was among four potential eventualities we had to work through.

Eddie had a yellow-card situation in mind when he introduced the sudden leadership dilemma into the equation. We were sitting in the boardroom at Pennyhill Park. I started to answer, but he stopped me and threw it out to the room, because he wanted to see who would step up to fill the vacuum. As it turned out, it was a wise precaution.

We were clinging to a four-point lead, with thirteen minutes remaining at the Stade de France, when I saw Uini Atonio, the France tighthead prop, coming round the corner. I can't remember lining him up but it's an instinctive action, ingrained since the days Dad told me to go as low as possible, in taking down a big man.

Within that fraction of a second, you have a decision to make. You either let him dictate, by sitting back on your haunches and letting him get a head of steam up, or you go after him. The best defenders in the world attack the attacker. I intended to take him out with a chop tackle, a high-risk move in which essentially you lead with your head.

I'd attempted it countless times, without a problem, before I met the self-styled 'Gorilla'. A Kiwi of Samoan descent, who qualified through residency as a La Rochelle player, Atonio is 6'6" tall and weighs in at 146kg (23 stones in old money). A profile in *L'Équipe* revealed that the kit man, Hervé Didelot, had to source a size 13 shirt, an XXXXXXXXXXL, for him. It was the biggest ever made for a French player.

The back of my head hit his right knee, just below the kneecap, and I was knocked clean out. I recently watched the incident in a slow-motion sequence, captured by French TV. The commentator exclaimed 'Oh là là . . . impact énorme!' in instinctive alarm. I hit the deck, face down, arms splayed in front of me, and received treatment for several minutes before being stretchered off.

I was out cold, unable to savour the satisfaction of dislodging the ball with my backside on impact. Forcing that knock-on was probably my best contribution in the second half. My plight gave the rest of the team time to connect, come together, and revisit a training scenario that had become all too real.

Owen Farrell, who went on to confirm the 31–21 win by kicking two further penalties, stepped into the breach. When I eventually came around, he was standing over me, smiling, and saying 'You all right, lad?' I mumbled 'Yeah, yeah', though in truth I was thinking 'Where am I, and what have I done?'

I have a sketchy memory of feeling the coldness of the turf, and hearing the buzz of the crowd. I can't recall doing the cognitive test for concussion in the doctor's room, beneath the main stand, which probably proves the point that I failed it. I was conscious that I needed to let Jo, who was watching on TV at home, know I was OK, so asked for my phone, but they weren't keen to allow me to watch the end of the game, and join in the celebrations, without supervision. They had no choice when I left of my own volition.

Lifting the Six Nations trophy remains a blur, a bit of fuzz. No face is symmetrical, and each one of us has our own self-image. Looking back at photographs and the video of the ceremony I can see, better than anyone, that I am not right. There is a distant look in my eyes, and a distinctive tilt to my head. I'm smiling, but there's no one at home.

The immediate symptoms of concussion are easy to identify, hard to overcome. I recoiled from bright lights that night, and struggled to maintain conversations. Stringing a sentence together required a conscious act of will. Owen did me a great favour, in agreeing to do the speech at the post-match dinner.

The worst thing was I had to retreat to the team hotel as the rest of the boys headed out to a Parisian nightclub, to unload after a long campaign. It was our first big night as a team, the fulfilment of a long-held promise to one another that we would celebrate suitably, and there I was, with nothing but the trophy for company. There was no way that was being used as a rugby ball, or a pint pot, in the early hours.

It was depressing; I sat in the team room, with a few members of the support staff. I knew I couldn't drink, had burger and chips, and went to bed. I couldn't sleep, which is perhaps as well, since it is not advisable in such a state. It was my second concussion of the season: I had been out for forty-five days following a clash of heads with Billy Vunipola in a Premiership match against Saracens the previous November.

I felt very lonely; my thoughts wandered across a long night, but I kept returning to my family. Wasn't it about time that I got my priorities in order? What was I in danger of sacrificing to rugby? How could I justify ignoring the potential consequences of further damage, not just to myself but to my wife and daughter?

Jo deserves greater credit than she gets. She has shared my journey, lived through the success and the setbacks, but I kept our relationship at arm's length from rugby, because I always considered it as work. I saw players worrying about ticket drop-offs for their girlfriends, and felt, selfishly, that it was an avoidable distraction.

Jo has never attended an away game; watching matches at Twickenham was a means to an end, since it meant we were able to spend time together with Thea, following the self-imposed isolation of a training camp. As I look back on my career, I realize I should have been more inclusive. Rugby institutionalizes you, especially when you are single.

A false reality is built around machismo. I obviously could not train with the Saints because of concussion symptoms, but my condition had sufficiently improved to accept an invitation to appear on the Jonathan Ross chat show, with Billy Vunipola, Danny Care and Jonathan Joseph, on the Tuesday after the win in Paris.

I was politically savvy enough to check with Eddie that he didn't think I was being Bertie Big Potatoes. Like me, he saw it as recognition of an important achievement, an indication of national pride in the completion of the Grand Slam. When I returned to the club on Thursday morning it was immediately obvious that Dorian West, our coach, didn't share his worldview.

My relationship with Dorian ran hot and cold, and in this case he was positively frigid. 'Think you're big time?' he muttered under his breath. 'How can you not be fit to train, and fit enough to be on TV?' He walked off before I could answer. It was immature of him, unworthy of a guy I respected, despite our increasing differences. I was thirty, and he was still treating me as if I was nineteen.

But that's the voice of old-school sourness. It says you should not visibly enjoy success in rugby. I have never forgotten my debt to Northampton for the support they showed me in times of personal strain; that sense of loyalty, and a determination not to exclude myself from England contention, led to me turning down a big-money offer to join Montpellier from the 2015 season onwards.

I wasn't going to rush back to play. There was far, far too much to lose.

# 12

# Shadowlands

I didn't recognize the man I had become. I craved sleep and didn't want to get out of bed. I would put my kit on, fill my water bottle with the intention of exercising on the indoor bike, and retreat to the couch, with a bizarre combination of shame and relief. I was lethargic, resentful and old before my time.

My club coaches thought I was an England captain with an agenda. They were under pressure because of poor results, and in time-honoured fashion the sticky stuff slithered downhill. I couldn't train, but was obliged to attend team meetings, even though being in a dark room with a bright light, focusing on game film, was the last thing I wanted or needed.

I hated predictable reminders of my condition, the question, recycled countless times, 'How's the head?' from teammates, support staff and fans. The concern was wearing but well intentioned, since the type of concussion I suffered in the Grand Slam match is among the most severe. Only 10 per cent of cases involve a player who has been knocked clean out.

I was in the shadowlands, a place all players recognize, regardless of club loyalty and national allegiance. There are tantalizing moments of clarity and respite, but you live for long periods in a fine mist of anxiety and fatigue. You worry that the game has finally caught up with you, and confront the reality that rugby is only an element of your existence.

There is a hidden element of self-loathing. As someone who took pride in my independence of thought and my capacity to work, unbidden, in my own time, I found it very hard to reconcile my sudden lack of desire to commit to physical activity. The 10k evening bike rides and the sessions in my home gym, a fat lad's penance, were in abeyance.

I had no get up and go. We are an outdoors family, and love walking and cycling in the local countryside, but my world shrank. I shuffled between two rooms at home without purpose. Occasionally I would sit down, and wonder why I was there. The injury complicated the usual comedown from an intensive Six Nations campaign.

Even without the delicacy and uncertainty of rehabilitation, it is mentally difficult for an international player to come back to a quiet house. I had spent the previous ten weeks in an England camp, surrounded by around fifty people. There had never been a quiet moment. The buzz was constant and the day flew by in fast-forward.

My every need was met. If I was hungry, I was fed. If I was thirsty, someone would thrust a bottle at me. I didn't have to worry what to wear. Kit would appear, clean and fresh, in my room. Each minute of the day, every action, was accounted for. No wonder professional athletes have a sense of dependency.

They go home after a competition, open the fridge, and can't find the food they want. They rummage around, looking for a pair of clean pants. They have to go shopping, organize their laundry, because most are in two-income families, in which wives and partners work. They love their children, and have missed them immensely, but the attention they demand becomes irritating, because it is so unfamiliar.

Eventually, of course, equilibrium returns. Life is recalibrated by the school run and the supermarket trolley dash. When concussion is involved, and your absence as a senior player causes suspicion and frustration because it is not a visible problem, like a black eye, an immobilized knee or an ankle encased in an airboot, it is a much more difficult transition.

What are we dealing with?

Here is an official explanation, taken from the RFU's Headcase Education Programme: 'Sport related concussion is a traumatic brain injury resulting from a blow to the head or body which results in forces being transmitted to the brain. This typically presents as a rapid onset of short-lived impairment of brain function that resolves spontaneously.

'This impairment results from a functional disturbance, rather than a structural injury, and no abnormality is seen on standard hospital scans. A range of signs and symptoms are typically seen, affecting the player's thinking, memory, mood, behaviour, level of consciousness, and various physical effects.'

The last annual survey in Premiership rugby confirmed concussion as the most commonly reported injury in 2017–18. There were 140 cases in matches, the first fall in seven years since 169 were recorded in the previous season. Against that, the number of reported concussive incidents in training rose by 38 per cent.

Concussion accounted for 18 per cent of all injuries to the ball carrier and 37 per cent of all injuries to the tackler. Injuries in contact training with England rose to 6.1 per 1,000 hours, double the study average. Research reported by the

*British Medical Journal* suggested concussion was twice as likely in international rugby than in the club game. That's a lot to take in, even at your sharpest.

In my case, I paid particular attention to this extract from World Rugby's Concussion Guidance: 'Players with a history of two or more concussions within the past year are at greater risk of further brain injury and slower recovery and should seek medical attention from practitioners experienced in concussion management before return to play.'

The prospect of so-called 'second-impact syndrome', in which a second concussive blow is suffered before the brain has recovered from the first, is quietly terrifying. It is rare – a coroner ruled that its first known case in rugby caused the tragic death of Ben Robinson, a fourteen-year-old schoolboy from Carrickfergus in Northern Ireland, in 2011 – but relevant.

I understand the parent who worries for his or her son. As a player, I have been guilty of underplaying the risks, and ignoring warning signs because I so desperately wanted to make my mark, or keep my place. As a concussion sufferer, I finally realized the one person to whom you cannot lie is yourself.

Recovery must be self-policed, even if worthy reports help to contextualize the issue. An all-party parliamentary group found professional rugby union was second, in terms of the incidence of sports-related concussion, behind National Hunt racing. There were problems, on a descending scale, in American football, Flat racing, boxing, rugby league, ice hockey, amateur rugby union and football.

I followed the six-stage Graduated Return to Play protocol. This begins with a minimum of fourteen days' complete rest, and builds up through light aerobic exercise, undertaken at less than 70 per cent of predicted maximum heart rate. Running drills lead into more complex sessions, involving passing and resistance training.

The crunch comes, quite literally, in full-contact training sessions with the squad where, ironically, many concussions are suffered. Only then can you return to play; on both occasions in the 2015–16 season, I was out for forty-five days. Coincidentally, that is the upper limit for the mandatory timescale for recovery in boxing, following a stoppage or a knockout.

Recovery was a strange experience. Over a couple of days, I gradually felt as if a weight had been removed, and a veil had been lifted. I began to exercise, renewed my appetite for life, and eventually viewed my comeback, against Gloucester in the last match of the Premiership season, as a release. Before I knew it, I was back on the treadmill, literally and metaphorically.

In the immediate aftermath of the Grand Slam Eddie Jones had told us to use England's support staff in any way possible. This wasn't a power grab, or a dismissive reflection on trusted relationships, such as the one I had established over a decade with Matt Lee, Saints' brilliant chief physio. It was a reiteration of the principle of using any assistance possible, to become better.

Eddie wanted to be able to recognize our quality as England players whenever he watched us at club level. We had to prove to him that we could respond to his next challenge, a typically loaded public promise to become the first England team to whitewash the Wallabies in Australia by playing what he called 'Bodyline' rugby. No pressure, chaps . . .

My struggles in late spring had given me perspective. I returned determined to enjoy the experience of a demanding tour. I resolved not to get too caught up with the process of performance, because it is easy to forget why you are there, to play a game that you are blessed to be very good at. If you appreciate the privilege, and accentuate the positive, it is fulfilling.

Touring is hard enough, without being one of those people who finds the negative in everything. If you are constantly complaining that everything is shit, it will be. We had a team-first ethos, which acquired meaning beyond a motivational slogan in a three-week whirlwind, with Tests on successive Saturdays in Brisbane, Melbourne and Sydney.

The buy-in was complete. Everyone in the squad contributed, irrespective of game time.

Of course, in more contemplative moments, I pondered the potential consequences of another head injury. But I would never take the field if I wasn't willing to go for it. I am going to get stuck in. There can be no half-measures. It's rather like trying to hide in training when you've got a niggle; if you make a conscious effort to avoid contact, the game will find you. If you go full on, you get through it.

The mood of the series was set in the second minute at Brisbane, when James Haskell wiped out David Pocock. Hask made eighteen tackles in a 39–28 win, England's first at the Suncorp Stadium, as we overcame an early ten-point deficit. He prompted three turnovers, justifying Eddie's decision to remove him from Stuart Lancaster's naughty step. He even made a fifty-metre side-stepping run to set up a try for Marlon Yarde.

It had only been eight months since Australia knocked England out of the World Cup at Twickenham, on the way to being beaten by the All Blacks in the final, so a lot of ghosts were laid in Melbourne when we clinched the series with a huge defensive performance, in which we made more than 200 tackles, three times more than our opponents.

The intensity of the build-up was captured by our assistant coach, Paul Gustard, who recited the poem 'The Guy in the Glass', written in 1934 by Dale Wimbrow, an American singer and writer. It was a call to arms, a reminder that the man we saw in the mirror each morning would ultimately be our harshest and most gratifying critic. The final verse spoke to us, as a group on the verge of historic achievement:

> You may fool the whole world down the pathway of years
> And get pats on the back as you pass
> But your final reward will be heartache and tears
> If you've cheated the guy in the glass.

It was a redemptive night, on which I scored one of my four Test tries, peeling off from a rolling maul, which ground forward from within ten metres of their line. The pitch was terrible, with groundsmen having constantly to repair sandy divots left by the scrum, but the occasion was memorable. I felt so happy for Chris Robshaw, my predecessor as captain. What a way to mark your fiftieth England appearance.

It could have been so easy to get the deck chairs out before the final match, but Eddie had conditioned us to avoid the easy option. Only an unprecedented clean sweep would suffice. We played with freedom and aggression in winning 44–40 in Sydney. It was the perfect complementary performance; we scrummaged effectively and shared nine tries in an epic Test.

Appropriately enough, we clinched victory in the final minute through an Owen Farrell penalty, conceded at a ruck. He scored sixty-six points in the series, landing twenty-three of his twenty-six shots at goal, and consistently put his body on the line in defence. Little more than four months after I had wheeled out the flip chart in Scotland, we had moved up the world rankings from eighth to second with nine consecutive wins.

We had left the launch pad, and were aiming for the stars. The possibilities seemed endless, but momentum is finite. By the time I had my next experience of brain injury, in 2018, it was about to stall, temporarily. The wider issue, of concussive problems within the game on a global level, had never really gone away.

Soon after we clinched the 2016 series in Australia, James McManus, a Scottish-born winger with Newcastle Knights in rugby league's NRL, was forced to retire because of the lingering after-effects of an apparently innocuous knock on the head in a match against South Sydney the previous July. His unprecedented legal case, arguing that his club should have forced him into retirement in 2013 to prevent him suffering permanent brain injury, is still going through the courts.

The scary thing about concussion is it represents the unknown. There is no definitive cause and effect. Diagnosis feels like trying to pin a tail on an invisible donkey. Every case seems different. I'm sometimes pulled up short by an inexplicable hiccup in my speech. I get words mixed up, almost as a form of verbal dyslexia. Maybe I am thinking too fast for my own good, and consequently spit the words out randomly. It's weird.

The first obvious recurrence of problems with my head happened in the first minute of our second game of the 2018 Six Nations, against Wales at Twickenham. We had a defensive block to start the match; I just wanted to spring off the line and smack someone, to set the tone. Samson Lee, their tighthead prop, obliged by carrying the ball into contact.

He dipped his body to avoid me, but his shoulder made contact with my head. Jérôme Garcès, the French referee, saw me hit the ground and blew immediately. I had full recall of what was a clean shot; in my mind I saw myself falling in slow motion. I explained I had just gone off the line too hard, but they wanted me to leave the pitch for the statutory ten-minute Head Injury Assessment. I stayed calm, knowing that if I protested too vehemently it would be regarded as evidence of concussion.

'OK. Let's do it.'

I felt fine as I sat down in the dressing room, and played the medical game. The doctor's initial questions were familiar: what's the score? What day is it? How many minutes have gone? Where are we? Who are you playing against? The answers were pretty straightforward: 0–0, Saturday, one, Twickenham, Wales.

The test continued. I had to repeat a sequence of words: sugar, candy, paper, wagon, water, letter. Then, to check my mental dexterity, I had to rearrange a series of numbers in sequence. 316, for example, became 613. 4219 could be recycled as 9142 or 9124. They continued by examining my balance, asking me to stand with my hands on my hips, with my eyes closed.

The HIA is sufficiently intricate to identify the obvious victim, but has similarities to an eye test. If you've done a few you've got a pretty decent idea of which letters are on specific levels. I'm not saying I cheated, but the words are familiar (finger, penny and blanket also recur.) You know they will ask you to repeat the first sequence, to test your short-term memory.

Then, after one last test, usually to read the months of the year backwards, you are out into the noise and frenzy. It is a little like walking out into a thunderstorm; not to be taken lightly but strangely thrilling. We didn't know that our 12–6 win, earned through two Jonny May tries, would be our last in that year's championship. I had no apparent after-affects, and lasted until twelve minutes into the second half, before Jamie George, who had filled in initially, was summoned back.

It was only in the days after the match that I considered the significance of what I originally regarded as a slight knock on the head in a club game six weeks earlier. It wasn't an obvious incident. I shook it off quickly, and reported to a subsequent England training camp in Portugal without a moment's thought. I felt very tired, and slept a lot, but put that down to the intensity of Eddie's camps, and the cumulative fatigue of another overloaded season.

I was probably in more trouble than I realized when I took another impact in the first half of our final Six Nations game, against Ireland at Twickenham. It was another relatively mundane incident, in which someone hit the back of my head, and the top of my upper back, in a ruck. I stayed down to catch my breath when play broke up, and the doctor and physio ran in, to check my condition.

It felt like whiplash, probably triggered by the unidentified opponent's shoulder. It was just one of those things, rather than the result of anything illegal, or ill intentioned; another scratch, sustained by an old soldier in the turmoil of close-quarter combat. Rob Young, the doctor, saw that I was winded. 'I'm fine,' I told him. 'I just need a minute to clear my head and clear my lungs.'

I played on, without apparent problems, until replaced by Jamie midway through the second half of a chastening 24–15 defeat that gave Ireland their third Grand Slam in nine years.

It was only when we reached the dressing room, after post-match ceremonies had been completed and the usual patching-up processes had started, that things got seriously weird.

I lay on a bed for half an hour, icing my ankle and knee as part of my recovery protocol, before sitting up, with the intention of getting washed and dressed. As I went to stand I toppled off the bed, grabbing the edge before I was caught by physio Phil Pask and by Dan Cole, who was walking past on the way to the shower.

Dan thought I was mucking about, but changed his mind when he saw the look on my face. I lay back down, took some time to unscramble my senses, and fell once again when I tried to stand. Maybe I didn't want to admit the obvious to myself, but I suggested to the medical guys that it was probably an episode of the benign vertigo I had been suffering.

BPPV, or benign paroxysmal positional vertigo to give it its full medical title, is an inner-ear disorder that causes severe dizziness. It is thought to be caused by the displacement of collections of calcium crystals known as otoconia or otoliths, which move loosely into one of the ear's semicircular canals. This disrupts the body's sense of what position it is in.

It is associated with similar complaints, like labyrinthitis and Ménière's disease, and I had been taught to treat it simply, through a movement known as the Epley manoeuvre. This involves sitting on a bed, turning your head forty-five degrees to the right (if the problem is in the right ear) and then quickly lying back, with the head still turned.

Your shoulders should be on the pillow. You wait thirty seconds before turning your head ninety degrees to the left, without raising it. You wait another thirty seconds, and turn your head and body another ninety degrees to the left, into the bed. After another thirty seconds, you sit up on your left side, and the symptoms should be relieved.

I felt better, and went home with a sense of resignation, rather than real worry. That changed after a day or so, when my balance was still affected, and I had this disconcerting sensation of my eyeballs flicking continually, across the eye socket. I repeated the Epley manoeuvre, but felt really unsteady and extremely tired. I alerted the club to my condition immediately.

There had to be something more going on; I put two and two together and realized I was suffering from concussion. I was back in the shadowlands. I felt slow and lethargic, as if I was coping with permanent jet lag. My eyes were tired, and sensitive to light, so I wore sunglasses. I felt a form of pressure in my forehead. With the exception of low-level conversations, I was sensitive to extraneous noise.

I became irritable, and struggled to concentrate. Things had changed from the days when the prevailing advice to a concussed player was to stay in a dark room, remain inactive, sleep as much as possible and keep the heart rate down. That often led to deconditioning and depression, so my recommended regime included measured exercise, without triggering symptoms.

I would carefully get my heartrate up on an indoor bike, in increments of ten beats per minute, until I hit 150, and then feel completely spaced out. I know this probably makes no medical sense, but I felt as if there was a blockage, preventing blood being pumped around my head. I would go home, and sleep like a baby for at least two hours. I would often nod off, sitting upright in a chair.

My imagination took me on an uncomfortable journey. I thought most deeply about Thea, growing up with a dad who had played a little too much rugby. I watched her play, listened to her read, and was moved by her childish innocence, her inquisitiveness and sense of wonder. I had long conversations with Jo, in which I confessed to a feeling of despair, that I would never get better.

It was hard to explain. Every time I moved my head too quickly, it felt as if my eyes were running to catch up. There was a time lag of a couple of seconds before everything settled down. My mind was whirring. There were bigger things than rugby, but life was coming at me very quickly. I had just signed my most lucrative club contract, covering the next two years. How could I turn my back on that? Money isn't everything, though sometimes it seems so.

I spoke to Jo about retirement. She was hugely supportive, saying we had enough to get by. We would be OK. Our wedding was in a matter of weeks, and she didn't want to be married to a vegetable.

Eddie put absolutely no pressure on me. 'The body's got a funny way of dealing with things and it will heal when it's ready,' he said. 'Listen to the medics, and take their advice, because players are their own worst enemy.' I knew the harsh truth contained in his counsel, because I had just suffered another bout of dizziness during an unsanctioned weights session.

I was on my own in a local gym I had quietly signed up to, and was shit scared. I ignored common sense, that exertion involved in lifting means you hold your breath and prevent the flow of blood to the brain, because I was paranoid about becoming deconditioned. I was worried about my next skinfold test when I should have been concerned about the next twenty years.

I had a club season to complete. An England tour of South Africa was on the horizon. Mercifully, the decision to resume playing was taken out of my hands by the neuro-specialist. He showed me my brain scans, and pointed out 'signs that your head has had quite a tough time over the years'. He couldn't put a timescale on my recovery, but there was no way I would be on the summer tour.

He ordered me to rest properly, and come back to see him in six months, after another brain scan. As terrified as I was, entering that consultation room, his certainty gave me release. I felt as if a huge weight had been lifted from my shoulders. It had been a confusing time. Now I could hold myself back, not worry about maintaining short-term fitness.

I had been under pressure, trying to please too many people, instead of looking after myself. If I needed any further encouragement, it came from my imagination. I saw myself in Japan, lifting the World Cup. I reassured myself that dreams can come true, even in the midst of a nightmare. Little did I know that the rugby gods were having a quiet chuckle in their celestial changing sheds.

Gradually, the fatigue subsided. I regained my focus, enjoyed normality. I took a holiday, and rediscovered grass-roots rugby. I had the best time of my life at a testimonial match in Bedford, seeing former teammates for the first time in ten years. I mucked in without fear or favour. I pulled pints, sang songs, and was reminded that human connection is what sport is all about.

Professionalism can strangle you with its ceaseless search for perfection. The game moves so quickly you leave good friends behind. Jo saw a change in me; without a schedule, and the remorselessness of a fitness regime designed to throw me back into the fray before I was ready, I had a sense of freedom. I was the battery hen, allowed out into the clean, fresh air from clock-controlled twilight.

Time and rest did their jobs. I stopped to count my blessings. I had the safety cushion of still being paid at the end of the month. I reaffirmed my debt to the Saints, and owed it to them to be around, to fulfil my obligations. I ran for the first time in ten weeks, under supervision, around Franklin's Gardens and felt the familiar surge of endorphin-fuelled happiness.

The sun was out. Crikey. Maybe I did have a future in the game, after all. It took a conscious effort to calm down, and allow things to take their course. I lifted very light weights, and prepared a transitional fitness programme, which would be triggered only when the experts considered it to be beneficial.

I would take ten days off, between two three-week blocks of training, and have another ten days' rest before a month's training. I had a greater awareness of the importance of what I had been through. I felt obliged to share, especially with younger players whose ambitious nature inevitably invites them to take risks with their welfare.

I had been that poor bloody infantryman. I would see lads in corridors, or in car parks, and strike up a conversation. I knew how to pitch my questions about their approach to injury, without being patronizing or holier-than-thou. They knew I carried the scars, and had a natural curiosity about my capacity to cope. Some remained behind their shields; others lowered their guard, and admitted to private fears.

It takes courage for a kid who has had a couple of HIAs to challenge a coach who has little reason to care about tomorrow. I played down my seniority, saying that it was easy for an old 'un like me to push back against the man, without diluting my central message. Take your time, and take care of yourself. I've seen too many people come back too soon, and suffer the consequences.

All major sports exist in a risk-averse society, and rugby must be seen to be aware of its duty of care to participants. The intention of protecting a player's head is obviously central to that responsibility, but the strategic approach to doing so is flawed, and in danger of changing the nature of the game. I don't say that lightly, given my medical history, but I feel it strongly.

Every defence coach I have played for has taught the two-tiered approach to tackling. One defender goes in low, to tie up the attacker's legs and stop the move's momentum. His partner tackles high, to stop or slow the ball. Quick ball places the defence on the back foot, stretches the game, and enables an offensive unit to create and exploit space.

By seeking to lower the tackle height, to appease understandable concern about head injuries, the authorities are doing the wrong thing for the right reasons. There will still be two-man tackles, unless and until the pointy-headed zealots in the rules department complicate the game still further by decreeing that it must be a one-man job.

Relatively few tackles are attempted head on; most come in from the side. If both tacklers are forced to tackle low, it stands to reason that they will come round the attacker's body from different sides, right shoulder, right foot and vice versa, and meet in the middle. They will clash heads, with a fair degree of force, because they will be coming in at the same height.

According to a world players' conference I attended in Monaco (a tough gig, but someone had to do it), that so-called friendly fire collision between two teammates was responsible for the biggest upsurge in cases of concussion. It also led to big, athletic attacking players with good ball skills being able to offload with relative ease. Welcome to Harlem Globetrotters rugby.

As the boys left for South Africa, I was keenly aware of what I was missing. I visited them for lunch, at Eddie's invitation, with the intention of giving a philosophical team talk, but rugby life got in the way. Recovery over-ran, cars had to be ferried home, and families had to be accommodated. I ended up talking informally over coffee to a group of six or seven, mainly senior, players.

I spoke from the heart about opportunity and enjoyment, to men with whom I had gone through a lot. My emotion was unforced, but raw, because at that time I was still unsure of what the future held. I told them their last game could come at any moment, which might have been too close to home for some, but it needed to be said.

You don't think it is going to end, but it is inevitable. If it happens on your own terms you are blessed. Being on the outside, looking in, because of a twist of fate is more painful than anyone cares to concede. It hurts like hell, even if it does have its morbidly amusing side. At Twickenham the previous weekend I had been mistaken for Chris Ashton three times.

I was making my debut as a TV pundit, in the usual try fest against the Barbarians, because I knew the result didn't matter. I admired the professionalism of the guys around me in the studio, but felt a bit unclean. I still had a loyalty to the team, and that led me to turn down an invitation to cover the trip to South Africa.

Eddie had been generous in his praise in the build-up to the tour, calling me England's most successful captain. It was appreciated, even if it was not entirely accurate. Yet, when one of the journos tried to stir the pot by making a point of my TV appearance he reverted to type. 'Dylan's not in our team any more,' he said. 'He can do what he wants.'

That was me told. It was a classic piece of man management. I flinched from the stick, and could only hope he hadn't thrown away the carrot.

# 13

# Boys in the Bubble

When we talk about courage in rugby, it tends to be in physical form. It involves an element of self-sacrifice, a capacity to endure punishment and a willingness to lay your body on the line for others. That's an easy concept to grasp, because of the confrontational nature of the sport and the mythical status of the warrior. To be the best, though, you have to exhibit a singular sort of bravery.

You must possess the moral courage to overcome deeply ingrained scepticism. You must dare to be different. You must be sufficiently curious to ignore the scorn of the cynics, who find it easier to laugh at you than learn with or from you. In the case of the England team under Eddie Jones, you have to be sufficiently open-minded to study the secret life of fish.

I thought I had become used to Eddie's brain-training emails until I received a link to a scientific article, outlining the internal dynamics of a school of fish. That's different to a shoal, by the way. It's more intimate, because it contains a solitary species, rather than a variety of types. It operates on a different wavelength.

Each fish has its preferred place in the school. There are natural leaders, at the head of the group. Others follow obediently, but not blindly. They watch one another closely, and move in a synchronized manner, through instinct and inbred intelligence. They sense water stirred by their companions as they swim, through pressure-sensitive pores along their body. They speed up, or slow down, to leave two body lengths between them and their neighbours.

*What on earth does this have to do with the organized chaos of a rugby scrum?* I hear you ask. To be honest, at first glance, I thought exactly the same. It came from so far left field it originated from a different solar system. But the art of coaching involves having the courage to remove traditional limitations from players.

Eddie trusted us to think for ourselves, and used coaches from other sports to make his points for him. He taught us to look for method in apparent madness. That pioneering mentality was one of our core values as a team. We took pride in doing things differently, because routine can deaden the mind. A relatively minor detail like changing hotel the day before a game to mentally trigger the imminence of the match has a disproportionate effect.

The fish became relevant when he introduced us to an old friend of his, Lisa Alexander, head coach of Australia's netball team. They helped to reinforce her central message, of the power of interconnectivity, and a singular purpose. Her story was doubly relevant, because she had turned an underachieving team into world champions, in a four-year cycle.

Sound familiar?

There was an easily recognizable restlessness to her, a need 'to find the next challenge when you are on top of the mountain'. She sought 'more important measures of success' than 'back-slapping from the public'. She stressed a coach's relative impotence during a match, and looked to develop players as leaders capable of 'making the biggest decisions on their own, under pressure'.

Lisa had stepped outside her own comfort zone, early in her tenure with the national team, by bringing in the leadership consultant who had helped to change the culture of the Sydney Swans, one of the most successful Aussie Rules clubs. Incidentally, the Swans used to be known by one of the best nicknames in sport, the Blood Stained Angels. I can relate to that.

Australia's netball team, known as the Diamonds, was being strangled by a hierarchical structure, which gave senior players too much influence. Due respect was still paid to their experience, but Lisa empowered younger players, to break down internal barriers through their idealism and freshness of thought. The resultant 'sisters-in-arms' strategy proved to be unifying, and emotionally powerful.

That, in turn, led the group to be open to new ideas. Eddie, who like Lisa comes from a teaching background, saw the relevance of a netballer's fundamental skill in detecting and exploiting space. He adapted a four-minute warm-up drill with a hybrid ball, in which we had to scan the field, eyes up, looking for teammates running into space.

The rules combined elements of the codes. We couldn't move with the ball, or pass it overhead. All passes had to be sharp and quick, off the hip. To score we had to bounce the ball off a trampoline, and catch it. It took some getting used to, but it improved our dexterity, shortened our thinking time, and programmed us to look for the gaps.

Pep Guardiola, who obviously had a huge impact on Eddie when he visited him at Bayern Munich in 2015, is another fiercely driven coach who looks outside his sport, to the likes of handball and Aussie Rules, to refine his knowledge of the art of creating and capitalizing on space. He used intense, short-sided games to get his message across, often stopping players to teach the intricacies of body shape.

I'm no great expert on football, tactically, but it intrudes on all our sporting lives. I wore an England football shirt to the pub to watch their matches in the 2018 World Cup and even had a retro number, red with number 66 on the back, with me on my stag do in Hvar, an island off Split in Croatia. Since you are asking, it was the usual carnage; eight hours' sleep in four days.

I love the patriotism channelled through England's national teams. My hunch is that the history of the football team taught Eddie about the corrosive effect of a fear of failure. Gareth Southgate, who addressed and diluted that fear in the build-up to his World Cup in Russia, came to Penny-hill Park to watch us train, and share his philosophy, on the same day as Lisa.

Rugby is different to football, in that the national team still has prominence and priority. Our clubs are politically powerful, though damagingly self-interested, but they have a smaller constituency. The international game raises a player's profile immeasurably; it also increases earnings, which is something the modern international footballer doesn't have to worry about.

They deserve due credit for giving their England match fees to charity, and to be fair have always struck me as good guys, but as a breed they tend to have first-world problems, like deciding the colour of their second Ferrari. The boys loved the association; I'm sure some were tempted to bring their Premier League sticker books to training.

I found Antonio Conte, who was passing through Chelsea on the way to a return to Italy with Inter Milan, an intriguing character, respectful yet watchful. Top coaches are magpies; interest from such celebrated figures in their own field added to the impression that we must have been doing something right.

We equalled the All Blacks' record of eighteen consecutive victories by routing Scotland 61–21 at Twickenham to win the Six Nations in March 2017. It still irks that Ireland prevented us winning a consecutive Grand Slam in Dublin the following week. It was our only defeat in two full seasons; we had won 22 out of 23 before the wheels fell off the following year.

We were aware what was coming during the team's second transitional phase in 2018. There are some good guys in the press, and on the punditry platforms, but the nature of our media is to ransack the temple at which they once worshipped. There was a sense some couldn't wait to challenge perceptions of Eddie's effectiveness. His is a public-facing job, with all its attendant absurdities, but I loved the way he used the media for his own ends.

He has a fondness for big characters, and he took Tom Wood into his confidence when convenient. 'I'm going to fuck with the Press,' he told him, a month out from an autumn Test against South Africa. 'Don't tell anyone – not your mum or your mates and certainly not them – but I'm going to start you.'

Eddie's ruse was brilliant. Tom didn't get any training reps in his normal position. He wore the reserves' bib. He played the role of spare part to perfection. Once on the pitch, like a bulked-up supermodel, springing out of a hollowed-out birthday cake, he was freed to be himself. 'All I want you to do is smash the rucks,' Eddie told him.' That's your USP.'

He did as he was told. We all knew there was a flipside. Eddie spoke to us through the media. He had his private eyeballs-out moments, but if he wasn't happy he didn't necessarily need to strip the paint from the dressing room walls. If he bigged us up, by stressing how strong and sure we had become, we were given a lift, and responded in kind. We no longer tiptoed around the issue of our superiority; this was who we were.

Deal with it.

Northampton were struggling around that time. Believe me, when you're parachuted into a team that has lost twelve games on the bounce it is difficult to achieve an incredible lightness of being. You see people scuffling in the dark, suffocating from the negativity. That experience, and missing the summer tour of South Africa with concussion, taught me the importance of perspective.

I had been around long enough to strip the experience of representing my country back to basics. We are thirty boys, in a bubble. It is not until you leave that bubble that you understand the scale of things. In what other job do you have the goodwill of millions of strangers? That summer, getting my head together, I was struck by how many people approached me in the street, asking how I thought the team would get on.

We had reached a level with England in which perfectionism was in danger of poisoning the well. I addressed the group when I sensed some of them were too down on themselves, even after a victory: 'Boys, be self-critical, do all that, but don't have a face on. There's no point in playing if you don't want to win, but winning is hard. That's why we put the work in during the week. It's what we strive for. When we succeed, relax. Even if you played shit, enjoy it.'

Eddie was enthused by a meeting with Ken Ravizza, one of the pioneering sports psychologists, before his death, aged seventy, from a heart attack, in July 2018. He worked in base-ball, initially with the Los Angeles Angels and latterly to huge effect with the Chicago Cubs alongside a forty-year career as a kinesiology professor, teaching stress manage-ment at Cal State Fullerton University.

Baseball is one of those sports, like golf, that is rooted in failure. Even the best hitters are out two thirds of the time they go to the plate. Ken had a three-point survival guide for his athletes: forget the last game, forget the last play and for-get the excuses. To illustrate the point, he left a miniature toy toilet in the dugout, with a simple instruction.

'Flush it. Let it go.'

Our environment lacked for nothing, though it was phys-ically and mentally demanding. Eddie insisted on the RFU investing £16,000 in infrared leggings, which had an inner layer designed to retain body heat. He could be cranky, but was also prepared to ease personal pressure points, if con-vinced it had a performance benefit.

That advocacy usually fell to me as captain. To give a typical example, I once noticed that the message schedule for the following day, posted on the noticeboard and in our online drop boxes, began at 8am. It was meant to be a day for regeneration; we had been diligent in our work, so Eddie gave the squad an extra hour's grace.

He did so without altering the rhythm of the week. Mon-day was our installation day, set aside for learning. That involved input from external coaches, and confirmation of match specifics, such as new plays, set-ups from the kick-off and first moves from scrum and lineout. Any screw-ups would be ironed out just before dinner at 6pm, in a confer-ence room walk-through.

This was the rugby version of the Knowledge, the cab driver's bible. There was no going back from that point. Clarity and familiarity had to be established, because Tuesday was our physical day, in which those plays were executed under pressure. It was heavy-contact, live-scrum work, basically the re-creation of game intensity.

We went through phase after phase, ruck after ruck, and kept going until there was an outcome, positive or negative. It's known as contact conditioning; the very mention of the term makes me ache. You hit the tackle bag, get off the floor, carry the ball through the pads, accelerate, clear out a ruck, get up on your feet, and must be ready to repeat, between six and eight times a minute.

We entered the ice age on Wednesday, regenerating to be ready for a fast day on Thursday, where we would work on leg speed, with less contact. Invariably, this would focus on our first four moves of the match, topped up by repetitive lineout drills.

Friday was an individual day, in which it was down to everyone to do whatever they felt they needed at the stadium. I used it to throw some lineout balls; kickers gauged specific wind speeds and angles. The so-called Captain's Run was a thing of the past. The team ran itself, with the coaches assigned to the stands. Depending on circumstances, there would be walk-throughs to reassure certain players, and reaffirm specific initiatives.

We weren't trying to catch anyone out as senior players, posing questions to the group about what we wanted to achieve, and how we would go about it, but we all needed to know the answers when we ran out of the chute, into the madness of an international match, the following day. It was win–win. If there was doubt and uncertainty, it was cleared up before it could do damage.

There are layers to captaincy that people don't see. I paid particular attention to our body language when we were together. I hated people with their hoods up at the table. I took notice of who was sitting with whom; that's usually the first sign of the formation of a clique. I didn't make a show of disapproval; a quiet word about changing tables, usually at our Tuesday night meals in town, would be enough.

We had our standards, maintained through occasional friction. I once went down to the spa in the training centre, and was appalled by the mess we had left. Strapping tape and discarded water bottles were strewn around, and had to be addressed immediately in a players-only meeting. 'Fuck this,' I told them. 'There's shit all over the place. Boys, let's be mindful of cutting corners. If we cut corners off the field we're creating bad habits that will creep in on the field.'

I saw the stern faces of leaders like Owen Farrell, George Ford and Mako Vunipola, and knew the outcome. Sure enough, from that moment on, you could have filmed a sequence of *Made in Chelsea* in the spa's spotless surroundings. That might have not been a brilliant idea, come to think of it, but it was a natural process of self-supervision.

Standards matter. I learned as captain to deal with issues during a session, rather than waiting for the team huddle. If I saw things not being done properly, I called a halt. It was better to frame questions than bawl out a bollocking: 'Why are we offside at every breakdown when we know we'll get pinged for it on Saturday? What's the point in training if we have this attitude? Aren't we learning our lessons?'

Those reminders, not to waste a session, or toss off a day, added up. Over time, players developed the confidence to confide in me. Everyone has their own struggles, domestic tensions and complications often dealt with at a distance. I could buy credit with the lads by helping to sort such personal issues. They trusted me and Eddie; anything shared confidentially stayed with us.

Again little things, like giving someone an extra six hours' grace on a Sunday to see his wife and kids after a match, can mean a lot. Eddie was responsive, just as Sir Alex Ferguson, one of his coaching idols, had been, in giving a young Cristiano Ronaldo as much time off as he needed to visit his ailing father at a pivotal stage of the season. That type of gesture is never forgotten, and invariably reciprocated.

I've got a thing about living in the past. It's an unnecessary diversion from the present and future. In 2018 I asked Eddie to remove all references to our success the previous year from the training centre. We would walk up the stairs, see the Six Nations trophy, the Cook and Calcutta Cups, and be subliminally invited to luxuriate in our wonderfulness.

'Mate,' I said to Eddie. 'That's 2017. We can't have that. Every book I've read on leadership or high performance has told me to never celebrate the past, and to always look forward.' He thought for a moment, and said 'Good point.' The silverware and the printed eulogies had disappeared by the following morning.

Looking back, I reckon I iced the deal by mentioning this quote, from Bill Belichick, the fabled head coach of the New England Patriots: 'If you sit back and spend too much time feeling good about what you did in the past, you're going to come up short next time.' I could easily have added another zinger: 'To live in the past is to die in the present.'

Eddie was fascinated by Belichick, and North American sport in general. We would swap insights into the culture of

American football, both in the NFL and the College game, where coaches tend to be a cross between TED-talking gurus and TV evangelists. Remove the media hype, though, and they dispensed the type of theatrical common sense we could use.

Only an android would describe Belichick as a people person, but he has an amazing capacity for detail, delivered to his coaches and players over hours of intensive scrutiny of game footage. We were drawn to his weekly video insights on the Patriots website, under the title of the Belichick Breakdowns.

He would sum up half a dozen key plays from the previous week's match, without focusing on the obvious. Others would eulogize eye-catching athleticism, or decisive moments. He would draw out the hidden gems, the marginal gain in an under-appreciated defensive play, or the interception created from a player's memory of the final play of Friday practice.

This is the grunt work of coaching. Eddie doesn't believe in the narcissism of supposed genius. Like Belichick, he focuses on the minutiae of technique, the dedication to application. To adapt another analogy that's employed endlessly in performance sport, he is a fan of the man who sweeps the floor at NASA, in the hope of helping the first man to Mars.

Eddie introduced me to Urban Meyer, the Florida and Ohio State football coach, through his book *Above the Line*. This was a personal odyssey, a man who realigned his life after realizing his obsession with his sport was impacting on his health and relationships. The competitive drive instilled by his father, who gave a dinner in Urban's honour as a boy, because he had got into his first fight protecting his sister, was renewed.

Like Eddie, who re-evaluated personal priorities after suffering a stroke, Meyer consciously tried to avoid what he called 'below the line' behaviour, berating officials and screaming at fate. He wanted to live, and coach, above the line, through accountability and self-control. He felt success was impossible with a BCD – blame, complain, defend – culture.

The book uses the 2014 season, in which Ohio State won its first national championship, as a template. His star quarterback sustained a season-ending injury before it had begun. It does not shy away from waste and personal tragedy: another athlete took his own life. A third potential star was drawn back to the streets, and died of a drug overdose in his car.

Eddie was taken by Meyer's three core values, relentless effort, competitive excellence and the power of the unit. They were transferable, since they covered the purity of preparation, mental discipline and an unthinking commitment to the group. I was taken by the equation, $E+R=O$. In other words, Event plus Reaction equals Outcome.

Meyer's theory is that the management of reaction to events is critical. Occurrences might be uncontrollable, but response can be ordered. He calls that 'the R Factor'. This has six elements which, used sequentially and consistently, lead to success: press pause, get your mind right, step up, adjust and adapt, make a difference and build skill.

Eddie followed up with a series of texts, taken from the book.

'The foundation of our success is relentless effort. We go 4–6 seconds point A to B as hard as we can. Elite is not about how talented you are, it's about how tough you are.'

'Success is cumulative and progressive. So is failure, it's a result of what you do every day.'

'Relentless effort, not talent or intelligence, is the key to achieving great things in your life.'

'If you want to win in the future, you must win the grind today.'

I countered by sharing the principles of the youngest NFL head coach, Sean McVay, the so-called 'mad scientist' who has been in charge at the LA Rams since 2017. He's exactly two months older than me, for heaven's sake. As a high-school quarterback he went through a season disguising a broken bone in his foot to lead his team to a state championship.

He came from a famous football family, but took defeat to heart, and rejected favours. When his team lost, he would stand in front of the group, claim the blame irrespective of merit, and apologize. As a young coach, he cycled into work by 3.30am, so he could be on hand to learn from his mentor, Jon Gruden, who returned to the NFL in 2018 with a ten-year $100m contract as head coach of the Oakland Raiders.

Nice work if you can get it.

McVay is the geek's geek. He spent his summer studying substitution patterns for every NFL team, and sought academic advice in communicating with his players. He was taught to make eye contact from the left of the room, through to the middle and to the right, to give every member of the group the impression he was speaking directly to him.

Gridiron is a largely pre-programmed sport, based on the coach's supposed infallibility, but McVay is consultative. He approaches players, individually and collectively, for their input. He wants them to stretch themselves, but be comfortable with the execution of his ideas. Without that buy-in, he changes options.

Those players don't just turn up for work. I also shared a *Sports Illustrated* profile of Kurt Cousins, the Minnesota Vikings quarterback, that beggared belief. He came across as a bit of a nerd, but his was next-level commitment. He has a personal brain coach, fitness adviser and physical therapist. He consults with a naturopath, a biochemist and a kinesiologist.

He sleeps in a hyperbaric chamber that measures his heart rate and breathing patterns. He funds personal blood-profiling, saliva-testing and tissue rejuvenation programmes. He measures electrical activity in his brain, and monitors hormonal, adrenal and testosterone levels. He combats stress through a computerized film programme.

I could tell Eddie was impressed. He replied with a one-word text: 'Thanks.'

People used to draw parallels between our relationship and that of Belichick and his legendary quarterback, Tom Brady. They have worked seamlessly together at New England for twenty years, without fusing personal and professional lives. They have never, for instance, had dinner together. There is a creative tension between them.

Eddie and I had our moments, but he took me into his confidence, and would ask me to run over his training plans, for reassurance. I wish I had met him earlier in my career, if only because of the chance he offered me to become more clued up through a network of personally relevant coaches. They worked on my mind and body on England's behalf, and oversaw my working day.

Frank Dick, the celebrated track and field coach, came in once a week and followed me around with a notepad. He would float around at the back if I called a team huddle, listening and watching body language, before approaching discreetly, with words of guidance and encouragement. He pushed me to coax answers out of the players, rather than giving them solutions. I loved him, especially when he brought Arsène Wenger in to see us.

Michael Bisping, the UFC champion, allowed us to use his ground-wrestling coach on a training camp in Portugal. I did four one-on-one sessions with him, learning how to control an opponent's body, and how to get off the ground quicker. It was punishing, but practical work, because if you can get back in the defensive line 10 per cent faster you will hold a measurable advantage.

In one wrestling session, with Mako Vunipola and Henry Thomas, the Bath prop, we grappled with one another holding tennis balls in the palms of closed hands. The session taught us to compensate for the subsequent lack of grip on the opponent by keeping the chest and hips tight. Jason Ryles, defence coach of Melbourne Storm in the NRL, spent weeks at a time with us, teaching tackling technique.

He played 270 games as an NRL prop, and was capped fifteen times for Australia. He wasn't that fussed about coaching, but got the bug in the Illawarra Coal League with his local team in Wollongong, the Western Suburbs Red Devils. He's hailed as a master of rugby league's so-called hit-and-stick tackle move.

It's the classic two-man technique I mentioned in an earlier chapter: one goes high, the other low. The aim, as the name suggests, is to hit the opponent, and stick with him, wrapping up the ball to kill the offload. That gives us a chance to reset our defensive line, and apply pressure. If the flow of the ball is not slowed, their attack gathers momentum and we are on the back foot.

The information stream was constant. Knowing Eddie and boys like Jamie George, Elliot Daly and Joe Launchbury are huge cricket fans, I introduced Alastair Cook to the group. Cookie loves his rugby, and we became mates after meeting at Franklin's Gardens. He epitomizes the dedication of a largely self-made athlete; his informal lessons in longevity were brilliant.

I was mentored by Neil Craig, who became the RFU's head of high performance in October 2017. He's in his early sixties, a prominent Aussie Rules player and coach who worked as a sports physiologist for Cycling Australia in the 1990s and developed specialisms in strength and conditioning.

He's the Rugby Whisperer, a fascinating guy with a light-touch approach to leadership and teamwork. We didn't deal in speeches or sermons; he communicated through asides, like 'Make sure you train quality today, don't just get through the session', that sound like statements of the obvious but stick like superglue in the brain.

I wasn't daft. He was Eddie's emissary. He quietly set me a series of personal challenges. 'The captain should never come off due to a fitness-related issue,' he would say, somehow managing to avoid a nod and a wink. We spoke about players owning their performance, and the importance of what he called 'density of leadership' within the squad.

I came in on my days off and made sure I hit my targets. 'That's why you're "The King", mate,' Jonny May said during one of those piss takes that reveal the peer respect we all, as professional athletes, crave. 'The King is gonna work harder than everyone else.' If you'd like an insight into how hard, here is my timetable for a training camp in Portugal before the autumn internationals in 2017.

I reported to Pennyhill Park on the Saturday night, after being pumped by Saracens, who ran up fifty-seven points with Eddie watching. After a few 'fancy seeing you here'

handshakes with the likes of Jamie George and Owen Farrell, we flew out, all friends together, the following day. Two
intensive training days led to a temporary parting of the
ways.

The boys went out for their traditional Tuesday night
steak and chocolate fudge cake. Their Wednesday involved
regeneration, a gentle massage and a little sunshine. Eddie
and I flew back to England on Tuesday evening. We landed
at Stansted at 7.30pm, drove an hour to our hotel at Syon
Park, and I dived into the pool, for half an hour's recovery
work.

By 9.30 I was suited and booted for a two-hour dinner
featuring small talk and salmon breath. I was up at 6.30 the
next morning for a full day of media commitments. We then
jumped into a taxi for a referees meeting at a Heathrow hotel,
before flying back from Stansted, arriving at the training
camp at midnight on Wednesday.

You never show anyone that you are sore and tired, so no
one knew I was on anti-inflammatories. The easiest thing
would have been to wake in a foul mood the following morning, moan about fatigue, and have a shit day's training. I
forced myself to focus, and made a conscious effort to be
vocal, during both the session and the subsequent team
meeting.

It was my way of letting Eddie and the boys know I am
not one to sulk.

I knew I was not the only one under pressure to hit targets
and make the numbers sing. On one relatively rare Friday
night at home I received a phone call at 8.30pm. It was from
Graeme Close, England's lead nutritionist. He was told
Warrick Harrington, the sports scientist, needed my weekly
skinfold statistics.

As it happens, I'd been a good boy that day, removing my fish from a brioche, and eating all my veg. The only problem was that Graeme was going on holiday to Thailand on the Sunday. I gave him my postcode, and he drove for an hour, before doing the test in my living room. Within ten minutes, he was back off, out into the night.

The message had been received, and understood. Life in the bubble wasn't meant to be easy. Trust me, it wasn't.

# 14

# Own the Unexpected

I was on the clock from six in the morning until nine at night. Each day began with a text message from Eddie Jones, whose pre-breakfast meeting set the mood. On good days he was content to deliver a couple of key points he wanted me to pass on through senior players. On bad days, when the phone pinged at 4am, our world was a wasteland.

We were wasting our time. Training had been shit. I needed to be better. The team weren't doing enough. The litany of apparent incompetence went on and on. Anxiety gave way to resignation. This is how it was going to be, in the short term at least. Eddie saw his captain as an extension of his management team, so it was work, work, work.

It would be an exaggeration to suggest he created a climate of fear, since authority is, by its nature, intimidating, but my back was always straighter in his presence because of his unpredictability, and the respect in which I held him. I was continually conscious of the correctness of my body language, and my choice of words. I knew when not to waste time or oxygen trying to make him change his mind.

I was in the inner circle, but it wasn't a comfortable environment. You could never relax into the rhythms of the England camp, and enjoy the experience. It is not a question of whether that is right or wrong. That debate is the privilege of the outsider. If you can't cope, you don't stay. I saw plenty of people, players and staff, come and go. I never felt any less of them, or for them, if they weren't cut out for it.

Eddie worked his coaches and support staff extremely hard, to give his players the best chance to excel. I straddled the lines in a series of planning meetings and review sessions when the boys were having their downtime. I was the voice and face of the team; various departments, under pressure from the boss, quietly asked me to act as ambassador or adviser.

My room was my safe place. When I got the chance, I would lie coffin-straight on the bed and stare at the ceiling, trying to put my brain in neutral. I craved momentary oblivion. To relax, I would FaceTime my wife and daughter, whose domestic problems, priorities and enthusiasms might as well have been beamed in from a distant planet.

You have to be pretty strong, mentally, to survive in that setting. I'm proud of sustaining my England career for so long, until I physically could no longer do my job. I never forgot that high performance never forgives. Any weakness, however fleeting, had consequences. A good head coach is like a clever fisherman: he always keeps tension on the line.

To be honest, I wasn't entirely surprised when Kearnan Myall, the former Wasps lock forward, suggested several England squad members dreaded going to training camp because of the heavy workload and constant scrutiny. I was more concerned, on a personal and professional level, by the revelation he was driven to the verge of suicide by mental-health problems he felt unable to share.

We were roughly of the same age; he played, uncapped, for England against the Barbarians, toured Argentina in 2013 without making the Test team, and featured in Stuart Lancaster's Saxons squads. The secrecy surrounding his suspension for cocaine use was a commentary on the game's sensitivity to the issue of recreational drugs, and the implications of stress, but the wider points he made could not be ignored.

Scott Wisemantel, England's attack coach, before he moved to fulfil a similar role with Australia after the World Cup, argued in response that Eddie's routine was 'intense, but well structured'. He was realistic in saying 'The pressure is high at the pointy end of the stick', but I couldn't agree with his insistence that there was time 'for players to refresh, to get their heads right and to recover'.

I never had that time. I went through a phase of dreading going away, and know other England players felt similarly. It wasn't something that was discussed openly, because it is such an individual issue and no one wanted to be seen to be speaking out of turn, but we were honest in privately sharing the strain. The language was heartfelt, but pretty basic.

Two words recurred when we talked among ourselves: 'I'm fucked.'

We probably didn't feel that much different to some of the coaches, who were told one day they didn't have a good enough relationship with us, only to be told the following day they were too close to us. We were bonded by the ripples in Eddie's character and constrained by the ludicrous convention that athletes, like Victorian children, should be seen and not heard.

Rugby is played in a heightened state of emotion, because it is a physical game that arouses powerful feelings. It is not darts or snooker, an overtly mental challenge you can undertake in your slippers. To put your body where it literally hurts, on a daily and weekly basis, you have to rationalize the price, and commit to the prospect of punishment.

The kids, with careers to forge and reputations to build, tend to internalize the pressure, and shy away from speaking their minds. But, as senior players, we all sit there and say the same thing, especially when we return to our clubs in the long dark days of mid-winter: 'I'm fucked. I need a week off . . . Not going to train today, I'm fucked . . .'

Everyone is wired differently. Some players are ground down by the monotony of training. Others are picked apart by insecurity and insufficient game time; they die a quiet death at the first sign of a team sheet that doesn't feature their name. We are all looking for a new stimulus. Some find respite through yoga or meditation; others struggle to escape the 'big boys don't cry' culture.

We all need to realize that silence is a natural enemy. A ripped body often disguises a fragile psyche. We must ask more pertinent questions about what the game is in danger of doing to us. We are trained to push through pain and celebrate sacrifice. It gives us camaraderie, financial reward and a focal point in life, but what does it take away?

Kearnan is a bit of a thinker, more introverted than most. His type of voice can be lost in the noise of a dressing room, yet his intervention concentrated minds. I was struck by his selflessness; he put himself out there for others to benefit. No one will be able to question the authenticity of the PhD he is doing at Oxford University, where he is researching mindfulness and mental health in athletes.

I've never felt depressed or suicidal because of the world in which I've operated. I've never dabbled with drugs, other than the painkillers most rugby players gobble like Smarties. But, without question, I have suffered from mental burnout. More often than not, it was a cumulative problem that manifested itself when I returned from an international camp.

One week you are playing in front of a capacity crowd at Twickenham, pouring everything into a Test match followed by millions. The anthems, anxiety and analysis can suck you dry. The next week you are playing in front of 4,000 in a club game at Sale. You're beside a motorway on a ground that smells of sewage because it is next to the main waste water treatment works for the city of Manchester.

Trust me, that takes some getting used to.

It is a life of contrast, summed up in a weird way by Eddie's character. He's brilliantly sociable, loves a drink and is so well travelled he can talk about anything and anyone. He will sit on any table at lunchtime and draw people in with his rugby stories, insights and opinions. But when he flips into work mode, watch out.

I got the call to see him in the drawing room every day. Sunny Eddie would be as good as gold, and urge me to 'Stay on it, mate.' Cloudy Eddie would remember seeing a pair of discarded trainers around the spa and remind me that 'I don't want it looking like a landfill.' The rest of the lads didn't know who they were going to meet when they reported to him for their one-on-ones at the start of camp.

Anyone who looked even slightly out of shape had about as much chance of survival as a wildebeest wandering into a pride of lions. Luke Cowan-Dickie, one of my understudies, loved a beer on the quiet. He once drove up from Exeter to Teddington for a camp and was sent home within half an hour because his body-fat composition was poor. Rejection was brutal.

Marland Yarde, the Sale wing who made his comeback in October 2019 after being out for a year when he ruptured ligaments and dislocated his knee in a game against New-castle, once drove down to Pennyhill Park from Manchester

Martin Johnson giving me some advice at training in the run-up to my Test debut against the Pacific Islanders in November 2008 (Photo by David Rogers/ Getty Images)

With Tom Smith after winning the European Rugby Challenge Cup in 2009 (Photo by Mike Hewitt/Getty Images)

With Phil Dowson and Chris Ashton after Chris scored a try against Treviso in the Heineken Cup group stage in December 2009 (Photo by David Rogers/Getty Images)

With Lee Dickson after we beat Perpignan in the 2011 Heineken Cup semi-final (Photo by David Rogers/Getty Images)

Celebrating a penalty try against Ireland in the 2012 Six Nations with fellow front-rowers Dan Cole and Alex Corbisiero (Photo by David Rogers/Getty Images)

With Chris Ashton after we beat Ireland in Dublin in the 2013 Six Nations (Photo by David Rogers/Getty Images)

With Luther Burrell after beating Scotland at Murrayfield in 2014 (Photo by David Rogers/Getty Images)

After we beat Wales in the 2016 Six Nations, Prince Harry presented me with the Triple Crown trophy (Photo by Clive Rose/Getty Images)

suffered a concussion in the latter stages of our Grand Slam win in Paris in 2016. Afterwards,
was smiling, but there was no one at home (Photo by Pascal Rondeau/Getty Images)

ith Maro Itoje after the first Test of the June 2016 Australia series in Brisbane. We
me from 10 points behind to win 39–28 (Photo by David Rogers/Getty Images)

With Eddie Jones and the Cook Cup after completing our 3–0 series victory over Australia in Sydney in June 2016 (Photo by David Rogers/Getty Images)

It's easier to get Mum and Dad to a game in Australia, and it was great to celebrate with them and with Jo after our historic series victory (Photo by David Rogers/Getty Images)

With Owen Farrell after we beat Wales in Cardiff in 2017, en route to our second consecutive Six Nations championship (Photo by Stu Forster/Getty Images)

That's the Calcutta Cup in my hands, but when we beat Scotland 61–21 at Twickenham in 2017 we also clinched the championship with a game to spare (Photo by Laurence Griffiths/Getty Images)

Jo is the constant
in my life. She
and Thea are my
biggest supporters.

after a Sunday afternoon match, feeling a little bruised and battered. Eddie greeted him with a bright 'How are you feeling, mate?' and the conversation quickly went downhill.

'Oh, a bit tired.'

'Fuck off, mate.'

'What?'

'If you're tired, fuck off. I don't want tired players here.'

As you can imagine, that cosy fireside chat echoed around the halls within minutes.

I simply became used to being judged by a higher standard. On one of Eddie's good days, someone like Courtney Lawes could just about get away with strolling around in a vest, or wearing nothing on his feet in the dining room. If I did that, as captain, my cauliflower ears would burn.

The anxiety would begin to build even before I left home. I would pack slowly, fighting my conscience at leaving my family, yet again. Farewells would become sadder, because we knew I was going into a difficult situation, where I have to deal with constant stress and a very public sense of responsibility. Underpinning everything was the understanding that, because of the physical and mental challenge of international rugby, I would return home feeling like a dead man.

I'm not seeking sympathy, just a sharper understanding that elite athletes are human beings, too. I accept that, in some senses, I was no different to the businessman or businesswoman, preparing for a long-haul sales trip. The divergence, of course, is their negotiations are not broadcast, live, to a global audience. Their deals and decisions will not be examined minutely by the media.

This is not the release of leaving home for a jolly boys' outing, a weekend of golf and far too much beer. Though you will be renewing important friendships, the atmosphere is laced with unspoken uncertainty and transition is difficult. It's like breaking a horse in; it takes two or three days of constant self-evaluation and increased training loads before you accept the disciplines of the new normality.

To an extent, as far as family is concerned, it has to be out of sight, out of mind. Jo, my wife, saw the bigger picture, but I felt bad checking in with Thea, my daughter. 'You're at the rugby hotel, aren't you, Daddy?' she would say, and it would break my heart. The family had the option of seeing me at Pennyhill Park on what was nominally a day off, but it would have felt like a prison visit.

Joe Marler didn't try to hide his desire to break out whenever possible, even before he took a ten-month break from international rugby until the 2019 World Cup. He was an obvious home boy, who married his childhood sweetheart, doted on his kids, and drove three hours each day, to train and play at Harlequins, because he never wanted to leave his roots in Haywards Heath.

At heart Joe is the great lad who plays for the local team in the lower leagues. He was Eastbourne's player of the year for five successive seasons, and distinguished himself for a year by playing in a shirt with 'Physio' emblazoned on the back. Legend has it he asked to be known as 'Psycho' but someone misheard him.

He doesn't have great luck with rugby gear. He was one of the poster boys for the launch at Twickenham of an updated England kit, under the tagline of 'Own the Unexpected.' He looked the part, dominating promotional photographs like some sort of black-shirted Viking. Such a shame that he had 'retired' from the international game a week previously.

I couldn't resist sending him a text: 'You certainly owned that one, mate.'

We are all, to a degree, playing a role. By his own admission, Joe doesn't take himself too seriously in what is a very serious business. He increasingly questioned the one-dimensional nature of life as an elite athlete and spoke of missing basic pleasures, like helping his son learn to read and write, when he stepped away from the England team just before a training camp in September 2018.

The simplicity of his initial explanation, that he wanted to devote more time to his family, was understandable and persuasive, but I'd always suspected it told only part of the story. He went on to expand on the anxiety he felt in leaving home, and having to be coaxed into reporting for international duty by his wife, Daisy.

We got on well, which might not be too much of a surprise, since we are both used to being up in front of the beak. He was banned for three weeks for use of the elbow against Wasps in 2017, missing two autumn internationals. Eddie administered a well-rehearsed bollocking when he was forced to sit out the opening two matches of the 2018 Six Nations after being shown a red card for a dangerous clear-out at a ruck against Sale.

Joe caused a bit of a stir before clarifying comments that he deliberately picked up suspensions to avoid England camps. When he spoke about behaving irrationally, I understood where he was coming from. We would often console one another after a brush with the RFU disciplinary panel, and wonder whether the aggravation was worth it.

His decision to return, to play in the World Cup, wasn't a surprise. You have to manage a different set of frustrations in the club game, and he had all the time he needed to sort his head out. You notice the difference, financially, when you are outside the England squad. Standards are also not quite as high as those you become used to in the international game.

There's such a fine line between elation and misery. As captain, I knew that if we lost I would get a kicking from the critics and the cyber cowards. My compensation came in the sweetest release, the relief I felt for about half an hour after an England victory. Everything moved on pretty sharply; I was soon on parade, with another job list to work through.

In hindsight I should have enjoyed the wins, but I didn't have a drink because of my speech at the post-match dinner. I knew Eddie would be picking up on every word. He had drilled into me that whenever I spoke publicly it was a chance to communicate with the team. I couldn't just stand up there and spout empty platitudes; I had to make my message progressive.

I couldn't sleep after a game anyway, because of thoughts and images pinballing around my brain, so it helped that the analysts were quick on the draw. My first action, on returning to my room, was to switch on the computer and assess my numbers, which, despite the carping of those who loved to critique my game for long periods of my career, tended to be pretty damn good.

It was hard to quibble with the effectiveness of my workload. I just didn't do the shiny things people picked up on. I rarely provided eye-catching contributions for the highlight packages, but needed to know that when Eddie phoned on Sunday morning I had evidence that I had done my job. If his captain wasn't hitting his numbers, he wanted to know why.

Does the elite environment need to be so unforgiving? Again, it is a moot point. It is what it is. We are on firmer ground in asking, over the long term, whether it is sustainable. There were times when playing for England felt a bit like taking part in one of those brutal dance marathons in the Great Depression of the 1920s, where penniless couples kept going until they collapsed.

Our union, the Rugby Players' Association, is increasingly concerned about the relentlessness of the demands placed upon us. I wasn't in the slightest bit surprised when Damian Hopley, the RPA chief executive, estimated that around 10 per cent of Premiership players phone the RPA's confidential helpline each year to discuss mental problems.

Human beings are naturally adaptable, but we are being asked to play and train at the highest intensity for eleven months a year. Comparisons with the NFL, which have become more pertinent since they started to come to terms with their horrendous concussion problems, are valid because our sports share certain characteristics.

They play only sixteen regular season games. I wish . . .

Of course, I'm being a little facetious there, since retirement statistics are now more personally relevant, and incredibly worrying. The RPA's most recent survey found 62 per cent of past players experienced some kind of mental-health problem within two years of retiring. More than half did not feel in control of their lives. 99 per cent called for greater assistance.

In one way, that's a reflection of how self-worth is so closely linked to athletic performance. I play, therefore I am. But it also underestimates the complexity of the issue. It is not as simple as concentrating on the game's duty of care, and pushing for such advances as the availability of independent medical teams at all grounds, which, incidentally, I agree with.

Eddie and I were shattered to learn of Dan Vickerman's suicide in February 2017. Eddie had coached him with the Wallabies, for whom he won sixty-three caps as a second-row enforcer, and I had played briefly with him for Northampton, when he was studying at Cambridge University. The terrible irony of his death, aged thirty-seven, was that he killed himself on the day he was meant to be conducting a seminar on stresses on retired players.

He was trying to help from within the system, on behalf of the Australian Players' Union. He had taken inordinate care in building a new career, in personal development and fund management. Yet who knows what other lights go out when sport's spotlight fades? I only know that in my lowest moments, dealing with the aftermath of concussion, I couldn't bring myself to ring that helpline.

Is that healthy? Probably not, but resilience is revered. Is the cult of the sporting gladiator overblown? Certainly, yet it is attractive because its basic superficiality is supposed to make the pain go away. Ask the 23-year-old player who blows his knee out in his first match after a six-month spell rehabbing his other knee whether he feels like a hero.

The answer will be short, sharp and laden with pain.

Everything is wonderful when you are winning, and the body is behaving itself. But darkness descends when results deteriorate, or something breaks. I've seen the ill-disguised terror in a player's eye at club level, when he is released. You can try to console him, by telling him you will be there for him as a mate, but you both understand rugby's reality. He's damaged goods.

Here's another Catch-22 situation: successful teams tend to have stability, in terms of selection. Yet when there is no real rotation at club level, the reserves hardly play. Some become ticking time bombs. They want to rip into the starters in training. Grudges build, because the regulars have taken what they believe is rightly theirs.

Fringe players become gym freaks. They try to purge their frustration by lifting bigger weights, and doing longer, more demanding circuits. They're fresh for the physical session on a Tuesday. Starters will still be sore from the weekend, and thinking 'Oh fuck. This is the last thing I need.' Reserves will be salivating at the chance to make their mark. I'd never be so prissy as to accuse any player of lacking respect because he wants to take my shirt, but I have to confess I've smacked a few who had the temerity to try.

Old-school coaches love aggression. They see a scrap in training, usually after a defeat, and think 'That's sorted things out.' They go for quantity over quality, and are never happier than when their players are twatting tackle bags. Invariably you don't lose because of a lack of physicality; you are undone by technical shortcomings in the set piece, or a lack of imagination outside the scrum.

I'm fortunate that my latter years at Northampton, under Chris Boyd, were closer in spirit to the England set-up. Training is planned to the minute. Sessions are posted in the team meeting room; on a typical day we will have eight minutes of individual preparation, followed by fifteen minutes of specialist work for forwards and backs, before four-minute blocks of specific plays.

We train for forty-eight minutes, and the coach is almost umbilically connected to a sports scientist, who tends to be hyper-sensitive to fatigue. Instead of relying on the traditional two-word answer on a Monday morning – you've guessed it, 'I'm fucked' – he will greet us with a wellness survey in which we have to rate everything from soreness to quality of sleep out of ten.

Players zone out when the messaging remains the same. I'd grown out of the biff-bosh school of thought, and responded to the emotional intelligence of Chris's approach. It took some of the Northampton guys a while to thaw, to adapt to a new regime and philosophy, but I loved the difference in outlook and application.

He's sixty-one, and dispenses accumulated wisdom. He coached the Sharks in South Africa, ran Tonga's defence in the 2011 World Cup, when they defeated France, the eventual finalists, in the pool stage, and spent two years in charge of New Zealand's under-20s before turning Wellington Hurricanes into a dominant force in Super Rugby.

It's funny. I am a Kiwi by birth, but he's the first coach I've played under professionally who is a product of the New Zealand system. I've had to relearn the game tactically, philosophically and linguistically, because Chris uses a different terminology.

He has the Kiwi mentality of playing to space. I was brought up to kick it long to relieve pressure when defending in our own 22, but he argued against being so structured. A predictable team is an analyst's dream, so in that situation three or four players would be conditioned to dropping deeper, in anticipation of running the ball back. Chris countered that by encouraging us to maul, move the ball, and attack the space created by those guys dropping deep.

It is only by working closely with coaches that you can truly reach an informed opinion on their effectiveness. The relationship has a finite shelf life; my association with Jim Mallinder and Dorian West at Saints probably dragged on for a couple of years too long. I retain respect for and loyalty to them, since we grew together before drifting apart, but I needed new impetus.

People assume that senior players don't need coaching, but feedback and fresh ideas replenish us. Chris, like Eddie Jones, challenges me mentally, but Steve Borthwick is probably the best coach I have worked with. He was ridden very hard by Eddie, but his attention to detail extended to learning Afrikaans on the tour of South Africa in 2018 so he could decipher the Springboks' lineout calls.

His work ethic is unbelievable, and he doesn't hide from his own flaws. As an England player and captain, Steve was dour and uncommunicative. As a coach he is engaged and working continually on his interpersonal skills. Like anyone who has the resilience to work for Eddie on a long-term basis, he benefited from a crash course in what it takes to be the best. Part-timers need not apply.

Eddie oversaw an evolution in coaching in his initial four-year cycle with England. He refused to allow a meeting to extend beyond fifteen minutes, and limited them to the development of three key points, usually one positive, one negative and one general. He pressurized his coaches, but also expected them to empower the players. We, for instance, always developed and delivered the lineout options. No one went into a match wondering why we were doing something.

Chris Boyd's management style is also inclusive. On Saturday night the game is done. Win or lose, we are told to relax. Acknowledge the work that has gone in but be aware there is no point in carrying baggage. Be comfortable in your own skin. On Monday he calls a connections meeting, an exchange of views and ideas that aligns us for the week to come. He favours transparency in selection.

He once put a graph up, essentially telling people when they were going to play. Those of us in the red zone, who had played an hour or more on a consistent basis, were told to expect a holiday. 'I want you boys to go away and get some sun,' he said, to widespread amazement. This was not someone barking 'How much do you want it?' It was a mature, rational individual who believed in mutual respect.

Players aren't pieces of meat. We're not inanimate objects. Cut us and we bleed, profusely and regularly. Doubt or disparage us and we worry. Don't treat us like Orcs, created in the fires of Mordor. Don't insult our intelligence, as Saracens did with the systematic smashing of the salary cap that led to a 105-point deduction, the imposition of a £5m fine, and their eventual acceptance of relegation.

I'll return to the controversy in the context of what it says about the development of the professional game later in the book, but on a personal level I felt betrayed that such subterfuge undermined a central philosophy that involved continuity and caring for the individual. It was horrible to learn that someone had coldly cheapened the concept of contentment.

A belief in the power of positivity isn't tie-dye, hippy-dippy romanticism: research suggests teams that stay together longer, because of connection at a human level, tend to be conspicuous achievers. I was taken in by the smokescreen of academy players eating and training with the seniors, who were expected to share advice and experience.

More fool me, given the grotesquely hidden cynicism of the process, but I loved the way the circle of trust was extended to include players' families, who are often treated as unwanted baggage. I fell for the principle of a psychologist overseeing personal-development programmes, preparing players for life, after rugby.

Every player goes through spells of feeling vulnerable, and alone. I learned a lot about myself during my rehabilitation from concussion. I began at a low level, steady 100-metre runs and relatively light weights in the gym, and built gradually. The medical team's message was consistent, and bored into my skull: 'Don't be your own worst enemy.'

I had a setback just as I was on the verge of returning to rugby training. A small cyst was found in my hip joint, so I took the old man's New Age medicine, a Botox and cortisone injection. I surprised myself (and quite a few others) with my patience, in trusting the structures put in place for me but, just over a fortnight later, I announced my readiness to play.

It was only a twenty-minute cameo in a pre-season match, against Glasgow, but I felt like a little kid. I was excited, almost awestruck as the moments of truth multiplied. The first tackle led to the next; any conscious thought of the potential danger of going low, and leading with my head, quickly evaporated. The strain of the first scrum felt surprisingly comforting.

I wasn't avoiding contact. I was accepting it, even enjoying it. This was what I did, who I was. My head had healed and my soul was intact. All I needed now was for my body to keep its side of the bargain.

# 15

# The Shirt

A Northampton Saints shirt, number 13, hangs on its own in an open-plan locker on the right-hand side of the home dressing room at Franklin's Gardens. If you ignore the thin film of scum that tends to lap around the ice baths, it's a functional setting for a strangely suitable shrine. It is a powerful symbol of loss, a constant reminder of a friend, a fine man who didn't deserve his fate.

That shirt belongs to Rob Horne. It was his spare for the East Midlands derby at Leicester on 14 April 2018. He was captaining Saints for the first time, because I was at home going through concussion protocols. He was proud and excited, and chased a high kick-off hard, before going into a tackle he had made countless times before.

Sione Kalamafoni, their Tongan number 8, made a half-jump to catch the ball. As he landed, his full weight, 121 kilograms, came down on Rob, who was low, and advancing in the tackle position. He was crushed in a freak accident to which no blame can be attached. Thirteen seconds into the game, at the age of twenty-eight, his life had changed for ever.

Horney's first thought was that he had dislocated his shoulder. His instinct was to get up because he wanted to be true to how he played the game, and didn't want to worry his family, in the stands. Matt Lee, our head physio, had secured his head and neck in textbook fashion. Phil Dowson, our forwards coach, crouched beside him on his right side.

'I'm pretty embarrassed here,' Rob protested. 'I don't need any help.'

'It's OK,' Phil replied. 'Don't worry. Just stay down.'

'I don't want to show that I'm hurt.'

Matt, a calm, measured man who commands trust and respect, cut in: 'Rob, you haven't moved your legs yet.'

That was the moment Horney realized he needed to listen to the medical staff, probably for the first time in his career. He willed himself to move his right leg in a spasm of panic, before lying still as he was transferred on to a protective stretcher, and into a waiting ambulance. Watching on TV, I felt an icy stab of dread, and sent him a text, to which I have never received a reply:

'Tell me you're OK, mate.'

In medical terms, he suffered an avulsion of his brachial plexus in the collision. In layman's terms, he had damaged a network of five nerves that conduct signals from the spine to the shoulder, arm and hand, so badly they separated from the spinal cord. His right arm was completely paralysed, with no hope of recovery.

I'm not being maudlin or over-sentimental, but he is one of those people who enrich the lives of others. He's an energy giver, a contributor who prefers to give, rather than receive. He's a proper bloke. I'd got to know him well during his first season, when he moved into the next village with his wife, Simone, and two young kids.

He was named Player of the Year in the club's end-of-season awards, not through some understandable surge of misplaced sympathy, but because he was an outstanding centre, good enough to play for Australia in two World Cups and a home series against the Lions. It's amazing such injuries don't occur more often, given the physics and dynamics involved, but it should not have happened to someone like him.

Phil Dowson drove Ben Foden and me to see him in Leicester Infirmary the following day. I was in the back seat when Dows said 'I'd better give you a brief.' We had played together for years, so he didn't sugar-coat the news. I welled up. Rob didn't know the full implications of his injury. Paralysis was permanent, and we had obviously to be as upbeat as possible.

'How are you, mate?'

'Yeah, I'm good,' he said, smiling.

He was starving, and wolfed down the sweets and treats we had bought in Marks & Spencer's that morning. He had been lying flat since his admission, in the so-called settling period, but doctors had agreed that he could sit up and scan the room. We gossiped light-heartedly and chatted inconsequentially about the derby, which we won 27–21, while making a conscious effort not to look at his damaged arm.

He was not daft. He knew, from the reaction of the staff on his admission, that something serious was wrong. Exploratory surgery, undertaken after his transfer to the Royal National Orthopaedic Hospital in Stanmore, confirmed the worst. There were tears in the dressing room when the squad was told the following weekend. It was as if a close relative had died.

We had an informal meeting, and decided to hang his shirt in his locker for the duration of his three-year contract. New players don't need to be told of its significance, and the rest of us find it a comfort. The locker is directly in my eyeline. It provides perspective for anyone who is having a tough day, worrying about selection or struggling with rehab. I've seen the change in a couple of lads, who were notorious for their negativity.

We had to maintain the pretence of ignorance for the next three weeks, while the damage was assessed by a series of specialists before an announcement. Rugby is a global village, and players from all over the world were texting to ask after Horney. The club is central to the community, so I was continually stopped in the street. I had a standard reply: 'He's up, awake and in good spirits, but due to medical confidentiality I can't say anything about his injury.'

When Rob came back to the club, he told us he didn't want us to feel fear because of his example. Paralysis tends to be a secret anxiety, rarely expressed openly, but the boys were shocked by his appearance, because he had lost a lot of weight. There was real warmth towards him, despite a little initial awkwardness in having to shake his left hand, rather than his right.

I acted as his driver. I knew he was in chronic pain, a symptom of nerve damage that will never lift, but it was only when we were alone that its full force hit me. 'How are you getting on?' I asked him one day. 'I'm fucking doing it tough, mate,' he replied, quietly. To hear a typical Aussie battler hint at the inner struggle made me more protective than ever.

I only just stopped myself punching a supporter when he came across us, in our club suits, after a game. He asked me for an autograph, which I gave happily, and then said 'Oh Rob, I don't suppose you're up for signing.' He meant nothing by it, and was in a bubbly mood, but by that time I had learned to read Horney's body language. He stiffened. If the fan knew what he was saying, he would have kept his mouth shut.

Rob has reordered his life through what he calls 'positive realism'. He admits to going through a rough patch immediately after surgery, but after speaking to fellow sufferers, in and out of sport, he rejects false hope that a miracle will occur. The pain is constant, 10/10 on a medical scale, but he works selflessly in his role as ambassador for the Australian Pain Management Association.

He has become closer to his father, a Vietnam veteran wounded in combat, and was inspired by Martin Hewitt, a former Parachute Regiment Officer who lost the use of his right arm, hit by a 7.62 calibre machine-gun round as he led an attack by his platoon in Helmand Province in Afghanistan. Martin has mastered what he calls 'the life unplanned'.

In his case, that means attempting the Explorer's Grand Slam, climbing the highest mountain on each continent and reaching the North and South Poles. He made the summit of Everest at the second attempt in May 2019 and has already scaled Kilimanjaro, Aconcagua, McKinley and Elbrus, the highest peaks in Africa, South America, North America and Europe respectively. He reached the North Pole with Prince Harry, and plans an expedition to the South Pole in 2020–21.

As teammates, we could never match the purity of that type of ambition, but we wanted to make our mark beyond the usual charitable gesture of donating signed match-worn kit. I'm nothing special but I used my natural advantage as captain to raise just over £20,000 by hosting a dinner for ten, a training session at Pennyhill Park, and a coaching clinic in a local school.

All told the boys made £200,000 for Rob and his family. Proceeds from a match against Leicester in his honour at Twickenham took the total beyond £300,000. He took some persuading to accept it, since he has a natural humility, but it helped to secure his future as he studied for a Master's degree in commerce.

To my admittedly jaundiced view, that says more about the spirit of rugby than any florid nonsense dreamed up by a committee man whose game is lubricated by gin and tonic rather than blood, sweat and tears. Players are attuned to the reality that rugby hurts. It's not smart to submit to the probability of punishment, but the positives, illustrated by the sort of solidarity shown to Rob, far outweigh the negatives.

The demands placed upon us are incessant, and increasing. It is a simple equation: the more matches you play, because of a union's TV strategy or a club's commercial imperatives, the more injuries you are going to sustain. It is only when confronted by retirement that you realize the cumulative damage is unreasonable, in all senses of the word.

One of my final acts, in preparing to call it a day, was to ask the club for my annual medical records, dating back to my first herniated disc, which kept me out for thirty-five days in the 2005–06 season, when I also picked up two knee injuries. The first page is a summary of so-called 'significant incidents' which led me to being out for more than four weeks at a time.

In all, including the unsuccessful 322-day battle to recover from my final knee injury, I missed 1,320 days, more than three and a half years out of a fifteen-year career. Take your pick of the causes.

A chest injury and a stress fracture of the third metatarsal in my left foot, sustained playing for Worcester, led to absences of thirty-one and thirty days respectively. I took 246 days to recover from three bouts of concussion. Lumbar problems kept me out for 184 days. A fractured right shoulder cost me fifty-four days. Ligament and cartilage issues in the left leg led to my being out for 118 days, and medial ligament damage in my right knee cost me another thirty days.

By the end I could have bluffed my way through a medical exam. I knew my arthroscopy from my chondroplasty, my pulmonary contusion from my ruptured extensor pollicis longus (that's a skeletal muscle on the forearm, *Casualty* fans). Even the bad times are good. Looking at the fine print for 2006, I only missed two days after what the notes refer to as 'systemic vomiting'. I didn't train on 28 September 2010, because I had a cold.

You've got to laugh, because you do cry.

One of the worst things to suffer is a popped rib. Scrummaging with it is horrific, bearing in mind you can't cough, fart or laugh without being in agony. Dressing rooms are like *M\*A\*S\*H* clearing houses after matches. People are being put back together with stitches and glue. Senior players have bits falling off them, but can accurately diagnose the severity of injury they have suffered.

'Going for an MRI, mate?'

'Yeah, think it's a Grade One. Three to four weeks.'

I don't think I could find you a player who consistently turns out in perfect nick. Guys cut the ends of their boots off, so they can play with broken toes. I've had huge gashes over my eye, which in any sane world would entail a visit to A&E. Stitched up in the changing shed, I've been sent back out without a whimper, with tape protecting the wound. There's always an optimist in the background saying 'Let's see how that goes.'

Thank heavens for a respected physio like Matt, who has the balls to tell a coach not to do his job for him, and the respect he needs to tell a player he is going to be protected from himself. We are our own worst enemies; I've had bulging disc problems for years and still tried to run through them when the drugs didn't work. They were anti-inflammatories, in case you are wondering, officer.

I am right-side dominant, with my throwing, tackling and scrummaging. I've fractured the shoulder blade, and sustained nerve damage. Every now and again I experience pins and needles. I've learned to pre-empt the pain by seeing the physio on a regular basis. It can be too easy to become used to soreness as an occupational hazard.

I creak, since I have to keep moving to minimize problems in my lower back and hip. I wince when Thea asks me to sing 'Head, shoulders, knees and toes' because it reminds me of the pain laced into those medical records. I walk downstairs sideways, most mornings. I'm constantly cricking my neck. I struggle to wipe my backside the morning after a match, because I'm so stiff.

For the benefit of readers with a hypersensitive imagination, I sort myself out by getting a leg up on the side of the bath. When there's a will, there's usually a way . . .

It is bizarre. Guys you see staggering into the club on a Monday, looking like extras from a zombie movie, are transformed into Tarzan tribute acts by the following Saturday, beating their chests and boasting about how they're ready to go again. It can be funny; a scab across the bridge of the nose is known as a 'Borthers' after Steve Borthwick, whose scratch would open up and ooze blood every time he played. It only healed when he took up coaching.

I had to glue a crease in my bald spot together after one match, but thankfully, front-row forwards with a taste for opposition earlobes went out of fashion in the eighties with

Bonnie Tyler and bubble perms. Players think short term; it can be too scary to wonder what's coming down the track, in ten or fifteen years' time.

Your world contracts when you are recovering from a significant injury. If you are prone to self-doubt, or intense insecurity, your mental health, already delicate, can easily decline, quickly and savagely. I think it is good to know why you hurt. I've been relatively fortunate. I'm probably paying the price for my determination to disguise injury earlier in my career. Knocks take longer to heal.

My fingers ache, continually. My left thumb doesn't work because it has no tendon in it, and I suffered ligament damage in a match against the Springboks. I've had six different types of injury related to my hands and wrists, and have learned to strap them, like a boxer. It's not that difficult, but it is something I would not even have thought about ten years ago.

The game is getting faster, more physical, increasingly athletic. It cannot regress because that defies physiological evolution, and chief executives start twitching, since they see profit margins contracting. Players are trapped between the intended consequences of better preparation, and the inevitable concentration on the bottom line.

A week off is a distant dream for international players whose clubs are fighting on all fronts. The lads who come into the Premiership from Super Rugby in Australia, New Zealand and South Africa can't get their heads around our workload. They are used to a sixteen-match domestic season; we reach that at Christmas, and ours is only halfway through.

I once caused a bit of a ripple at a promotional event for Premiership captains, by suggesting we should be given two

weeks off for the festive season. Players 'joke' among themselves about arranging their own holidays through a timely
dead leg, concussion or disciplinary, though I've never been
cute enough to manipulate my brushes with the law.

Playing in what tends to be a tasty local derby on Boxing
Day, usually on a frozen pitch, is no one's idea of fun, apart
from that of the club treasurer, who hears the sound of jin-
gling tills rather than jingle bells. A break, at a traditional
time of devotion to family and friends, would provide the
perfect pit stop.

Physios and doctors are dealing with more traumatic
injuries to necks and shoulders, caused by higher forces, than
ever. Injuries are broader in nature than in other sports, and
there has been an increase in degenerative conditions, such
as the left-knee injury that ended my career. At least we don't
have the so-called 'front up' injuries sustained in rugby
league, which are closer in character to those suffered in the
NFL.

Ben Franks, Saints' former All Black prop, told me
recently that he weighed 110 kilos when he broke into Super
Rugby with Crusaders in 2006. Those considered big men in
that era weighed around 120 kilos. Now, after more than a
decade of weightlifting, Ben comes in at a leaner, meaner 120
kilos. Modern monsters are around 140 kilos.

It is not just about size. Players are so much fitter. They
can carry greater weight at greater speed around the park.
Their body composition has changed, to become more muscular. Impacts are, logically, more punishing. Support teams
are bigger and more professional, but expecting a player to
perform for nineteen weeks in a row, which is the new normal, is unsustainable.

Modern players are becoming accustomed to looking after themselves more thoroughly, but the natural instinct is still to dig in, and keep up with what is required. The inevitable struggle to maintain a level of performance can lead to mental-health issues. Fatigue leads to a lack of awareness under pressure, and a larger susceptibility to injury. It only takes one misalignment, through tiredness, to put you in harm's way.

Until the Covid-19 pandemic brought an extended halt to all sport, there were to be only four months without competitive rugby – August 2020, 2021, 2022 and July 2023 – for elite players until the start of the next World Cup, in France, on 8 September 2023. Good luck getting enough natural Vitamin D from the odd fortnight on the beach to get you through that little lot. It will mean less time for conditioning, and greater vulnerability.

This is not like Premier League football, where two matches a week can be balanced by less rigorous, more technical, training sessions. This is not life according to Dan from Accounts, whose world shuts down if he has a sore knee. This is about having necessarily hard midweek practices, which add to existing pressure on limbs, muscles and joints.

We are expected to deal with some big units on a daily basis. Eventually, that takes its toll. The specialist dealing with my knee injury summed it up starkly: 'You've been trying to manage this for too long,' he told me. 'Everyone does it. You're trying to cope, and tell yourself "My knee's all right." You try to power through it all until you fall off the edge of the cliff.'

Hope can be a hateful word, a damaging sentiment in the wrong circumstances. Anyone who goes into one game too many, hoping for the best, isn't doing himself any favours.

The decision is going to have to be taken out of his hands. I would like to see contact training be pared down incrementally over several seasons, so that it virtually becomes non-existent.

A senior player doesn't need to learn how to tackle. He doesn't need to batter a bag, because it is inanimate and feels different to the body of a ball carrier, advancing with aggressive intent. He needs to pause, and get over the stingers that occur all too often in high-intensity matches. He needs to be taken out of the firing line if he shows signs of taking too many elbows or knees to the head.

Careers are going to be curtailed. The age profile of leading players will reduce. Someone like Paul Tupai, playing to a high standard in his forties, belongs in the Natural History Museum. I was thirty-three when I called it a day in November 2019; in the future most internationals will ease out of the game by their thirtieth birthday.

Professional rugby union is still in its infancy. My generation of players have been crash test dummies for a sport in transition from semi-professionalism. It is being reshaped, subtly but relentlessly, by money men, geo-politicians, talking heads and television executives. They treat us as warm bodies, human widgets. But here's the thing: powerbrokers are neutered if there is no one prepared to play the sort of game they envisage.

The NFL, with such widely accepted and corporately expensive welfare issues to address, provides an indication of best practice. They have more than a dozen health and safety committees, which report into a Competition Committee. That reviews injury data and video evidence of how serious injury occurs. A Player Safety Advisory Panel submits recommendations for protective rule changes.

Over the top, maybe, but it can be practical, and effective. To give a transferable example, a review of the kick-off, covering all games between 2015 and 2017, found players were four times more likely to suffer concussion during that sequence than in running or passing plays. The kick-off represented only 6 per cent of action, but led to 12 per cent of concussions. Rules were amended accordingly, to outlaw the so-called two-man wedge. In essence, this entailed two of their biggest players linking arms to clear a path for the kick-off returner. They are now penalized if they are within two yards of each other.

On average, there are thirty healthcare professionals in the stadium on game day. Contact is monitored and managed in high-maintenance periods such as pre-season training camps, with franchises expected to cooperate for the collective good. Practice is filmed by drones, analysed, and relayed on a position-specific basis to a central information centre that seeks to educate through the pooling of knowledge.

It might smack of Big Brother, but the unseen eye is focused on the right things.

Given a clean sheet of paper, I would centrally contract England players. It works well in cricket, and has been fundamental to the health of the international game in New Zealand and Ireland, whose provincial teams have been powerhouses in European competition. Wales is trying to follow a similar lead.

I'm not naïve. Give a player a choice, and he will want to be paid as much as possible, for as few matches as he can get away with. He's cynical because he believes the system is stacked against him. Equally, leading clubs would fight any plan to distribute central contracts with everything at their disposal. They have considerable political power, and television deals to protect.

Civil wars tend to be nasty, and an outbreak of hostilities would be uncomfortable. Pioneering players would have to put up with moral blackmail about their perceived selfishness, and supposed willingness to abandon the grassroots of the game. The trick will be to work out who is compensated, and how. Forget the posturing; everyone knows why change is required.

I place great store by the history and traditions of my club, Northampton. I am in Saints' debt, because of the sense of purpose and direction they gave me, but I am not a hypocrite. In essence, once made captain of my country, I was England property, 365 days a year. That didn't prevent me giving the club a contractual bang for its buck, or loosen my ties to a town I still cherish, as home. I realize that, in any brave new world, such institutions would have to be looked after.

I'm not saying it would be easy, and without natural friction. A six-month elite season, which is probably the optimal amount of world-class competition required to maintain standards and give players sufficient room to breathe, would probably damage the club product, because of the dilution of quality. Hard-nosed decisions about prioritization would be inevitable.

There are obvious differences between rugby and cricket, but I've seen it work in the case of Alastair Cook, England's greatest batsman. His loyalty to his county, Essex, never diminished during an extended international career. His appearances were limited, but he remained close to the dressing room, and sustained the spirit of the county club's links to the community.

I know, from personal experience, that not many of us are able to write our own script, but Cookie has managed to come out on the right side of the deal. He followed the perfect retirement from Test cricket, having scored that valedictory century at the Oval, by winning the County Championship with Essex in 2019.

Talking to him about it, I was struck by how he relished the dynamics of the Essex dressing room. He loved playing with a bunch of mates who worked hard, and played hard. Opposition bowlers were still of high quality, but he could enjoy the challenge, without being compromised by the intensity that defines international sport.

The example of Irish rugby is contrasting, but equally instructive. Take Leinster, for instance. They have a bread-and-butter squad for domestic PRO14 fixtures, augmented by half a dozen centrally contracted players in blocks of matches, around their European Cup commitments. That is a workable compromise, though there will always be those who complain at such starkly divided loyalty.

Internationals, introduced in those circumstances, would be fresh, mentally and physically. They would be gagging to play, and in peak condition. They would be the human equivalent of a showroom-clean sports car, rather than a borderline MOT case, with 150,000 miles on the clock. Something usually breaks when you are stuck in sixth gear, speeding down the outside lane.

Attitudes would have to change. We've reached the stage where no one bats an eyelid at reports that something like sixty players are injured over the course of a Six Nations Championship. There's a quiet desperation to take the positives: sure, we might be missing key performers, but this is our chance to discover the depth of our talent pool.

Scheduling would have to be examined. We began the 2018 Six Nations by playing in Italy, late on a Sunday afternoon. There was only a six-day turnaround to the next match, an attritional low-scoring contest against Wales at Twickenham. It takes three days to put your body back together after a Test match, so in essence you roll into the following game without due care and attention.

The RFU would have to recognize their wider responsibilities by offering a form of get-out clause from the central contract, permitting England players to appear in the European Cup, with a warm-up window in the Premiership. I would envisage a successful club having their elite players for between twelve and fifteen matches a year.

That would require compromise from the home union. No one has ever accused me of being guileless; I'm as keenly aware as the RFU treasurer that Twickenham is a gold mine. They'd get 70,000 to watch fifteen England shirts, drying on a washing line, so long as the bars were open. I'd envisage between ten and twelve internationals a year, five in the Six Nations, three or four in the autumn, and two or three Tests on tour.

Less would be more. That's a good amount of rugby. Training would be sacrosanct, a sporting equivalent of the green belt. The bedrock of the club game would be protected, and the alickadoos on the RFU Council would have to lift their eyes from the buffet table. Everyone, to be blunt, would have to raise their game.

Administrators have got to be smarter, and balance their ability to generate income, through their commercial expertise, with the reality that the players, the game's raw material, must be looked after. Clubs must have greater pragmatism, and understand where they are in the pecking order. Their traditions deserve to be respected, but not at all costs.

A more assertive players' union has to be developed, to fight on their members' behalf. Our representatives should not shy away from using their financial muscle, to threaten strikes if required. That has worked in the NFL, NBA and Major League Baseball in the States, though not without media bleating about the spirit of the game being sacrificed.

Everything has to start at the top. Ian Ritchie, the former RFU chairman, is now straddling the fence in a similar role with the Premiership. I worked relatively closely with him when he was at Twickenham, and found him a great guy. He was a constant presence at games and training camps. I've no experience of him in a boardroom setting, but when he came into my world he had an air of approachability.

I have never forgotten a gesture, made before I became England captain. I was injured, and watching training from the sidelines, when he asked whether I was still going to the match at the weekend. 'Probably not,' I replied. When he asked why, I told him I wouldn't be able to get a ticket. He was dumbfounded. 'That's outrageous,' he said. 'Leave it with me.'

He was true to his word. The tickets arrived without the normal rigmarole of having to behave like a latter-day Oliver Twist, or badgering teammates to put you on their allocation. It cost Ian nothing, but typified his commitment to the players, since he never blinked at Eddie's budget demands. He was in danger of giving alickadoos a good name.

Incidentally, the dictionary definition of that term, which is unique to our sport as far as I know, is 'the hangers-on around a rugby club, usually ex-players who've an inflated opinion of their own sporting prowess.' Pretty harsh, and, in my experience, extremely fair, but do you know what? They tend to have the last laugh.

They'll still have their noses in the trough, when we are waiting for our knee replacement operations.

# 16

# The Long Goodbye

It was just another day in purgatory. An hour devoted to the manipulation of my right shoulder, right hip and both ankles was followed by a session of low-impact, ground-based conditioning, designed to increase my mobility. Shuffling along on my backside, in a movement known as shrimping, was not exactly dignified, but I got a sweat on.

The mind wanders when the body is being put back together. It's too easy to lose yourself in a labyrinth of ifs, buts and maybes. The uncertainties of long-term injury are an invitation to self-pity. On that particular day in Northampton, a hazily remembered figure with only a physio and conditioning coach for company, I was uncomfortably aware I was missing another England training camp.

I knew what would be happening, when and why. I knew others would be wearing my shirt, taking my responsibilities. I knew worrying about my knee injury was ultimately pointless, but it nagged away at the base of my brain. One thing I was in danger of forgetting, until Lucy and her son Jenson came into my life on that Friday afternoon, was how lucky I am.

Lucy was rapidly going blind because of a degenerative retinal condition. She described her field of vision, at the time, as looking out at the world through a five-pence piece. She had accepted her fate with greater courage than I could ever possess, and wanted to create a series of memories that would sustain her when she lost her sight.

The thought of those images was powerful. Jenson, her six-year-old, loved rugby and wanted to meet me. He was a little lad, who gave me a big hug. I was hobbling around on one leg, but spent half an hour with him, kicking a ball around on the pitch at Franklin's Gardens, and letting him tackle me. As we played together, I got a glimpse of his mum's face, and could see how much it meant to her.

It was emotionally overwhelming. I sat and chatted with them as a dad, rather than a supposed hot-shot sportsman. I was aware of the sensitivities, but felt I could be unashamedly honest, in telling Lucy how much I admired them both for putting a brave face on it. I spoke about my own family, since we had daughters of a similar age, and was reminded of the privilege of parenthood, which is sometimes taken for granted.

Sure, I was busy. I had a constant backlog of messages to catch up on. My career was in abeyance, and my future was uncertain. I had my own doubts and fears to contend with. But problems? When you meet people like Lucy, because you happen to make a living doing something that engages millions, you realize you have no problems at all. I invited them to meet the team as my guests at the following day's game, when Harry Banks was due to lead the Saints out, as mascot.

Harry is eleven, and suffers from relapsed neuroblastoma, an aggressive and rare children's cancer diagnosed in 2014. Two years of intensive chemotherapy, radiotherapy and immunotherapy, on top of major surgery, were rewarded when he went into remission. In November 2018, the disease returned to his central nervous system, forcing an emergency operation to remove a tumour from his brain.

Neuroblastoma has one of the lowest survival rates of all childhood cancers, and a remission is rare, but he remained bright and bubbly as his parents staged a fundraising campaign to underwrite a groundbreaking clinical trial in Barcelona. It was a community effort, involving everything from sponsored schoolboy fun-runs to set-piece promotional events. I chipped in where I could, as did Alastair Cook.

You hear of so many similar cases, and naturally feel sympathetic, but it is not until they are close to home that you are catapulted out of the bubble of professional sport. It brings everything down to basics, the importance of health and the gift of children. It's pretty humbling to discover your presence means something in those circumstances.

As players we are almost conditioned to expect people to come to matches, to cheer and get behind the team. When the shoe is on the other foot and you are expressing your support for young lads like Harry and Jenson, it feels good to feel valued. I went home, after that match, grateful that my family were well, and my life was relatively straightforward in comparison.

I'd gone through a pretty rough spell with concussion, and was just over a month into my rehab programme for the knee injury that would end my career. The cards were yet to fall. With less than nine months remaining until the World Cup, I couldn't countenance failing to make it back for at least a couple of the nine internationals leading into the tournament.

My immediate consolation was greater perspective, a bigger picture into which I could insert rugby, Eddie Jones and England. In my more reflective moments I could see my time in the game drawing to a close. I kept my thoughts to myself, but honed in on what I wanted to achieve. Being successful with England remained a driving force, but I also began to focus on how I could contribute to the club's evolution.

Though my circumstances were far from perfect, injury couldn't take away my experience in a specialist position. I began working with a good crop of young hookers on what was becoming one of my specialist subjects, lineout throwing. I'm no one's idea of a geek, but I got special pleasure from one particular statistic, a 93 per cent accuracy rate in the four-year cycle from the 2015 World Cup. That was the best of the fifteen hookers from Tier One nations who threw more than 150 times in that period.

Ultimately, I had little option but to trust fate and professional expertise. I took out a little insurance by playing a cute political game. Eddie believes rugby is a 'feel' game, 60 per cent art and 40 per cent science, but he placed great store by his principal sports scientist, Warrick Harrington. Shrewdly, I thought, I arranged for him to visit me twice a week, to oversee core strengthening work.

Phil Pask – a physio and another trusted lieutenant – conducted a weekly MOT test, and kept an eye out for signs of rust. Graeme Close, England's main nutritionist, checked in once a week, to make sure I wasn't in fat-boy mode. Putting on weight is my USP: I joked to one of the other hookers that I could end his continual struggle to weigh more than 100 kilos in a single weekend. Come on the pints with me, get some takeaway down your neck, and we'll get heavy.

My legs were a little chunkier, because I wasn't running, but my skinfolds were pretty good, if I say so myself. Obviously that was a physical manifestation of my commitment, but it also sent a subtle psychological message to Eddie, that

I was not prepared to compromise my standards. I wasn't daft: I knew every last scrap of information was being fed back to him.

In common with many recovering athletes, I found it hard to escape the feeling of being an outsider. I missed competing desperately, and realized just how much satisfaction I gained from the leadership role I had, with both club and country. My schedule was dictated by the fluctuations of rehabilitation, so I wasn't aligned to either team.

At Saints I made a point of attending the Monday morning connection meeting, which set the new week up. There was no point in me being in more immediate tactical and technical discussions, which inevitably centred on a match I had no chance of playing in. I was unaware I had already made the last of my 251 appearances for Northampton; we were working on an unspoken agreement that I would get back on script about a fortnight before my comeback match.

I knew I would be able to help England in the event of returning to fitness, and Eddie spoke publicly about me being available midway through the 2019 Six Nations. I got the impression he valued my transparency; I called him in the build-up to the championship and told him not to waste a squad place by taking me to a training camp in Portugal. It was far better to take the opportunity to look at another candidate on the fringes; I would go stir crazy if I was there without being able to contribute.

I like to think we both knew what I offered. One of the benefits of seniority and longevity as a player is greater confidence in a team environment. I was an old head, a good professional. I could still be a positive influence within the group, as someone who offered balance and perspective. Sport reflects society as a whole: the concentration on the individual, and instant gratification, is a threat to the common good.

I was secure in my maturity, conscious of the inevitable insecurity of emerging players. I didn't want to waste anyone's time, but when I spent a couple of days back at Pennyhill Park after the opening 2019 win over Ireland, I sat down with a couple of the new guys, if only to act as a sounding board. I talked about priorities, training and playing well, but being relaxed when appropriate.

Chris Boyd, my coach at the Saints, told me he had noticed my tendency to nurture. It was something I did naturally, without a lot of conscious thought. In hindsight, it was why the two-Test tour of Argentina in 2017, with a squad shorn of thirty senior players and British Lions, was one of the most satisfying of my rugby life.

It's a beautiful country, but things can turn ugly because it is a difficult place to play. Their forwards have the mentality of Mexican boxers in their own backyard: come and have a go if you think you're hard enough. We were up for a hugely physical challenge, which helped define a new generation of England players who, in rugby terms, were barely out of playschool.

Eighteen of the touring party were uncapped. Two of the bolters, Tom Curry and Sam Underhill, would go on to excel as Eddie's 'Kamikaze Kids' in the 2019 World Cup, where Henry Slade, who only had five caps at the time, would also make his mark. There was a sense of renewal; the kids contributed through the purity of their ambition, and the visibility of their hunger.

A successful rugby team ideally needs three influencers, rounded individuals who can accept responsibility for small groups of up to five less experienced players. It is the sort of job that doesn't need to be advertised by an armband; senior guys, whose bread-and-butter skills have been sharpened at international level, lead by example.

That group had high-quality ballast, since it included battle-hardened individuals of the stature of Chris Robshaw, Danny Care, Mike Brown, George Ford, Joe Launchbury and Jonny May. Their positivity of spirit helped no end. They knew when to rip the piss out of the situation, by making fun of the difficulties, and they knew when to work.

I saw young players with their shoulders back and their eyes wide open. They wanted to learn, and helped us to generate a real sense of momentum. Once a last-minute try by the Sale winger Denny Solomona, one of ten debutants, helped us to win the first Test, 38–34, we were on a roll. It was a breathless game, in which the lead changed hands six times. They are the best type of victories.

Underhill made his debut in the second Test, in the so-called Elephant's Graveyard, Estadio Brigadier General Estanislao López in Santa Fe. It's a football setting, with high fences, topped with razor wire. A moat separates excitable locals from visiting teams, who are often so intimidated they decide discretion is the better part of valour, and lose diplomatically.

Not this England group. We reclaimed the lead five times in another topsy-turvy match. Appropriately enough, given his inspirational performances in both Tests, George Ford sealed a 35–25 win with a forty-metre drop goal, set up by Danny Care after good work by Alex Lozowski. He might, just might, stop talking about it sometime in the next decade.

I played every minute on tour and Eddie was pumped. He didn't need the back of a fag packet to calculate that he suddenly had sixty-one viable candidates for his forty-man elite squad. He was in his element, and had given Denny just enough time to enjoy his match-winning try in the first Test before reading him his fortune.

A rugby league convert, Denny had made two horrendous defensive errors before his scene-stealing twinkle. Jones decided to introduce what he jokingly refers to as 'a bit of old-time Eddie'. He's the fierce-eyed taskmaster who picks his moment 'to ruck them up a bit'. As he told the press boys: 'If you see someone tackling bags in the street next week, it'll be him.'

Coaches are not clones, chiselled out of the same mould. The best have an ability to communicate cleverly and effectively in a way that reflects their character. Chris Boyd is one of those favourite teachers you remember as a kid; he's very smart in his rugby, and connects easily with people by showing that he cares. It doesn't matter if that's a superficial, highly calculated impression; a player instinctively returns the love.

Eddie reckons he has mellowed from his days as a bristling, whisky-drinking madman, who went in hard on his players. He eats really well, loves his greens, juices and herbal teas, and drinks a lighter wine in a Pinot, always backed up by glasses of water. He's an attack dog, kept on a long leash. He evaluates people constantly, without excessive emotion. Like Boydy, he's an expert at keeping tension on the line.

That tension must be appropriate. Every angler knows that if the line is too tight, the hook is liable to be ripped out of the fish's mouth. If it is too loose, the fish shakes it off, and swims away. As captain, I had to monitor that tension. If rules were applied blindly, without compassion or context, the group would switch off. If the atmosphere was too lax, with people going on the lash or training sloppily, the group needed reining in.

There's a lot of talk these days about developing a 'leaderful' team, in which a spine of senior players set and impose personal and professional standards. The concept was adapted by Clive Woodward from Ric Charlesworth, a brilliantly innovative Australian coach who has had unprecedented success in Olympic hockey and international cricket, in addition to graduating in medicine and operating as a Federal MP for ten years. It has the benefit of simplicity, and spreads the load.

The media likes to place the captain on a pedestal. He is an obvious presence on match day; he leads the team out, does the coin toss, liaises with the referee, and takes the press conference before pulling on a blazer and going through the formalities of the post-match speech. The unseen work is no less valuable, but it is rarely done alone.

I had been captain in twenty-six of Eddie's first thirty-one Tests in charge. He considered it the most onerous individual role in the global game, because of the magnitude of media commitments, and spoke to Owen Farrell and me for a couple of weeks about sharing leadership duties. He had done something similar, in sanctioning John Eales and George Gregan as co-captains, when he coached Australia.

Some of the press pack couldn't wait to add another line to my professional obituary when Eddie formalized England's co-captaincy arrangements before the autumn internationals in 2018, but I followed his logic. We were long-term roommates, and I had spent time with Owen earlier that summer, familiarizing him with the practicalities of captaining England, prior to the tour of South Africa.

Owen disproves the fashionable theory that the best player doesn't make the best captain. He's the star who inspires by example. He conducts himself impeccably, is diligent with personal preparation, and has the stones to do his day job, as an unerringly accurate place kicker under the most intense pressure. He's the sort who takes a step forward when others are taking a step backwards.

He is quiet and thoughtful, but comes alive in a rugby environment, whether that is leading a team meeting off the pitch or acting as a subsidiary coach on it. He commands attention and respect when he stands in front of the room because of what he has done, and who he is. A fly half is a quarterback by nature, so it is vital he sees all aspects of the game quickly and intelligently.

A number 10 tends to be instinctively attack-minded and is typically assertive as captain. If you play at 7, and especially 12, you are much more likely to be a defensive captain, whose strength comes in meticulous analysis of the threats the opposition presents. There's no one way to lead; different folks, different strokes.

No one really knows what Eddie is truly thinking, but we came to the conclusion that all he was doing was acknowledging reality. If outsiders grasped the dirty end of the stick, fine. We had been increasingly collaborative over the previous year or so, when our relationship grew organically. Whenever I had a problem or an idea, Owen was the first person I ran it by. Equally he would come to me if he was unhappy with something, or had spotted areas of potential improvement.

If you've come this far in the book you'll appreciate I have my faults, but an inflated ego isn't one of them. I did well, commercially, out of being England captain but I've never been a poster boy. I was in a specialist position, with a closed skill, throwing, so was not the type to be showered in stardust, or given a seven-figure contract.

I never wanted to be the highest-paid player; I merely wanted to be recognized for my service. I've liked to be seen as someone who loves coming in every day, and is a good influence on down days, where rugby life gets in the way, and morale can take a hit. I hate it when someone who is paid shedloads of money doesn't really give a shit.

That's where Owen sets himself apart. He's probably paid handsomely, in rugby terms. He can buy the flash car, the latest computer games, and the high-end headphones. He loves trainers, so it helps that he is sponsored by Nike. But he's not chasing money. That doesn't motivate him. He jumps in the car once a week to see Jonny Wilkinson, to work at his craft. They share an internal drive to be the best.

Athletes are becoming a bit like politicians; there are not that many genuine ones around any more. Just as MPs are conditioned to look after number one, instead of concentrating on being a force for the common good, there aren't many kids coming into our game who want to leave their mark, beyond the superficialities of smartarse posts on Instagram and photographs of their bling.

Blimey, when did I turn into my dad?

I suppose what I am saying, at the risk of coming across as a clubhouse bore, is that it is OK to care. In fact, it is essential, providing you are mature enough to keep your frustrations in check. I felt irritated and undermined by the gradual decrease in my playing time as starter, which seemed to go down in two-minute increments from sixty minutes, but I never challenged it because I didn't want to rock the boat.

I still did most of the formalities of captaincy; Eddie liked me to be the one who met the referee beforehand, since I would be in closer proximity to him for much of the match. Believe it or not, I was a more soothing character, when it came to dealing with the officials. Owen's relative inexperience in that area had been exposed in South Africa, where he badgered referees instead of subtly getting them onside.

That assertiveness works both ways of course. Owen was already a vocal presence when I was taken off, so he was able to assume authority seamlessly. I lasted fifty-seven minutes before being substituted in the opening match of that autumn campaign, against the Springboks, and Owen became the game's central character.

The boys absolutely loved two challenges he made, late in the game. We were under siege when he dispossessed Lood de Jager close to our line, and the countdown clock had reached zero when André Esterhuizen tucked the ball under his right arm and set off on a run from near halfway. Owen was in harm's way, and determined to protect a one-point lead by any means possible.

Owen charged into the South African centre, who fell backwards, with his legs splayed, and lost the ball, which was kicked dead. Esterhuizen looked as if he had run into a wall. Come to think of it, he had: it was a drystone wall, made in Wigan. I instinctively saw it as a brutal but fair collision. It was only when the referee confirmed it wasn't a shoulder charge, through the TMO, that we could celebrate.

Eddie loved what he called 'the arm wrestle' and immediately set his sights on the following week's match against the

All Blacks. I shared his sense of anticipation, not because of the well-worn backstory of my heritage, but because you don't get many chances to test yourself against the best. It's a special challenge and at half-time, with us leading 15–10, I felt pretty content with my contribution.

I'd scored a try from a powerful rolling maul, supplemented by Owen, Jonny May and Henry Slade. I'd had a high level of involvement and showed durability in a game played in driving rain. There's always a lot of hustle and bustle in the changing room at the interval, but you learn to find your own head space. I was immersed in thought and totally unprepared when Eddie came across to me.

'Mate, we're going to bring you off. We're going to make a change.'

'OK. Fine.'

I was determined not to allow shock, and a degree of anger, to influence my body language. I played the political game, knowing people would be looking to gauge my reaction. I put my shoulders back, got my head up, and slowly walked to my peg, where I towelled myself down and changed into a fresh set of kit.

I'm a big boy, but felt a bit demeaned. I knew the media loved the narrative of me being hunted down by Jamie George. I had nothing against him, and understood the principle that he is a high-energy player, an ideal replacement when I had poured everything in. I'd like to take this opportunity to dispel any lingering rumours that I couldn't do the full eighty, if required.

No prisoners are taken in professional sport, so the texts from mates, hailing me as 'the forty minute man' were taken in the spirit intended. I zoned out from external critics, who didn't see the selfless stuff I did for the team while Jamie was winding down during the week, having a coffee with the rest of the players. But, deep down, being replaced in that manner hurt because I knew how it would be interpreted.

We lost, 15–16, after what would have been a match-winning Sam Underhill try in the final minute was disallowed when TV replays suggested Courtney Lawes was fractionally offside when he charged down T. J. Perenara's kick in the build-up. Owen did most of the media duties, and talked a good game as far as the forthcoming World Cup was concerned. We were back on an upward curve.

I was playing well. I knew I wouldn't be there unless there was a use for me. Coaches don't waste time in international rugby. They don't risk a result on players they don't trust. Respect is a bit nebulous – it tends to be transmitted through quiet gestures rather than moist-eyed admissions of admiration – but I felt wanted and needed in the England environment. I knew my value.

Jamie started the next match, against Japan. I consoled myself that it was against second-tier opposition, and got on with it. Eddie made eleven changes for a game that had obvious personal relevance. He spoke about 'emotionally smashing' his former team, who gave an indication of the threat they would pose as World Cup hosts by leading at half-time through some inventive, attacking rugby.

I spoke to the group during the interval, as did George Ford, to try to trigger a momentum shift, and it was not until midway through the second half that we established a measure of control. Owen was a pivotal figure off the bench, and I trundled on for the last seven minutes. That's a blink of an eye in rugby terms, and a measure of the strength of Jamie's performance, but it was long enough for me to score another try off a driving maul in a 35–15 win.

Competition for places is the essence of sport. At international level selection is a business decision. Yet it felt dauntingly personal when Eddie approached me in the build-up to the final match of the year, against Australia, and said, with trademark directness, 'You're gonna come off the bench this week.' It gave me the chills, because I recognized the significance of the decision. This was the first Test, against top-tier opposition, from which I had been excluded under him.

I was determined not to flail around, asking for answers and retreating behind a sense of grievance. I didn't want to show any chinks in the armour. I parked it, concentrated on my wider role as co-captain, and trained with the usual intensity. Let's face it, I would have been a massive hypocrite if I prepared with less rigour, because I had been asking the group to be selfless for several years.

Beneath the surface I was churning. You convince yourself you are conditioned to concentrate on the immediate challenge in Test footie, but it is difficult to prevent the mind racing. Had Eddie reached a tipping point, and come down in favour of the other fella? It certainly felt that way. All I could do was seize whatever opportunity he offered.

International rugby is a 23-man game, but there are moments, as a replacement, when you feel a bit of a gooseberry. I was desperate to get on and began clock-watching in earnest after the break, reached at 13–13. Mentally, I had prepared myself to come on somewhere between the fiftieth and sixtieth minutes, but that private deadline came and went.

I didn't quite turn around and look imploringly up at the coaches' box, to the right of the tunnel at Twickenham, but I did my best to mime my enthusiasm. I started moving, swung my arms around with implied purpose, and generally looked busy. Jamie, to his credit, was playing well and showing few signs of fatigue.

I was given the final eight minutes, with the game already won. It was Australia's eleventh defeat in fifteen matches; they had no answer to our set-piece strength. I went through the celebratory rituals, lifting the Cook Cup with Owen in front of the royal box, but it felt hollow. There's a revealing image of me in the aftermath, sitting on a box in front of a sponsor's hoarding.

I'm not looking at the photographers. I'm smiling, but my eyes are downcast. I've taken off my winner's medal, and draped its green ribbon around the lid of the cut-glass trophy. A penny for my thoughts? Here you go, then: 'What's next? Shit happens. I'm going to start the Six Nations on the back foot. I'll be on the bench. I'm going to have to fight for the shirt.'

If only.

I had won my final cap. I would go down to see the lads in the changing room during the Six Nations the following spring and be inspired by a sense of loss and a gnawing hunger, to push myself through the frustrations of rehabbing the knee injury I sustained just before Christmas. But then, on another cold, lonely morning, hope would ebb away.

I'd look at my two companions in the club gym, Mike Haywood and Harry Mallinder. My empathy was tinged with a strange envy. They were also enduring the insecurity and discomfort of long-term injury, but were six and ten years younger than me, respectively. Their aches and pains were not as wearing, and they had a better chance to play.

They didn't have a specialist telling them to think about being able to walk properly or play with their kids, once rugby is over. They weren't being told about the consequences of losing muscle mass in retirement, and warned to avoid putting on weight to reduce the stress on their knees. They didn't need to accept the reality of those two words that every professional athlete uses, but secretly dreads.

I'm done.

# 17

## Outside, Looking In

I would invariably wake just after 2am. I'd lie there for hours, listening to the silence and letting my imagination illuminate the darkness. Sleep was impossible, since I was coming to terms with my mortality as an athlete. We all know the quiet death of retirement is inevitable in high-performance sport, but acceptance takes time.

My energies had been sapped. I had been worn down. I didn't have a timeframe to work to, because no one, least of all me, knew with any certainty if, or when, I would be able to play again. I couldn't see an end to the drip, drip, drip of deception; my continual insistence that I'd be 'back in six weeks', to anyone who asked, became increasingly incredible.

I talked through my options and emotions with Jo, my wife. We had spoken often of my original intention to play until I was thirty-five. It was a milestone on the map of our family life. After too many restless nights, I finally recognized that falling a season short, and bowing out on my own terms, would give me peace.

I owed it to Chris Boyd, my gaffer at Northampton, to be direct and transparent. I told him my knee was probably as good as it was going to get. That wasn't good enough to carry me through three hard training sessions a week, topped off by a high-intensity match. I had reached a plateau that seemed to stretch interminably in front of me.

Contractually, the club could have called time had I not made it back before Christmas 2019. Saints were brilliantly supportive, and there was never any hint they would take advantage of such legal leeway. There was no pressure on me to make a decision, but I recognized my responsibility to them, and the futility of further hesitation.

I was starting to feel fraudulent. I wasn't being fair to my teammates. There was no chance of me being pushed, but I jumped. I felt liberated the moment I told Boydy that I was done. No regrets, no recriminations. Looking back on my playing career, I hadn't done that badly for a fat lad with zero athletic ability and a bombproof mindset.

After weeks of feeling miserable, because I felt guilty listening to the little birdie on my shoulder, whispering 'be selfish', I could release positive mental energy, and plan for the future. I've never wanted rugby to define me, but it is all I have known, as a working life. I didn't want to rush into full-time coaching, but mentoring attracted me.

I had stepped away but, because of my technical role helping the Saints' hookers, I had left the door ajar. I was still in my habitat, and around like-minded people. I continued to lift weights in the gym with the lads. I retained the instinct to demonstrate my value, which had sustained me as a player. In short, I had the privileges without the pressure.

I remained in the players' WhatsApp group, Banter Central, but withdrew from the technical groups. With their training plans, analytical clips and performance profiles, they seemed a little too close to home, as reminders of what had been. By removing myself, I achieved a significant degree of separation and respected the unwritten rules of relevance.

It took three weeks or so to sort the formalities, so there was still an element of Secret Squirrel in my everyday activities. It was mildly annoying not being able immediately to confirm my retirement, and I had better take this opportunity to apologize to the lads at BT Sport for fibbing my way through a live studio interview before the details of my departure were confirmed.

When I came back from my eighth ban, I often talked of being on my ninth life. Eddie warned me that 'You're not a fucking cat, mate', but I quite liked the image, to be honest. Now the curiosity of others wasn't going to be fatal or even mildly inconvenient; because my mind was made up, I could afford to be almost flippant.

My answer to the same old question, trotted out by friends and strangers alike – 'How's the knee?' – became revealingly more light-hearted as the countdown to truth and reconciliation accelerated. I took to replying 'Watch this space' with a quizzically arched eyebrow, instead of regurgitating ritual optimism. Nudge, nudge, squire. Know what I mean?

They would do soon enough. A burden was lifted around midday on 7 November 2019, when I stood up and, in the words of my Instagram post, announced that 'It's time for me to take off the playing boots and limp off into the real world.' All that was left was the weird sensation of seeing the world react, through the lens of social media.

That post got 858 replies, many from teammates and former opponents. A lot of people said a lot of nice things. Some of my fiercest critics, who made a handbrake turn at the sight of my funeral cortège, might even have meant them. I wanted to share the mood of sweetness and light. I even thanked those who called out my 'horrific' facial hair and summed up my career in a single word: 'thug'.

The mind, predictably, had one final, fiendish trick to play. My knee suddenly began to feel a whole lot better, once I had given up on it. As weak as it sounds, I was tempted to scratch the itch. I got as far as wondering about the practicalities of testing it in a couple of training matches before I saw sense. If there's one thing I've learned about professional rugby, it is that you can't toy with it.

I'm comfortable with the truth. All my blemishes are there, for people to see. I have made that journey, from shiny new thing to old nag, without making too many comprom-ises. I've seen people try to be something that they are not, and the charade seems pretty constricting. Change is con-stant; players get injured, have families, move clubs and ultimately retire. My cycle was complete.

Of course, I would have loved to have made the World Cup in Japan. It was there for me, if I had been able to play a hand-ful of matches in the build-up. The squad contained seventeen survivors of Eddie's first playing group. It was natural to think 'What if?' when I watched a team I had helped to develop run out on the biggest stage, but if sport teaches you anything, it concerns the pointlessness of bitterness.

In a perverse way, those sixty weeks of suspension, over sixteen years, were not wasted. They weren't particularly pleasant to deal with, but they taught me to swallow my pride, accept the setback, and deal with difficult circum-stances. Anyone who can't accept fate, and attempts to avoid the inevitability of moving on, is flirting with a very sad life.

I found it amazing that so many people asked me whether I still wanted England to win. Why wouldn't I? The tourna-ment might not have had a fairytale finish, but I enjoyed their performances, right from the start. I had fun having breakfast with the family at home, bouncing around the living room during what I called the 'will win' group games against Tonga and the United States.

I started mentally reprioritizing my life. I had bills to pay, and an eye on the future, so I began to focus on life outside rugby. That involved dipping my toe in commercial waters, by hosting bigger matches for sponsors. I couldn't be completely candid about my intentions, since they were yet to be confirmed publicly, but I fed off the interest and enthusiasm of the audience. Understandably, they wanted the inside line, but I was in control of the narrative.

I'd always been wary, as a player, about cashing in on my experience. I lost count of the number of TV, print media and promotional opportunities I turned down when I was injured, even when they involved shooting the breeze for half an hour at Franklin's Gardens, at a match that I was already going to attend.

I knew Eddie's all-seeing eye would be on me, even when I was enduring the drudgery of rehab, and I'd become accustomed to his ways. He equated work on the punditry circuit, or the studio sofa, with a marginal reduction in commitment, and had acquired Sir Alex Ferguson's knack of asking seemingly throwaway questions to which he already knew the answers.

I never forgot one particular enquiry about James Haskell, whose plan to join Northampton in the summer of 2018 for a season dedicated to securing a World Cup place was undermined by persistent injury. Eddie loved his physicality, enjoyed his sense of fun, and awarded him fifteen of his seventy-seven England caps, but was always aware of the distractions of a player's brand development.

'How's the big Hask?' he asked me.

'He's good,' I replied. 'He's trying to get fit.'

'Nah, he's retired, mate.'

'No. He's working hard, he wants to play.'

'No, mate, he's fucking retired.'

'What do you mean?'

'Well, any player that plays on a Saturday and then does TV on a Sunday is retired, because he's not recovering properly. He's thinking about other things.'

At the time Hask was still optimistic he could beat the odds. He spoke positively to me about his latest conversation with Eddie. It wasn't my place to shatter any illusion. He's my mate, and I couldn't bear to crush his spirit with the truth; I had a delicate balance to strike. Influence can never be taken lightly; trust must be honoured.

I knew that as soon as I broke Eddie's confidence our relationship would founder, and I owed him for throwing me a lifeline. He had implicit faith in me. I had to leave all manner of problems in his office, go back to my room, and keep private issues to myself. Even when Owen Farrell asked me what was going on, before we shared the captaincy, I had to tell him: 'Don't ask me and I won't have to lie to you.'

That didn't mean all information was classified. I had the authority to lead through hints and, occasionally, as in the case of the young flanker Lewis Ludlam, something a little more urgent, with the proviso that they carried little chance of causing harm or offence. Eddie was still Santa, delivering presents, but I was his most valued little helper.

Lewis was fretting about his future in the summer of 2018, when it seemed a move to Europe was his best option. Boydy, with characteristic honesty, told him he couldn't visualize his progression at Northampton. He had struggled with ill-timed injury since starring in the Junior World Cup in 2015, and was restricted by the club's depth of talent in his position. No one doubted his resilience, since he had survived initial rejection by Saints' academy, but he needed a break.

It arrived, with typical irony, with Hask's fitness problems. Though it never seemed as if he was on the international radar, Lewis's no-nonsense style and consistency in taking an unexpected opportunity quietly impressed Eddie. He was drafted into the training squad for England's end-of-season try-fest against the Barbarians in June 2019, when Teimana Harrison, our clubmate, was called away to the birth of his son Wolfe.

I was close to Teimana, since I had recruited him from Rotorua Boys High School. Eddie must have thought I was his agent, since he continually asked me about his development. 'How's Mince?' he would say, knowing I would respond positively: 'He's a bloody good player, mate.' He had given him five England caps in 2016, before appearing to rule him out, but in his case never doesn't always mean never.

Teimana kept his hopes alive by returning, starting and starring in a 51–43 win. Lewis didn't even get his boots on; he was in a tracksuit, running water on a warm day. He must have been some delivery boy because I quickly picked up a rumour that his attitude was so spot on he had a very good chance of being invited to the pre-World Cup training camp.

The only problem was that he was on a three-week holiday at some potato-head beach club in Bali. I couldn't blame him for giving it a lash, since he had enjoyed a breakthrough year, and felt the realistic limit of his ambition was to start against the Baa-Baas in the 2020 version of the showcase fixture. Thank heaven for Instagram.

I messaged him, trying a little too hard to be casual: 'Looks awesome bro. I've been there. Enjoy.'

He replied: 'Yeah, it's sick. Having an amazing time.'

Here was my chance: 'Now I've got you, Luds, I've heard you might be in the World Cup camp. Just make sure you're doing some running and staying relatively fit.' Instead of pressing send, I deleted the message.

He was a kid I cared about, and I knew how demanding an environment he was being lined up to enter. But what if my information was duff? What right did I have to ruin his R&R? I decided Captain Sensible needed to take the day off: 'Have a good time, mate,' I replied. 'See you when you're back.'

The very next message I sent, when he returned to find my sources were spot on, had a smiley face emoji: 'Time for panic fitness . . .'

I was on the outside, looking in, but felt quite paternal towards the younger boys. Sport is routinely sensationalized, and distorted by the star system, but in the main you are dealing with good kids, going through the same process of hope and fulfilment that shaped you as a player. Lewis turned out to be a classic bolter; he excelled in two warm-up matches against Wales, and before he knew it he was on the plane to Japan.

There was a lovely element of innocence in his story, of a lad with Egyptian, Palestinian and Guyanese heritage. On the day I was getting my brief 'Thanks, but no thanks' call from Eddie, he discovered his selection when he was suddenly added to England's WhatsApp group. That's how the wheel turns in our business.

Squad development is not an exact science, no matter how many seminars are conducted in an attempt to prove otherwise. I represent the ever-present danger of long-term injury. Chris Robshaw, a brilliant bloke, was told hard track that he was not quite quick or mobile enough to survive in an over-stocked position. Danny Care, a hugely talented, richly experienced scrum half, found his face didn't fit, for whatever reason.

No team in the World Cup was flying from the get-go. Everyone was finding their feet. England, a bit rusty, stuttered early on, where the performance carried greater weight than the near-certainty of the result. It is very rare that a champion is announced with the 100-point fanfare of the perfect game; if we needed any reminder, South Africa began by losing to the All Blacks in Pool B.

Mistakes are inevitable, easily contextualized and countered. Tom Curry, for instance, dropped a couple of balls in the first couple of games. That was an indication of understandable distraction rather than a fundamental problem. From England's point of view, it was simple to rectify. Other indicators, such as decision making under pressure, were good.

It probably helped that England were spared the physicality and emotional toll of the group game against France, one of three cancelled because of Typhoon Hagibis. It ensured they were rested before the quarter-final against Australia, and sustained the feelgood factor of the formative 39–10 win over Argentina in Chōfu.

You know what you are going to get from the Pumas. I realize I'm not one to climb on the soapbox about this, but occasionally it comes in the form of rank indiscipline. The game didn't exactly hinge on the seventeenth-minute sending off of the second row Tomás Lavanini, for shoulder-charging Owen Farrell's jaw, but it hardly helped Argentina's cause.

Eddie took full advantage of the scope to rest Billy Vunipola's dodgy ankle, replacing him with Lewis Ludlam at half-time. Eddie, too, was growing into the tournament, where a coach is expected to be a bizarre combination of priest, politician and stand-up comedian. He uses humour cleverly and, occasionally, provocatively.

The media is a monster that demands to be fed in a World Cup. Any drama, real or imagined, is sliced and diced. There's a lot of second-guessing, because there are a lot of websites, newspapers and chat shows to fill. Asked, inevitably, about Billy's fitness, Eddie defused speculation with the throwaway line: 'I think he had too much Kobe beef, mate . . .'

It might not have had them rolling around the aisles in the Tokyo Hippodrome, but it got the job done. The last thing a leading coach wants to share is the truth, unless it is convenient. Eddie was on top form leading into the knockout match against the Wallabies, summoning the Samurai spirit in reminding his audience that 'Someone is going to live and someone is going to die.'

These are the occasions I will miss most, in the years to come. Big matches demand physical and psychological durability. They do not come around too often, by definition. In my experience, the bigger the occasion, the simpler, and more starkly defined, your game needs to be. Emotion needs to be shed, like a second skin.

Of course, passion has its place. A lot of that is expressed before you climb on the coach, in the hermetically sealed environment of the team room at the hotel. When the human chemistry is right, it is there that you speak honestly, openly and expressively about what it all means to you. Things get a lot more real, and intensely concentrated, at the stadium.

You can't buy entry into the dressing room in the final countdown. You have earned your right to be there. You make eye contact with your mates, and channel your commitment to one another. It's a crazy kind of love. You see people breathing heavily, gulping air. You hear the machine-gun rattle of studs being tapped nervously and relentlessly. You feel alive, but must deaden those senses, strip everything back, and trust in your processes.

Big players respond to big occasions and big decisions. A few of the press lads got over-excited when Eddie picked Owen Farrell at fly half, and kept George Ford in reserve. The captain had kicked poorly against Argentina, but when it mattered he was laser-locked in. Twenty points from his boot, counterpoint to four tries, must have felt like water torture to Australia.

Just as winners write their own history in war and in wider life, a victorious Test team has the right to interpret statistics as it sees fit. England lost out in possession, 64 per cent to 36 per cent, in ball carries, 151 to 71, and in defenders beaten, 21 to 12. But the scoreboard, which recorded a 40–16 win and a first World Cup semi-final for twelve years, was more eloquent.

The numbers that stood out for me were unprecedented for England in World Cup history. Sam Underhill and Tom Curry made thirty-six tackles between them. Mako Vunipola put in eighteen tackles, one more than Jamie George and Owen Farrell. I also loved the less quantifiable example of Kyle Sinckler's spirit, and the ferocity of the England pack.

Respect, chaps.

Man-of-the-match awards tend to be regarded as part of the furniture, but the one given to Tom Curry against Australia was special. I was a little less than 6,000 miles away, but felt especially close to him in his moment of recognition. I thought back two years, to when we roomed together in Argentina, and marvelled at how far he had come.

It was obvious, even then, that he was going to be ten times the player I ever was. There was no rugby tuition I could give him; my job was to offer wider counsel about the world in which he would grow up. Dispensing such advice was one of the most enjoyable aspects of captaincy, not because of any shallow boost to my ego, but because it gave me the chance to have enduring influence.

In essence, I wanted to show Tom right from wrong. That didn't necessarily involve the lessons of my various run-ins with authority. It was more about the power of example, the way in which the top player holds himself, and those around him, to account. I hope I got through to him, in the way I conducted myself. I like to think my pride, at playing for my country, shone through.

Even at such a distance, I could see belief within the England team multiply as World Cup wins were accumulated. It was an ideally blended group, which grew before our eyes. The vigour and hunger of the young guns were complemented by the steeliness of scarred old guys, who had been through the wringer. It is a heady thing to be part of; players get to know one another as people. Suddenly, strangely, it seems to matter more. It's personal.

Eddie was on a roll, recycling his Samurai shtick, but he knew what was coming. The All Blacks are not merely a rugby team, or a marketing phenomenon. They symbolize the might of myth, and are assumed to be in a permanent state of grace. I love what they represent, since to an extent they are in my DNA, but Eddie had it right when he insisted they were 'neither gods nor monsters'.

I wished him well in the build-up to the semi-final, when he texted me to see how I was faring. I told him of my retirement plans, and he agreed to provide a testimonial for the announcement. We knew my race had been run, but I still couldn't help myself when he asked if there was anything else he could do: 'Three more caps and a World Cup winner's medal would be lovely, mate.'

Harking back to our conversation at Wimbledon, in what seemed to be another century, I mentioned how impressed I was by the way in which the entire squad had bonded. He had generated an inclusive atmosphere in which those who weren't selected were presented with their shirts, numbered 24 to 31, by the playing group.

That's a simple but smart solution to a potential problem of resentment and alienation. Those guys usually celebrate their isolation. They give themselves a daft name, like the dirt-trackers, the mixed veg, the bin juice or the leftovers. The thirty-one might not have the same resonance as the 300, that legend of Spartan defiance, but the warrior spirit was strong.

I spoke with Eddie about the importance of intensity, for what seemed like the trillionth time during the four-year cycle. A lot was subsequently made of the defiant nature of England's challenge to the haka, and Owen's supposed smirk at its height, but the substance of the game plan was infinitely more significant than theatricality.

The boys fronted up, as part of a pattern of behaviour, rather than as a result of pre-match pageantry. They were an exceptionally difficult team to live with if they immediately imposed themselves, physically and mentally. They got into the All Blacks' heads by unexpectedly switching the direction of the kick-off, and pounded their way through the phases to take the lead through a Manu Tuilagi try within two minutes.

This was one of those occasions where the senses aligned. You could feel the performance was at the perfect pitch. You could smell the alarm England had created. You could see, in the resolute body language and the fiery eyes, that desire burned, but was under control. From 1 to 15 – on second thoughts, 1 to 23 – the boys were in the zone, on the edge, at their best.

You could also hear their superiority. The referee's microphone captured a dominant team, cajoling and chirping. The volume of such background noise may dissipate before it filters into the stands, and rarely carries reliably through the TV, but it is a barometer of enjoyment and effectiveness. A vocal team is set on doing good things. A silent team is waiting for those good things to happen.

I prided myself on being a communicator as captain. I recognize that must have got on the referee's wick, and wound up the opposition, but I loved the call-and-response routine, which told me my team was on the same wavelength. That's the sound of empowerment. It signals confidence, initiative and determination.

It took more time to put the All Blacks away than was entirely comfortable, but the reaction to the final whistle was in keeping with the mood of the evening. This wasn't a time for tears of joy and grand celebratory gestures. Sure, the guys were visibly delighted by their work. But they knew the job had not been done. They kept their discipline, and their sense of solidarity.

The rugby gods take fiendish pleasure in setting you up for a fall. What they give, they invariably take away. The golden boot was on another foot in the final, when the

Springboks were inspired by the magnitude of their mission. All their vital signs, collectively and individually, were good, from the kick-off.

By the third minute I had an awful feeling in my gut that things were not going to go England's way. Instant experts might have concentrated on the misfortune of Kyle Sinckler's concussion, and cited the immediate discomfort of Dan Cole, his replacement at tighthead, as a pivotal weakness, but that was crass, disrespectful and wrong.

South Africa's domination was total, a result of cohesive coaching and the underlying wisdom of their tactical strategy. The fact it was based on my sphere of influence, the tight five, didn't make England's defeat any easier to digest. The failure to dismantle the Bomb Squad was fatal. A better team, driven by a higher sense of purpose, deserved their win.

Rassie Erasmus, the coach who created the Bomb Squad by splitting his bench between six forwards and two backs, instead of the usual balance of five and three, was fully vindicated. A World Cup final, stage for the ultimate experiment, proved his theory that a well-rotated front five would come to the fore in the later stages of a match, when bodies are tired and brains are dulled. The Boks ran away with the trophy in the closing stages.

Geeks had their justification in the numbers. England played one match fewer because of the cancellation of the qualifier against France, but Jamie George slogged his way through 317 minutes of pitiless physicality. Demands placed on the six front-rowers used by the Springboks during the tournament were more constant. The Saracens tighthead prop Vincent Koch, who played 230 minutes, was the most lightly raced. The Beast, Tendai Mtawarira, had the most onerous workload, but was used for only forty minutes more.

Sport needs such cold calculation, but it runs on emotion and the universal currency of hope. When they come to make the film of the World Cup win it will inevitably focus on the triumph of the human spirit embodied by Siya Kolisi, the kid who kipped on the floor of his grandmother's township shack and played in his boxer shorts in his first provincial rugby trial, because he had no kit.

Personal memories crowded in when I watched him lift the Cup, as South Africa's first black captain. I lost count of how many times I envisaged myself in that role, before reality intervened. Our paths had diverged since we had last spoken, swapping shirts in the home dressing room after our 12–11 win at Twickenham the previous November.

I was as entranced as anyone by his dignity and humility, his insistence that 'It is a privilege, not a burden, to fight for the people.' I could not claim to match the scale of his achievement, in offering hope to a fractured nation, but I knew where he was coming from. We are both sons of the soil, who owe rugby everything.

# 18

# Hurting, Healing

Chris Ashton loves sticking it to The Man. He takes pride in the independence of his thoughts and actions, whether he is prioritizing his family over his England place at the World Cup, or winding up colonels, coaches and the critics by celebrating a try with a swallow-dive that often has all the grace and beauty of a belly flop.

He's a good mate, who takes liberties with my reputation by referring to me as 'The Motive'. He came up with that pet name because he decided that I was a natural actor, who followed a private agenda. There's an element of truth in his playful dig, because I consciously played up to my role as captain and leader, but very few survivors in top-class sport are straightforward personalities.

There's a script to follow, an image to project. You climb into character when you are knackered, and drive yourself through another gym circuit or contact session because you are aware of the wider influence of your commitment. People take notice of the example you set, the standards you uphold, and are not overly concerned that you might secretly hate the experience.

Endurance is not exclusively physical; those who lack the mental strength to accept personal sacrifice tend not to be around for long, in sport or business. Doing the right thing, accepting short-term pain for long-term gain, might be wearing, but it has relevance beyond rugby. Playing the political game by projecting my professionalism brought out the best in me.

Eddie Jones told me he wasn't going to change my nature as a player, but he delivered the kick up the backside that enabled me to squeeze the last drop out of my career, by improving physically and growing as a person. I know that sounds like I've ripped a page from the self-development handbook, but there's some truth to the corporate cliché.

I'm still hustling in my new world, which blends the familiar rituals of part-time coaching with the novel uncertainties of commerce. I've a diverse range of interests, from printing to property. The unknown is exciting, even if the day-to-day whirlwind has echoes of my past. I've retained that basic incentive, to provide a good life for my family, even if I am rebalancing my priorities.

Retirement gives an athlete time to think. You're told to pause and reflect, which is against everything you have been brought up to believe because you are conditioned by the knowledge there is always someone, somewhere, waiting to exploit the merest hint of complacency. I know, because I was that kid, scheming and dreaming in the background. Freedom can be scary, and it is no wonder many seek refuge in the sport that produced them by moving into coaching.

Things will develop organically in that area. A lot of time goes into being a great coach, and I want to be present for my kids. I've learned to cherish the school run and sports day. I want to keep animals, drive a tractor, and take things as they come. I know how to spot talent, analyse a player, and devise a game plan, but have yet to discover how my life will be recalibrated.

Chris Boyd advised me to avoid over-promising and under-delivering, but I've still got the smell of the changing shed in my nostrils. I'm in familiar territory, liaising with commercial partners and rugby contacts. I'm using recently honed skills in public-speaking engagements, and have scope to do more charity work. I've got the opportunity to engage and enjoy myself. The bottle of red with a Sunday roast is no longer off limits.

Do I miss playing? Of course. I loved being in the thick of it. Moving into the media is a conventional option, but to do so properly involves jeopardizing friendships. I would find it difficult to critique people I've played with. They're my brothers, my soldiers. The life cycle of elite sport is accelerating quickly, but it probably still takes five years to get to the stage where personal loyalty becomes irrelevant.

Today's pundits, like Brian O'Driscoll and Lawrence Dallaglio, don't know the current internationals. They're generally fair, extremely knowledgeable and consistently professional, but they haven't got a clue about modern players, as people. That's not a criticism, by the way; there is no reason why they should invest emotionally in them.

Coaches, rather than critics, shape a player's career and, despite our ups and downs, guys of the stature of Martin Johnson, Stuart Lancaster and Eddie saw past the rough edges, and recognized the potential of my work ethic at international level. I'm fortunate to have a new set of mentors, good people like Stephen Etheridge and Brad Piercewright. They open my eyes to what else is out there.

Brad, who played football for QPR, Darlington and Northampton Town, has successfully made the transition from professional sport to the real world. Stephen has been through it all with me, as a Saints fan, sponsor and director of the club's Foundation. He has recently retired as chairman of Church's shoes; in the latter stages of my career I would regularly pick his brains after training over coffee in his factory around the corner from Franklin's Gardens.

I have learned that, though there are different ways of thinking and acting in a new environment, people matter most. I'm getting the benefit of my open-mindedness as a player. I was never intimidated or bored walking into a room full of strangers in post-match functions. Instead of hiding in the corner, counting down the minutes and regarding the occasion as a chore, I forced myself to introduce myself to people.

Every occasion is an opportunity to learn. I study keynote speakers at conferences. How do they engage with the audience? Is their tone of voice authentic? Do they stand in a certain way, to promote assurance and authority? What other tricks do they use to get their message across? It doesn't necessarily matter whether they are good or bad; there is something to take from each and every one of them.

I cut through the waffle in self-help books, and look for nuggets of insight. Without being disingenuous, how can you influence people? I know this sounds bad, but how can you make someone like you? I'm fascinated by the mechanics of body language, and the subtlety of communication. Everyone likes talking about themselves; ask them three questions about their world, and you establish a bond, a bridgehead. The next time you see them you will have a mutual point of reference.

The rough-arse kid who came into professional rugby at sixteen changed through circumstance. He began to understand the choices, recognize the consequences of his actions, and appreciate the rewards. The shaggy hair has been tamed, through time and fashion; the dress code no longer involves board shorts and gumboots. He learned the truth of a famous statement by the legendary US College basketball coach, John Wooden: 'Success is never final. Failure is never fatal. It's courage that counts.'

Fatherhood inevitably changed my perspective. At the time of writing, in late November 2019, Jo and I are awaiting the birth of our son, due in March 2020. Just as I did with Thea, I am trying to envisage the world in which he will grow up. God willing, he will have the freedom to be himself, irrespective of what I happened to do for a living for much of my life.

I'm not one of those dads, like my best friend, Paul Tupai, who lived for the moment he could play alongside his son, Connor, in his testimonial match at Bedford. For me to achieve that, I will have to be bionic, the beneficiary of a quantum leap in medical science. I suppose, though, that a betting man would put a few shillings on my son being introduced to junior rugby through the local club.

How would I describe rugby to him, should he show signs of gravitating towards my sport? It's a bit like a three-tiered birthday cake; each level has the same ingredients, but can be enjoyed by different people for different reasons at different times. A lot of guys derive huge pleasure from the grassroots game, which offers a physical release and a ready-made friendship group.

There are distinctive levels within the professional game. Someone who lasts five years will have a different mindset to a player who goes the distance, and survives for fifteen years. The veteran has greater pain tolerance, a more natural acceptance of mental attrition, created by the monotony of reaching and exceeding acceptable standards, day in, day out.

Even within those narrow boundaries, there are divisions. As someone who played for one club for the majority of my career, I struggle to identify with a player who might have moved between five or six clubs in his decade or so of professional relevance. Did different scenery, certain variations in club culture, avoid routine? I doubt it, on balance. Small details may vary, but we are all slaves to the coach's stopwatch and the club's strategy.

The demands on me as an established international, an England captain, were onerous and came with the territory. That, in part, explains the appearance of The Motive. I was piggy in the middle. I had to keep everyone happy, balance conflicting priorities. My face had to fit. I needed to say and do the right things at the right time. I had to relate to the right people, in the right places.

It was about as far from a sinecure as it is possible to be, since there was no special treatment. I had to be self-aware, from Monday morning, when I would impulsively grab my midriff before breakfast to make a mental calculation of my body fat, to Saturday or Sunday evening, when I would lead my team off the field and into the inevitable inquest.

International rugby is bloody hard. It hurts, constantly. People are coming for you, every week, in concentrated bursts of hyperactivity. You can't be comfortable. But it is not a relentlessly negative experience. It provides special memories, unique life lessons. The good times tend to be a blur, and the bad times play out in slow motion, but the sense of achievement outlasts difficulties and disappointments.

I find myself wondering how I will feel when I read this book in ten years. How will I have changed? Will I appear naïve, or over-assertive? How will my opinions and experiences stand up to scrutiny by a new generation? Will they be aghast at the punishment I accepted as part and parcel of the game? You don't need to be a social scientist to imagine rugby being reshaped by a more risk-averse society that promotes health and safety above tradition and enjoyment.

I understand why the rugby authorities are acting, in introducing tackle laws that underline their awareness of their duty of care, but suspect we will reach a point where we recognize the futility of trying to change the nature of the game. I want my sport to be pioneering and innovative, in terms of player welfare, without being over-sanitized. I realize it's difficult to square that particular circle.

I look at the way professional football is taking rugby's lead, by introducing concussion substitutions, and recognize the wider sporting world is changing. Heading the ball is being banned in the younger age groups. As research into head injuries becomes more detailed and persuasive, the case for something similar, like mandatory head guards in junior rugby, is likely to be irresistible.

There are signs that individual sports recognize concussion, in particular, as a common problem. This may, of course, be due to the shared threat of legal action, emphasized by the £700m paid out by the NFL's 'concussion settlement' programme to families of former players, following a class action suit pursued through the US courts.

I found it encouraging and significant that the NFL met the football authorities last December to share best practice in protecting players. Former footballers are known to have died from brain damage sustained during their sporting careers. Coroners have described them as victims of an industrial disease. That concentrates the minds of anyone in a contact sport.

Rugby has yet to be part of that wider conversation, so I can only use football's example as a guideline, but it seems logical that kids who grow up without heading the ball will accept it as normal as they mature into young adults. The tiny minority who beat overwhelming odds, and progress into the professional game, will have known nothing different.

They will look at recordings of today's Premier League matches with the same sense of fascination that today's footballers have towards twentieth-century games, played with almost comical aggression on mud heaps by guys who might have had serious issues with a sports scientist or an analytically inclined coach.

Rugby, though, is intrinsically different to football. It is raw, gladiatorial and brutal. Let's be honest, that's why it is entertaining to watch, and fun to play. It is a blockbuster, served up on global television platforms. It features a series of individual physical confrontations within a collective contest in which the loser is left in an undignified heap, but has the capacity to fight back.

Take tackling out, and it is not rugby. Our challenge is to keep rationalizing the risks, making a player's continuous search for domination of his opponent safer while protecting the integrity of the game's basic challenge. People are already more aware of tackle technique, and justifiable areas of contact on the body. They accept the sanctions for transgression.

I'm not a dinosaur, bellowing at a meteorite that is about to wipe it out. I appreciate the outsider's temptation to condemn, and to usher the innocents towards calmer pursuits. It would be wrong to attempt to skirt the unavoidable truth that as players become bigger, faster and stronger they will be chewed up, and spat out, quicker. It is a given, therefore, that we need to insist on the highest standards of care.

You don't have to look too far below the Premiership to see guys playing for the glory, rather than a sustainable wage. They'll put up with a lot to have 'professional rugby player' in their Instagram bio. I don't recognize their names, but I identify with their hunger. They deserve to be supported by a better infrastructure, which at the very least guarantees the highest level of medical provision in the event of serious injury.

All too often, a blown-out knee is a one-way ticket back to the building site. Insurance is seen by some club owners as an optional extra. Ambition is exploited, because of the law of supply and demand. It takes unusual bravery and self-assurance to reject a skinny contract, because there are plenty of aspiring players who will sign first and worry about the financial implications later.

Money was secondary to me in the early days because I was desperate to be admitted into the brotherhood. The team ethic was important to me. I wanted to put my body on the line for my mates, regardless of personal risk. That was not out of any misplaced sense of machismo, but because I wanted people to come with me into what can be a horribly forbidding place.

The best teams are able to look one another in the eye and recognize the glint of mutual respect. I have played with talented guys known dismissively, within the group, as 'Peaheart'. They didn't last long, because they failed to convince the dressing room they were a credible person. I didn't want to spend time with someone with that sort of character trait.

I'm aware of the contradictions. I have few really close friends, but many teammates and acquaintances. Most of the guys with my age profile have now left the game, because professional sport has a high level of natural wastage. I was cap number 1802 at Northampton; the two latest recipients, All Blacks Owen Franks and Matt Proctor, are 2020 and 2021 respectively.

Maths has never been a strong point, but even I can calculate that I've played with more than 200 blokes at club level, and probably 100 or so more for England. We're on individual trajectories, but share a life cycle. The boys on the back of the bus, bonded by the certainty of being on the booze, win or lose, mature. They become family men, with a vested interest in prolonging their career.

They don't go out, because they don't want to expose themselves to temptation. They count the calories, and court the fitness coach. They play against kids they don't recognize, and feel old because they are confronted by a vision of themselves a decade earlier, trying to make a name. Then, like me, they loosen the ties, and let go. They try to compensate for friendships put on ice, for birthdays, christenings, funerals and weddings missed due to rugby commitments.

No one wants to be the former player who balloons up, through inactivity. Some will have a new lease of life; most will suffer with joint pain and be pretty immobile. We will all romanticize the big wins, and pretend we enjoyed the suffocating experience of playing in a pressure cooker. Stories will be exaggerated, but savoured. Selected statistics (did I mention that I was one of England's most successful captains in terms of victories, with a winning percentage of 85 per cent?) will be trotted out.

Medals are treasured mementoes, but what happens when they are tarnished? That was one of the many questions raised during the firestorm created by Saracens' unprecedented punishment for systematically breaking the salary cap between 2016 and 2019. Two of the five Premiership titles they have won since 2011 were in that timeframe.

Let's get one thing straight: the culture they created was based upon an unfair financial advantage. Belief and a sense of mental superiority, created by winning on a consistent basis, can take you to a different place. But is it right for that confidence and certainty effectively to be purchased, through three years of cheating? The damage is done. They should have been stripped of those tittles.

I am happy for the players who benefited financially. Seven of my mates in England's World Cup squad were involved, to a greater or lesser degree. No player is going to return the pay cheque because his conscience is troubled. I'm not prepared to be a hypocrite: in the same situation, I would want the club to find a way to get me the best deal possible.

Being brutally honest, the detail would be secondary. I wouldn't want special treatment, but if my teammates were profiting, I wouldn't ask to be excluded. In principle, such benefits as the co-investment schemes apparently set up for certain players by Saracens' owner, Nigel Wray, are a good thing because they provide an additional layer of post-retirement insurance.

But it is correct that others should question underlying injustices. I'm a big boy and didn't cry at the hidings we took from Saracens in recent years. They stung, even before the revelation they were fuelled by an artificially enhanced con-fidence and a well-funded squad strength those playing within the rules struggled to match.

We were bringing on Academy front-row forwards to play in the back row against them when they were using internationals as replacements. Is it any wonder we were gubbed by fifty points? I felt for our younger players, who didn't have the opportunity to be eased into senior rugby in the sort of all-star team Saracens were able to field.

Put a kid in a team sprinkled with British Lions and seasoned England players. Guess what? He's going to play pretty well. I don't intend to cast doubt or decry the talent and professionalism of those who launched international careers in the Saracens set-up, but don't tell me they did so from a level playing field.

Players talk, and there had been persistent whispers and moans about certain privileges their guys enjoyed. All we really needed to do was study the team sheets. Their squads were so deep they could afford to give players a week off in pressurized sequences, when we were trapped in the trenches, and held together by duct tape. For years they were the shining lights of rotation. Now we know why.

Let's remove the emotion, and look at this in a measured way. Rugby is increasingly competitive and becoming highly commercialized. The trend towards elitism in modern sport is an inevitable consequence of increased interest and enhanced levels of financial jeopardy. The temptation to do everything to win is ever-present. Equally, I have learned to accept my punishment when I have done wrong, and move on. Saracens have nothing to whinge about.

I suppose what we are talking about, at the heart of this debate, is something less tangible than a trophy or a league table. It's about the spirit of a sport, its essence. In my view, that's something too sacred for someone in a suit to pontificate about. It's for the players to acknowledge, respect and share. After all, they are the ones closest to the action, and most aware of the pleasures and punishments involved.

I've tried, in this book, to be realistic and authentic. I've not shirked some of the harsher aspects of my trade, and hope I've given some insight into why we do what we do or, in my case, did. Rugby has given me a head start, through the people I have met and networks I have been able to form. The pain has been manageable and the lessons have been invaluable. I'm done with looking back. I'm now focused on the future.

Rugby hurts, but I am healed.

# Acknowledgements

Books are not created overnight. This one has been five years in the making. When I first got together with Michael Calvin, who has put my words in the right order, we set ourselves the challenge of providing an authentic insight into the realities of rugby at the highest level. I'll leave it to you to decide whether we have succeeded.

Mike's constant reminders that these words have permanence, once they are placed between the covers of a book, concentrated my mind. God willing they will be read by my grandchildren, and pass into family history. That's why I have to begin my expression of thanks with Mum and Dad, for the upbringing they gave me, the values they instilled and their unwavering support.

Rotorua Boys High School set the bar high and made success in sport an achievable dream. I know the truth of the school motto, *Ad astra per aspera*: through hardships to the stars. Uncle Phil and Auntie Christine opened their home and gave me the opportunity to come to England and change the course of my life.

Dave Pass, my coach at Beacon College and Crowborough RFC, put in endless miles driving me to trial matches around the country. He always fought the rugged Kiwi kid's corner. Graham Smith made the move to semi-professional rugby happen even though it was on fuel expenses and in shit student accommodation. He taught me what it meant to be an uncompromising English front-row forward.

James Sinclair went above and beyond to make the move to Northampton Saints Academy a reality. The following year he awarded me my first professional contract, not knowing I'd be hanging around fourteen seasons later. All the things that made Dorian West a good player made him a great mentor and coach. Hard-nosed, uncompromising and loyal, he gave me countless hours of physical coaching, mindset lectures, counselling and bollockings. Cheers, from a fellow jarhead.

I thank Eddie Jones for seeing good in me and backing me till my leg fell off. Sure, he's always pushing for more, always making life more uncomfortable, always raising the bar and shifting the goal posts, but I'm grateful for being part of his team and tasting high-performance culture. If it was easy, everyone would do it.

The Tupai family ensure the door is always open, food is always on the table, and there's always a couch to sleep on. I thank them for giving me my second family here in the UK, something that a kid needed and still does. I couldn't have made all those comebacks without their help.

Jo, my wife, is the constant in my life. She has seen it all unfold and understands the nature of the beast, making sacrifices in her life to let me chase my career. I can't adequately express my thanks for her patience and selfless support. I know Mike thinks similarly about his wife, Lynn. He drives her mad when he is immersed in a book.

When Mike and I first met, I made a smartarse joke about a good book being a good doorstop. The Big Fella has taught me otherwise. I like to think, in return, I gave him a lesson in my trade when he asked me to go through a one-on-one session on scrummaging techniques in the kitchen. We made a decent team, all things considered.

ACKNOWLEDGEMENTS

We owe thanks to Michael McLoughlin, our publisher at Penguin, for his faith and foresight. Brendan Barrington and Mark Handsley have been meticulous and insightful in their editing. Christine Preston made Mike's life so much easier with her fast, accurate transcription of our interviews. Just as I value the support of my representatives at YMU Sport, Rob Burgess and Ryan Shahin, Mike appreciates the assistance of his literary agent, Rory Scarfe at the Blair Partnership.

And finally, thanks to you, the reader, for taking the time and trouble to investigate what makes me tick. I appreciate it.

Dylan Hartley, January 2020

# Index

*DH indicates Dylan Hartley.*

academy players, modern 35, 161–2
Alexander, Lisa 211–12, 213
alickadoos (hangers-on around a
    rugby club) 125, 259, 260–61
Alred, Dave 129
Altitude Bar, Queensland, New
    Zealand 126–9
Anderson, Ned 57
Andrew, Rob 102, 124
anti-inflammatory drugs 83, 226, 251
Argentina, England rugby team tour
    of (2017) 267–9
Argentina (national rugby team) 78,
    90–91, 109, 126, 150, 287, 289,
    290
Armitage, Delon 106, 132
Ashton, Brian 102, 105, 124
Ashton, Chris 102, 126, 127, 128, 130,
    131, 133, 140, 157, 169–70, 208, 295
Askew, Tosh 39
Atonio, Uini 188
Australia
    British and Irish Lions tour of
        (1989) 94
    British and Irish Lions tour of
        (2013) 101, 138–9, 141–2, 147,
        148, 149, 151
    England rugby team tour of
        (2016) 196, 197–9
Australia (national rugby team) 230,
    245–6, 270
Autumn Internationals (2008) 108
Autumn Internationals (2009) 110
Autumn Internationals (2012) 136

Autumn Internationals (2013) 150
Autumn Internationals (2018)
    276–7
Battle of Ballymore (second Lions
    Test against Australia in
    Brisbane, 1989) 94
British and Irish Lions tour of
    Australia (2013) and 148, 151
England rugby team tour of
    Australia (2016) and 196, 197–9
World Cup (2015) 165, 166, 169, 197
World Cup (2019) 287, 289–90
Australian Players' Union 238
Autumn Internationals 259
    (2008) 106–7, 108
    (2009) 110
    (2012) 136
    (2013) 84, 150–51
    (2016) 97
    (2017) 225, 235
    (2018) 214, 270, 273–7, 294

Balotelli, Mario 13–14
Banks, Harry 263–4
Barbarians 109, 147, 208, 229, 285
Barcelona FC, *rondos* training
    element 117
Barnes, Wayne 141, 143, 144, 146,
    148
Barnum, P. T. 1
Barwell, Keith 139, 154
Barwell, Leon 139–40, 151, 154
Bath Rugby 39, 41, 54, 63, 68, 91, 108,
    152–3, 167, 224

Battle of Ballymore (second Lions
    Test against Australia in
    Brisbane, 1989) 94
Batty, Grant 30
Bay of Plenty rugby team 30, 33
Bayern Munich FC 212
Beacon Community College,
    Crowborough 38–9
Bedford Blues 33, 46, 54, 299
Belichick, Bill 219–20, 223
Best, Rory 93, 147
Betsen, Serge 63
Biarritz Olympique Pays Basque 63,
    109
Bisping, Michael 224
Blackett, Jeff 88, 148
Blaze, Richard 43, 45
Borthwick, Steve 111, 112, 153,
    182–3, 241, 251
Bosch, Marcelo 153
Boyd, Chris 239–40, 241–2, 267, 269,
    279, 280, 284, 297
BPPV (benign paroxysmal
    positional vertigo) 202
Brady, Tom 223
Bristol Bears 62
British and Irish Lions 7, 12, 39, 41,
    62, 91, 94, 97, 129, 246, 267, 306
    Australia tour (1989) 94
    Australia tour (2013) 101, 138–9,
        141–2, 147, 148, 149, 151
    New Zealand tour (2017) 149–50,
        151
    South Africa tour (1974) 94
    South Africa tour (1997) 149
    South Africa tour (2009) 109
Brive, CA 110
Broad, Stuart 11
Brookes, Kieran 166
Brown, Mike 157, 268
BT Sport 281

Burgess, Sam 167
Burrell, Craig 30
Burrell, Luther 151, 154, 167

Callaghan, Mr (DH's school coach)
    30
Cameron, Sam 48
Campese, David 151
Cane, Sam 30
Captain's Run 140, 217
Care, Danny 78, 98, 191, 268, 287
CAT scan (using crossbar and
    touchline as reference points)
    80
Championship, RFU 46, 54, 65, 74,
    83, 88
Charlesworth, Ric 270
Close, Graeme 226, 227, 265
Cockerill, Richard 95–6, 143
Cohen, Ben 56
Cole, Dan 145, 182, 186, 202, 293
Colston's Collegiate School, Bristol
    54
concussion 5, 189–91, 192–6, 197,
    199–209, 215, 238, 243, 244, 249,
    253, 264, 293, 301
    cause and effect, no definitive 199
    Concussion Guidance, World
        Rugby 195
    contact training with England
        and 194–6, 255
    explained 194
    friendly fire collision and 207–8
    Graduated Return to Play
        protocol 195–6
    Head Injury Assessment (HIA)
        200–201, 206–7
    Headcase Education Programme,
        RFU 194
    international rugby, twice as likely
        in 194–5

most commonly reported injury
(2017–18) 194
NFL and 237, 255–6, 301
recovery from 195–7, 203–9, 243,
244, 249
'second-impact syndrome' and
195
Six Nations (2016), DH and
189–91
Six Nations (2018), DH and
199–203
substitutions 301
symptoms 189–94, 199–209
tackle height and 207–8
World Cup (2019), Sinckler at 293
contact training, injuries and 194–6,
255
Conte, Antonio 213–14
Cook, Alastair 225, 257, 258, 264
Cook, Captain James 21
Corbisiero, Alex 151
Cornish Pirates 83–4
Cousins, Kurt 223
Cowan-Dickie, Luke 165, 186, 232
Cowley, Garrick 28
Cowley, Jerry 27–8
Cowley, Oliva 27, 28
Cowley, Ritchie 28
Cowley, Sarah 28
Cowley, Talaia 27
Craig, Neil 225
Croft, Tom 39
Crowborough RFC 38–9, 48
Curry, Tom 267, 287, 289–90
Cuthbert, Alex 136

Dachau concentration camp,
Germany 20
Dallaglio, Lawrence 123, 297
Daly, Elliot 224
Davey, Sean 96

Davies, Kevin 51–2
Dawson, Matt 123
Dick, Frank 223–4
Dickson, Lee 55, 147, 151, 155, 156
Didelot, Hervé 188
double rucking 79
Dowson, Phil 153, 154, 245, 246
Doyle, J. P. 96, 154
drinking culture, rugby 39, 65–6,
106–7, 110–111, 120, 126 see also
Hartley, Dylan: alcohol/rugby
drinking culture and

Eales, John 270
Easter, Nick 127
Einstein, Albert 18–19
Elliott, Jamie 96
England (national rugby team)
Argentina tour (2017) 267–9
Australia tour (2016) 196–9
Autumn Internationals (2008)
106–7, 108
Autumn Internationals (2012) 136
Autumn Internationals (2013) 84,
150–51
Autumn Internationals (2016) 97
Autumn Internationals (2017) 225,
235
Autumn Internationals (2018) 214,
270, 273–7, 294
Captain's Run 140, 217
captain's speech at post-match
dinner 236
central contracts for players 256
club loyalties and 104–5
coaches see individual coach name
DH appointed captain 87, 132,
171–3, 177
DH career with senior squad
see individual coach and tournament
name

DH co-captaincy of 270–73
DH final cap 276–7
DH first cap 106
DH first joins up with senior
  squad 102–3, 104–9
DH in under-18 squad 38, 40
DH joins under-19 training camp,
  South Africa 39, 43, 54–5
DH plays for England Saxons 102
drinking culture within 106, 120,
  126
Johnson management of *see*
  Johnson, Martin
Jones management of *see* Jones,
  Eddie
Lancaster management of *see*
  Lancaster, Stuart
match fees 119–20
media and 1, 134, 214–15, 288
New Zealand tour (2008) 102–3
New Zealand tour (2014) 156–61
player personal appearances in
  sponsors' lounges 119–20
Six Nations (2003) 187
Six Nations (2009) 108–9
Six Nations (2010) 110
Six Nations (2011) 125
Six Nations (2012) 92–3, 133, 135
Six Nations (2013) 136, 169–70
Six Nations (2014) 151
Six Nations (2015) 167, 169–70
Six Nations (2016) 174, 176, 177,
  178–9, 182, 184, 185–6, 187–91,
  192, 193
Six Nations (2017) 214
Six Nations (2018) 94–5, 99–101,
  199–203, 235, 259
Six Nations (2019) 9, 266, 267, 277
South Africa tour (2013) 136
South Africa tour (2018) 205,
  208–9, 215, 241, 270, 273

World Cup (2003) 52, 59, 99, 105,
  110, 124, 125
World Cup (2007) 17, 39, 88, 99
World Cup (2011) 17, 32, 39,
  99, 108, 120, 121–32, 156, 159,
  240
World Cup (2015) 17, 39, 52, 101,
  102, 159, 163, 164–9, 170, 177,
  186, 197, 265
World Cup (2019) 1–2, 4, 10, 12,
  17, 40, 99, 141, 150, 160, 205,
  234, 235–6, 264, 267, 275, 282–3,
  286–94
World Cup under-19 (2004) 55
World Cup under-21 (2005) 53, 55
England Saxons 102, 133, 229
English Premier League (EPL) 231,
  254, 302
Enright, Sean 164
Epley manoeuvre 202–3
Erasmus, Rassie 293
ESPN 183
Esterhuizen, André 273
Etheridge, Stephen 297–8
European Rugby Challenge Cup
  (2014) 152–3
European Rugby Champions Cup
  258, 259
  (2007) 63, 109
  (2011) 93
  (2014) 153
  (2016) 97
  (2018) 133
European Shield 55
Evans, Rob 185–6
Exeter Chiefs 28, 56

Facebook 99
farmer's walk 43
Farrell, Owen
  Australia tour (2016) 198–9

Autumn Internationals (2018) 273,
274, 275, 277
character 271, 272
DH captaincy of England and
218, 226, 284
DH shares captaincy with 270–71,
272, 273, 274, 275, 277, 284
Lancaster and 133
Premiership (2014) 154
Six Nations (2016) 185, 189
Six Nations (2018) 95, 99, 100
South Africa tour (2018) 273
World Cup (2019) 11, 287, 289, 291
Farr Jones, Nick 94
Ferguson, Sir Alex 219, 283
Ferris, Stephen 92–3, 136
Fiji (national rugby team) 151, 152,
164, 166, 287
First World War (1914–18) 18–19
fish-hooking 91–2
Flannery, Jerry 109
Flood, Toby 125
Flutey, Riki 106
Foden, Ben 55, 65, 126, 127, 130, 133,
143, 146–7, 153, 246
Ford, George 95, 133, 218, 268, 275,
289
Ford, Ross 109
Foster, Ian 160
Fox, Grant 160
France (national rugby team) 63, 78,
81, 108, 122, 132, 164, 187–8,
240, 287, 293
Francis, Piers 99
Francis, Tomas 186
Franklin's Gardens, Northampton
3, 51, 56, 65, 109, 136, 152, 206,
225, 244, 263, 283, 298
Franks, Ben 159, 160–61, 253
Franks, Owen 159, 160, 304
friendly fire collision 207–8

front row 68–85, 87, 91, 148, 182, 251,
305, 309
brotherhood of 40
DH role in 79–81
earlobes and 82, 251–2
high-impact tackles and 81
injuries 76, 81–5
pain and 59, 81–2
scrum and 68–79 *see also* scrum
World Cup (2019) and 293–4
'front up' injuries 253

Garcès, Jérôme 200
Gatland, Warren 147
George, Jamie 162–4, 165, 177, 178,
186, 201, 224, 226, 274–5, 289,
293
Georgia (national rugby team) 125,
128
Ghaut, Luis 154–5
Gibson, Jamie 81
Gloucester Rugby 39, 54, 196
Goode, Alex 154
gouging 86, 88–90, 186
Graduated Return to Play protocol
195–6
Grayson, Paul 59
Gregan, George 270
Grewcock, Danny 91
Grinter, Chris 31, 32, 38
Gruden, Jon 222
Guardiola, Pep 212–13
Gustard, Paul 77, 111, 198
Guyan, Dave 100

Hahn, Jason 27
Haimona, Kelly 26
haka 29, 30, 291
Hallam, Chrissie 46, 49–50, 57
Hamilton, Tom 183
Hampson, Matt 51, 76

Hamurana, New Zealand 21–2
Hansen, Steve 160
Harlequins 77, 89, 234
Harrington, Warrick 226, 265
Harrison, Teimana 32, 285
Harrison, Wolfe 285
Harry, Prince 248
Hart, John 59
Hartley, Alex (brother) 21, 22
Hartley, Blair (brother) 21, 22, 32–3
Hartley, Caroline (mother) v, 20–21,
    22–3, 27, 29, 36, 46, 47, 50, 143,
    146, 174
Hartley, Dylan
  accent 26
  alcohol/rugby drinking culture
    and 4, 39, 62, 65–6, 106–7,
    110–111, 118, 119, 120, 121, 122,
    126–32, 156, 157, 176, 190, 233,
    236
  anti-inflammatory drugs and 83,
    226, 251
  authority, early issue with 50, 53
  back problems 3, 6–7, 9, 83,
    249–50, 251
  banned for eight weeks for biting
    Stephen Ferris (2012) 92, 136
  banned for eleven weeks for
    comments made to Wayne
    Barnes (2013) 148–9
  banned for a fortnight for
    punching Rory Best (2012) 93
  banned for four weeks for
    headbutt to Jamie George 164
  banned for three weeks for
    elbowing Matt Smith in the
    face (2014) 95–6
  banned for 26 weeks for making
    illegal contact with the eyes of
    Jonny O'Connor and James
    Haskell (2007) 88–90, 102

bicycle, attempts to steal a 110–11
body fat 3, 300
BPPV (benign paroxysmal
    positional vertigo) 202–3
brain scans 205
Calcutta Cup match (2018), fracas
    following warm-up for and
    94–5
CBD and 3
charity work 297
chest injury 249
childhood 21–34
club rugby see individual team name
coaching work 296
commercial interests 296
concussion see concussion
diet 3, 8, 297
disciplinary issues 7, 86–103
ears 82, 233
Eddie Jones and see Jones, Eddie
England captain, appointed (2016)
    24–5, 87, 132, 171–3, 177
England career, end of 1–17,
    274–9, 282–6, 296
England co-captaincy 270–73
England, final cap for 276–7
England, first cap for 106
England, first joins up with
    104–9
England management and see
    Johnson, Martin; Jones, Eddie;
    and Lancaster, Stuart
England match fee 119–20
England matches see England
    (national rugby team) and
    individual opponent and tournament
    name
England under-18 squad 38
England under-19 training camp,
    South Africa 39, 43, 54–5
family background 18–21

family life *see individual family
member name*
finances 10, 13, 40, 46, 48–50, 54,
55, 57, 58, 272, 303
first organized games of rugby
27–8
front row and 68–85 *see also* front
row
hands and wrists, injuries related
to 84, 252
harm with malice, never
consciously set out to inflict 89
high-impact tackles and 81
high-school rugby 28–34
hip joint, cyst in 243
hooker role 38, 53, 55, 57, 59,
70–72, 74, 75, 102–3, 171, 172
initiation ceremonies and 45, 65,
106–7
injuries *see individual body area*
joint aspiration 4, 15
knee injuries 1–7, 10–16, 40, 81–2,
136, 249, 250, 253, 254, 262, 264,
277–8, 279–82, 303; rehab 9,
11–17, 247, 264, 283
ligament damage 250, 252
lineout throwing 28, 42, 59, 72, 78,
84, 111–14, 165, 216, 217, 241,
265
long-term injury and disciplinary
action, parallels between 87
love life *see* Hartley, Jo (wife)
lung, punctures 84
media and 25, 101, 111, 127–8, 134,
149–50, 165, 174, 180, 191, 214,
226, 233, 270, 274, 275, 283, 297
medical records 249
mental burnout 231
metatarsal stress fracture 249
mind maps 87–8
New Zealand, leaves 34, 35–7

New Zealand, roots in 17, 18–19,
21
nurture, tendency to 267
one-dimensional thinking, hatred
of 115–16
pain, conditioned to 43–4, 81–2
painkillers, use of 3, 7, 231
pool work 3, 16, 110, 226
popped rib 250
public-speaking engagements 297
punches Kevin Davies 52
purposeful walking 14
retirement 249, 255, 277–8,
279–86, 291, 295–9
scrum and *see* scrum
sells England kit on eBay 48–9
shoulder injuries 81, 82, 249–50,
251, 262
skinfold tests 8, 205, 226–7, 265
sledging 38–9
sleeping on Saturday nights,
difficulty 82
social media and 86–7, 88,
99–100, 118, 130, 149, 272, 281
son, birth of 299
spitting at opponent, accused of
99–100
sponsors and 119–20, 129–30, 149,
283
straight-arm tackle on Sean
O'Brien 97–8
suspensions 86–7, 88, 89, 97, 148,
165, 166, 169, 282
'The Motive' nickname 300
'The Talisman' nickname 78
trigger thoughts or movements 114
TV punditry 208, 209, 283–4, 297
VA (veteran athlete)/JCA
(joint-compromised athlete) 16
wedding 10, 204, 213
weight 265

Hartley, Guy (father) v, 21, 22–6, 33, 36, 46, 47, 49, 143, 146, 174, 188, 272

Hartley, Jo (wife) v, 4, 10, 11, 12–13, 23, 82, 84, 132, 145, 148, 174, 189, 190, 204, 206, 229, 234, 279, 299, 310

Hartley, Thea (daughter) v, 5, 10, 12, 13, 23, 34, 56, 60, 169, 190, 204, 229, 234, 251, 299

Haskell, James 55–6, 57, 88, 109
  Australia tour (2016) 197
  DH's 26-week ban for making illegal contact with the eyes of 88–90, 102
  Eddie Jones and 283–4
  Six Nations (2016) 182
  Stuart Lancaster and 133, 168
  World Cup (2011) and 126, 127, 128, 130, 131

Hatley, Neal 111

Haywood, Mike 9, 153, 277

Head Injury Assessment (HIA) 200, 206

Heineken Cup see European Rugby Champions Cup

Henry, Graham 23

Hewitt, Martin 248

Hill, Paul 182

hit-and-stick tackle 224

Hitler, Adolf 20

Hodgson, Charlie 153

Hongi (traditional Maori greeting) 47

Hopley, Damian 237

Hopley, Mark 45–6

Horne, Rob 244–9

Hughes, Graham 154

Hughes, Nathan 95

Hunter, Rob 56, 57

Hyland, Eamonn 2–3, 9

Instagram 86, 272, 281, 285–6, 303

Ireland (national rugby team) 7, 113, 164, 256
  Six Nations (2009) 109
  Six Nations (2011) 125, 126
  Six Nations (2012) 92–3
  Six Nations (2014) 151
  Six Nations (2015) 170
  Six Nations (2016) 184
  Six Nations (2017) 214
  Six Nations (2018) 201–2
  Six Nations (2019) 267
  World Cup (2015) 168

Italy (national rugby team) 26, 102, 108, 134, 182, 259

Itoje, Maro 11, 99, 112, 182–3, 186

Jager, Lood de 273

Japan (national rugby team) 170, 275, 286

Jenkins, Garin 90–91

Jenner, Jeff 49–50

Jenner, Jim 49–50

Johnson, Martin 104–5, 106, 107–8, 110, 111, 122, 123, 124, 125, 126, 127–8, 133, 134–5, 297

Johnson, Nick 142

Jonathan Ross Show, The (TV show) 191

Jones, Alun Wyn 11, 99

Jones, Eddie 1, 97, 98, 126, 150, 153, 226, 264, 281
  Argentina tour (2017) and 268–9
  Australia tour (2016) and 196, 198
  Bill Belichick and 219–20, 223, 241
  Bill Knowles and 12, 13, 16, 17
  Billy Vunipola and 186
  brain-training emails from 210–211
  British and Irish Lions tour of New Zealand (2017) and 150

captain as an extension of
management team, views 228
captaincy, offers DH England 132,
171–3, 177
captain's speech at the post-match
dinner and 236
coaching evolution under initial
four-year cycle with England
241
co-captaincy of England,
introduces 270–73
concussion of DH and 204, 208–9
continual development of player
and 111–12, 181–2
cricket and 224–5
dedication 179–80
detail, attention to 6, 185
discipline under 176
disciplinary problems of DH and
97, 98, 100
drops DH, Autumn
Internationals (2018) 274, 275,
276
eases personal pressure points, if
convinced it has performance
benefit 216–18
end of DH's England career and
1–2, 4, 5–6, 7, 10–12, 13, 17, 274,
275, 276, 282, 284–6, 296
England coach, appointed 170–85
faith in basic qualities of DH 166
first advice to DH on becoming
England head coach 170–71
first meets DH 171–2
James Haskell and 168
Joe Marler and 235
Ken Ravizza and 215–16
knee injury, DH's and 1–2, 9,
10–12, 13, 16, 17, 18, 265–6
Lewis Ludlam and 284–6
Lisa Alexander and 211–12, 213

'lovely guy' 13, 172
Marland Yarde and 232–3
Martin Johnson and 108, 111, 133
media and 1, 214–15, 288
mellowing of 269
monitors England players by
proxy 9
naturally communicative coach
185
Neil Craig and 225
Pep Guardiola and 212–13
pre-breakfast meeting 228
recovery and 180
relentlessness of contact 175–6
replacements as finishers, recasts
186
RFU and 260
self-reliance and 161
Six Nations (2016) and 176, 184,
187
sociability 232
South Africa tour (2018) and
208–9
spitting incident, DH and 99–100
spotting of global trends and
tailoring them to player
requirements 185
statistics, use of 184–5, 265–6
Steve Borthwick and 153
stroke 221
Stuart Lancaster and 134
texts with DH 8, 170–71, 174, 175,
221–2, 228, 290–91
thinking processes of DH and
179
training camps, intensity of 201
turnovers and 115
TV appearances of DH and 191
TV punditry, outlook on 283–4
Twickenham Syndrome/player
dependency on 8, 166

Urban Meyer and 220–22
unforgiving atmosphere of life under/imposition of pressure on those around him 228–38, 241
Vickerman and 23
Wimbledon meeting with DH 10–12, 291
working day under 176–7
World Cup (2019) 1–2, 7, 12, 13, 18, 267, 288, 289, 290–91
World Cup squad (2019), selection of 1–2, 4, 5–6, 7, 10–12, 13, 17, 282, 284–6
Jones, Hiroko 11
Jones, Robert 94
Joseph, Jonathan 182, 191

Kahukura RSC 26, 27
Kalamafoni, Sione 244
Karma group 142–3
Kennedy, Nick 106
Knowles, Bill 12–17
Koch, Vincent 293
Kolisi, Siya 294
Kruis, George 112, 186
Kydd, Robbie 63

Lampard, Frank 80
Lancaster, Stuart 124, 133–5, 150, 157–8, 165–6, 167, 169–70, 171, 177, 180, 197, 229, 297
Land Rover 129–30
Laulala, Nepo 160
Launchbury, Joe 112, 133, 224–5, 268
Lavanini, Tomás 287
Lawes, Courtney 81, 99, 112, 151, 233, 275
'leaderful' team 270
Lee, Matt 196, 244–5, 250–51
Lee, Samson 185, 199–200

Leeds Tykes 55
Leicester Tigers 51, 53, 58, 95–6, 104–5, 107, 110, 111, 137, 138–47, 152, 153, 244, 248
Leinster Rugby 97, 133, 258
Leonard, Jason 106
leopard crawl 43–4
Lewis, Michael: *The Blind Side* 71
Lomu, Jonah 22, 31
London Irish 160
Lord, Josh 63
Lord, Matt 63–4
Louw, Francois 30
Lozowski, Alex 268
Ludlam, Lewis 284–6, 288
Lutner, Herman (maternal great-great-grandfather) 20

Ma'afu, 'Apakuki 151–2
Ma'afu, Campese 151
Ma'afu, Salesi 151, 152
Mallett, Nick 135
Mallinder, Harry 9, 277
Mallinder, Jim 53, 55, 65, 66, 83, 93, 140, 145, 240–41
Mamaku, New Zealand 33
*Mana* (Maori powerful, mystical force) 29
Maori culture 17, 21, 22, 26, 27, 29, 30, 31, 47, 61
DH childhood and 22, 26, 27, 29–31, 47, 61
haka 29, 30, 291
Hongi (traditional greeting) 47
*Mana* (powerful, mystical force) 29
Marae (communal meeting place where culture is celebrated) 29–30, 47
Tangihanga (ceremony in which the group says farewell to the dead) 30

Tūrangawaewae, concept of ('a place to stand') 21–2

Marae (communal meeting place where Maori culture is celebrated) 29–30, 47

Marler, Daisy 235

Marler, Joe 185–6, 234–5

maul 41, 42, 67, 72, 78, 81, 82, 91–2, 93, 163, 172, 198

May, Jonny 9, 99, 119, 201, 225, 268, 274

McBride, Willie John 94

McCaw, Richie 23, 84

McGeechan, Ian 149

McGregor, Shane 27

McManus, James 199

McVay, Sean 222

Meakin, Gary 41

Mears, Lee 102, 108, 109, 165

'meerkating' 77

Melbourne Storm 224

mental health, rugby and 231, 237, 238, 252, 254

Messam, Liam 30

Messam, Sam 30

Meyer, Urban: *Above the Line* 220–22

Millfield School 39, 54

Mobbs Memorial Match (2019) 33

Monye, Ugo 106, 109

Moody, Lewis 124, 125, 126

Morgan, Oli 39

Mtawarira, Tendai 293

Mujati, Brian 74, 137

Munster Rugby 7

Myall, Kearnan 229–30, 231

Myler, Stephen 96, 143, 144, 153, 154

naked-bus policy 65–6

Nazi Party 18, 19, 20

NBC 151

New Zealand

British and Irish Lions tour of (2017) 149–50, 151

DH childhood in 21–34

DH high-school rugby career in 28–34

DH leaves 34, 35–7

DH roots in 17, 18–19, 21

England tour of (2008) 102–3

England tour of (2014) 156–61

Maori culture 17, 21, 22, 26, 27, 29, 30, 31, 47, 61 *see also* Maori culture

New Zealand (national rugby team) (All Blacks) 22, 23, 24, 25–6, 30, 56, 59, 61, 62, 63, 77, 84, 103, 107, 108, 116, 127, 136, 156, 159–61, 177, 197, 214, 240, 256, 304

Autumn Internationals (2008) 108

Autumn Internationals (2012) 136

Autumn Internationals (2013) 84, 150–51

Autumn Internationals (2018) 273–5

central contracts 160

coaching 159

community links 25–6

DH childhood and 22, 61–2

DH father and 224

eighteen consecutive victories record 214

England tour of (2008) and 102–3

England tour of (2014) and 156–61

grounded nature of players 159–61

scrum and 77

unstructured, instinctive play 116

World Cup (2011) 159, 197–8

World Cup (2015) 159

World Cup (2019) 287, 290–92

Newcastle Falcons 39, 40, 49, 54, 232
Newcastle Knights 199
Newton, Annabel 130, 131
NFL (National Football League) 16, 25
  coaching in 220, 222–3
  Competition Committee 255
  concussion and 237, 255–6, 301
  'front up' injuries 253
  left guards 71
  Player Safety Advisory Panel 255
  players' union 260
Ngongotaha RFC 27
Northampton Saints 2–3, 9, 33, 40, 46, 56, 60, 62, 76, 81, 83, 86, 109–10, 111, 118, 151, 157, 160, 164, 182, 191, 196, 215, 238, 239–42, 257, 262, 266, 267, 279–80, 283, 284, 297, 304
  Academy 45–6, 56, 60, 285, 310
  Chris Boyd and see Boyd, Chris
  DH concussion and 190–91, 192, 203, 206
  DH debt to 191, 206, 257
  DH disciplinary record and 89, 97, 98
  DH joins 56–67
  DH knee injury and 2–3, 4, 9, 40
  DH made youngest captain (2009) 87
  DH retirement from 266, 279–81
  DH technical role at 280
  Dorian West and see West, Dorian
  European Cup (2007) 63
  Foundation 298
  Horne injury and 244–9
  Jim Mallinder and see Mallinder, Jim
  Leon Barwell and 139–40, 151, 154
  Premiership (2013) 136–7, 138–49, 152

Premiership (2014) 151–5, 156, 157
Premiership (2015) 163, 190
Premiership (2016) 196
  relegation to Championship 88, 102
  Teimana Harrison recruited by DH for 32
North, George 3, 4, 151
NRL (rugby league) 177, 199, 224

Oakham School 53
O'Brien, Sean 97–8
O'Connor, Jonny 88, 89
O'Driscoll, Brian 126, 297
Oher, Michael 71
Olympics
  (2008) 30
  (2012) 28
  (2020) 41
Ovens, Laurence 54–5
Owens, Nigel 92

Pacific Islanders 106
Paice, David 103
Palmer, Tom 127
Parra, Morgan 81
Pask, Phil 12, 16, 202, 265
Pass, Dave 38
Pass, Jon 38
Paterson, Michael 89
Paxton, Jeremy 170
Pennyhill Park, Surrey 98, 106, 169, 171, 187, 213, 225, 232, 234, 248, 267
Perenara, T. J. 275
Phillips, Zara 128
piano fingers (initiation game) 45
Pienaar, Francois 91
Piercewright, Brad 297
Pisi, George 154
Poblenou, CN 41

Pocock, David 197
Poite, Romain 129
Pountney, Budge 59, 60
Powley, Rob 22
Premiership 9, 41, 54, 58, 65, 102,
    104, 115, 136, 260, 303
    (2005–6) 58
    (2012–13) 136–7, 138–49, 152
    (2013–14) 151–5, 156, 157
    (2014–15) 163, 190, 196
    (2015–16) 196
    (2017–18) 215
    concussion and 194
    DH debut in 58
    mental health and 237
    salary cap 242, 304–5
    workload in 252–3, 259
PRO14 133, 258
Proctor, Matt 201

Rae, Alex 46
Ravizza, Ken 215–16
Recaldini, Alberto 92
Redman, Nigel 'Ollie' 41, 47, 55
Rees, Matthew 109
Regan, Mark 62
Reihana, Bruce 61, 62, 63
Retallick, Brodie 30
RFU 13, 16, 39, 53, 87, 99, 100, 122,
    123, 124, 126, 127, 130, 131, 141,
    148, 163, 175, 194, 216, 225, 235,
    259, 260
Riley, Phil 13
Ritchie, Ian 260
Robinson, Andy 124
Robinson, Ben 195
Robinson, Mark 'Sharky' 62
Robshaw, Chris 136, 177, 198, 268,
    287
Robson, Allan 89
robustness training 76

Romania (national rugby team) 129
Ronaldo, Cristiano 219
Rotorua Boys High School, New
    Zealand 29–32, 37, 38, 103, 285
Rotorua Review 24
Rowntree, Graham 93
ruck 52, 62, 63, 75, 80, 81, 89–90,
    92, 93, 96, 98, 114, 198, 201, 217,
    235
Rugby House 102, 175
Rugby Players' Association (RPA)
    237
Ryan, Eugene 100
Ryles, Jason 224

Safford, Rev. Jez 4, 5
Sale Sharks 232, 235, 268
SAQ (Speed, Agility and Quickness)
    training 37
Saracens 46, 115, 137, 153, 163, 172,
    183, 190, 225, 242, 293
    breaking of salary cap 242, 304–5,
    306
Schwarzschild, Alfred (great-
    grandfather) 18, 19, 20
Schwarzschild, Bettina 19
Schwarzschild, Henrietta 18
Schwarzschild, Karl 18–19
Schwarzschild, Luise 19
Schwarzschild, Moses 18
Schwarzschild (née Lutner),
    Theodora (great-grandmother)
    19, 21
Schwarzschild Metric 19
Scotland (national rugby team) 59,
    64, 93
Six Nations (2009) 109
Six Nations (2016) 176, 178–9, 199
Six Nations (2017) 214
Six Nations (2018) 94–5
World Cup (2015) 125, 131

scrum 28, 37, 51, 59, 68–79, 80, 83,
    84, 89, 91, 94, 105, 144–5, 171,
    172, 180, 198, 211, 216, 217, 239,
    243, 250, 251, 310
  changes in over the course of
    DH's career 69–70, 74–5
  dangers of 68–9, 76
  earlobes and 82, 251–2
  face and 72
  France and 78
  getting a shove on in, feeling of
    76–7
  headbutts in 69–70
  hooker and 71–2, 74, 79
  loosehead prop and 70, 72
  'meerkating' 77
  mental element 72–6, 79
  New Zealand and 77
  punching in 91
  scrum pox (*Herpes rugbiorum*) 72
  tighthead props 70–71, 72, 74
  wheeling the scrum 72–3
second-impact syndrome 195
Shaw, Simon 127
Shelford, Wayne 30
Shingler, Aaron 99
Sinckler, Kyle 88–9, 289, 293
Sinclair, James 56, 310
Six Nations 6, 116, 167, 169–70, 219,
    258, 259
  (2003) 187
  (2009) 108–9
  (2010) 110
  (2011) 125
  (2012) 92–3, 133, 135
  (2013) 136, 169–70
  (2014) 151
  (2015) 167, 169–70
  (2016) 174, 176, 177, 178–9, 182,
    184, 185–6, 187–91, 192, 193
  (2017) 214

  (2018) 94–5, 99–101, 199–203, 235,
    259
  (2019) 9, 266, 267, 277
Sky TV 102
Slade, Henry 267, 274
Sloane, Peter 59–60
Smith, Graham 40–41, 46
Smith, Matt 95–6
Smith, QC, Richard 98–9, 100–101
Smith, Tom 64
Smith, Wayne 135–6
social media 86–7, 88, 99–100, 118,
    130, 149, 272, 281
Solomona, Denny 268, 269
South Africa
  British and Irish Lions tour of
    (1974) 94
  British and Irish Lions tour of
    (1997) 149
  British and Irish Lions tour of
    (2009) 109
  DH joins England under-19
    training camp in 39, 43, 54–5
  England tour of (2013) 136
  England tour of (2018) 205, 208–9,
    215, 241, 270, 273
South Africa (national rugby team)
    24, 30, 55, 74, 78, 91, 94, 109,
    273
  Autumn Internationals (2009) 108
  Autumn Internationals (2013) 136
  Autumn Internationals (2018) 214,
    252
  World Cup, under-19 (2004) 55
  World Cup (2007) 102
  World Cup (2015) 170
  World Cup (2019) 287, 293–4
Southgate, Gareth 11, 122, 181, 213
Spence, John 142–3
Spencer, Carlos 61–2, 63
Spreadbury, Tony 76

Stanley, Andrew 41
Stoke-on-Trent RUFC 41
Straker, Christine (aunt) 36–7
Straker, Holly (cousin) 37
Straker, Jamie (cousin) 37
Straker, Phil (uncle) 36–7, 39
Straker, Robin (grandfather) 21
stretcher carries 44
Strettle, David 135
Stridgeon, Paul 129
Super Rugby 240, 252, 253
Sydney Swans 212

Ta'avao, Angus 160
Tait, Matthew 39
Tangihanga (Maori ceremony in
    which the group says farewell
    to the dead) 30
Taylor, Phil 42
Teague, Mike 94
Thomas, Henry 224
Thompson, Steve 56, 109–10, 125,
    164
Tindall, Mike 99, 126, 128
TMO (Television Match Official)
    96, 135, 143, 154, 273
Tonga (national rugby team) 74, 152,
    240, 244, 283
Tonga'uiha, Soane 74, 137
Toulonnais, RC 153
Tour de France 161
tractor tyre carries 43
Tuilagi, Manu 129, 132, 133, 166, 292
Tupai, Connor 33, 60, 299
Tupai, Leah 33
Tupai, Mary 33
Tupai, Nadine 33
Tupai, Paul 'Toops' 33, 60–61, 63, 83,
    139, 147–8, 174, 255, 299
Tūrangawaewae, Maori concept of
    ('a place to stand') 21–2

Tu'ungafasi, Ofa 160
Twitter 99

Underhill, Sam 267, 268, 275, 289
Uruguay (national rugby team) 39

Vickerman, Dan 238
Vickery, Phil 91
Vunipola, Billy 115–16, 133, 186, 190,
    191, 218, 224, 288
Vunipola, Mako 289

Wales (national rugby team) 11, 94,
    129, 151, 286
    Six Nations (2009) 109
    Six Nations (2012) 135
    Six Nations (2016) 185–6
    Six Nations (2018) 99–101,
        199–200, 259
    World Cup (1999) 90
    World Cup (2015) 165, 168,
        169
Waller, Alex 32, 154
Wannenburg, Pedrie 93
Ward, Dave 158–9
Warrington Wolves 151
Wasps 46, 88, 91, 102, 125, 229,
    235
Waugh, Steve 28
Webber, Rob 157, 165
Wells, John 105
Wenger, Arsène 80, 224
Wentz, Carson 16
Wesley College, Auckland 31
West, Dorian 52–3, 65, 66–7, 83, 191,
    240–41, 310
White, Julian 71
Wilkinson, Jonny 59, 110, 123, 125,
    129, 272
Wilson, Davey 39, 40
Wilson, Ryan 95

Wimbrow, Dale: 'The Guy in the Glass' 198
Wisemantel, Scott 230
Wood, Tom 125, 129, 151, 152, 154, 157, 158, 159, 163, 168, 214
Wooden, John 299
Woodward, Clive 99, 124, 270
Worcester Warriors 40–58, 59, 249
    DH at Academy 40–58, 59, 249
    DH first team debut for 55
    DH leaves 57–8
World Cup 74, 91, 245, 295, 305
    (1995) 22
    (1999) 90
    (2003) 52, 59, 99, 105, 110, 124, 125
    (2007) 17, 39, 88, 99
    (2011) 17, 32, 39, 99, 108, 120, 121–32, 156, 159, 240
    (2015) 17, 39, 52, 101, 102, 159, 163, 164–9, 170, 177, 186, 197, 265
    (2019) 1–2, 4, 10, 12, 17, 40, 99, 141, 150, 160, 205, 234, 235–6, 264, 267, 275, 282–3, 286–94
    (2023) 254
World Cup under-19 (2004) 55
World Cup under-21 (2005) 53, 55
Worsley, Joe 88
Wray, Nigel 305
Wyles, Chris 154

Yarde, Marlon 197, 232–3
Yorkshire Carnegie 182
Young, Rob 201
Youngs, Ben 156
Youngs, Tom 95–6, 136, 145, 151, 152, 156, 164, 165